CAMPING HAWAI'I

Camping Hawai‘i

A COMPLETE GUIDE

REVISED EDITION

Richard McMahon

A LATITUDE 20 BOOK
UNIVERSITY OF HAWAI‘I PRESS • HONOLULU

Printed in the United States of America
First edition 1994
Revised edition 1997
02 01 00 99 98 97 5 4 3 2 1

Library of Congress Cataloging-in-Publication Data

McMahon, Richard, 1928–
Camping Hawai'i : a complete guide / Richard McMahon. — Rev. ed.
p. cm.
"A Latitude 20 book."
Includes index.
ISBN 0–8248–1904–7 (pbk. : alk. paper)
1. Camping—Hawaii—Guidebooks. 2. Camp sites, facilities, etc.—Hawaii—Guidebooks. 3. Hawaii—Guidebooks. I. Title.
GV191.42.H3M36 1996
796.54'09969—dc20 93–36172
CIP

University of Hawai'i Press books are printed on acid-free paper and meet the guidelines for permanence and durability of the Council on Library Resources

Designed by Paula Newcomb

In memory of Eric Michael McMahon

28 May–1 November 1986

who left our family before we knew him well

but not before we loved him

CONTENTS

PREFACE TO THE REVISED EDITION

Since the publication of the first edition of *Camping Hawai'i* in the summer of 1994, extensive changes have occurred in the camping community: Some campgrounds have closed and others have opened. Jurisdictions have changed, along with phone numbers and addresses for obtaining permits, which otherwise have little effect on camping. (For example, on O'ahu, Waimānalo Bay and Kaiaka State Recreation Areas have become county beach parks, and Kahana Bay Beach County Park is now under state control and called Kahana Valley State Park). In a few cases, restrictions have been imposed on the issuance of camping permits to protect fragile areas or to curb overuse. Fee schedules have changed at state and national parks, resulting in small increases.

Some of the more important of these changes are as follows: Four campgrounds have closed on Moloka'i. Moloka'i Ranch no longer permits camping at Ranch Mo'omomi, Pu'uhakina Beach, or Hale o Lono Harbor, and Hawaiian Home Lands has withdrawn permission to camp at Mo'omomi Beach. Camping is no longer permitted at Kaumahina Wayside Park on the Hāna Highway on Maui. However, two new county campgrounds are opening on Maui, Kanahā and Pāpalaua Beach Parks. On Hawai'i, the Division of Forestry and Wildlife has reopened the 'Ainapō Trail, which extends from Highway 11 to the summit of Mauna Loa. A new cabin has been constructed at 7,750 feet, which opens new possibilities for traversing and exploring the mountain. On Kaua'i, camping permits for Kalalau Valley are now limited to sixty persons per day, and are further restricted as to where and how they may be obtained. Two campgrounds on military reservations have been added on O'ahu, not because they are new, but because I overlooked them in the first edition. They are located on Marine Corps Base Hawaii, in Kāne'ohe, and at Camp H. M. Smith, on the northwestern outskirts of Honolulu.

After discussions with state forestry officials, I have removed all reference to camping in Natural Area Reserves. While bedroll camping is technically permitted (no tents), the state is reluctant to issue permits except to those with a scientific or educational purpose. In most cases, there are no trails in these reserves, bushwacking through Hawaiian rain forests is destructive and certainly not fun, and sleeping without a tent in an all-night downpour is not restful. Seeds and soil carried on hikers' boots bring alien plants and other undesirable matter into the native forest. There are many fine campgrounds in Hawai'i that permit enjoyment of forested areas without disturbing these pristine places.

All in all, Hawai'i remains an outstanding place to camp, and camping remains one of the best ways to see and enjoy all that the Islands have to offer.

ACKNOWLEDGMENTS

Twenty-five years ago Lorin Gill first introduced me to the wonders and the pleasures of Hawai'i off the beaten path. I am still learning from him. The Sierra Club and the Hawaiian Trail and Mountain Club continued my education. Mountain Travel and REI allowed me to share Hawai'i's back country with hundreds of visitors who wanted something from Hawai'i other than Waikīkī. Ed Petteys, Curt Cottrell, and Bob Hobdy, of the state Forestry and Wildlife Division, provided much useful information and assistance. Daniella Lau and Alice Santiago, two very helpful ladies at the State Park Office, have cheerfully furnished me with information and assistance over the years. Jim and Pat Garrity, visitors from Florida, ferreted out three military campgrounds that I had missed and provided updated data on others. Eileen D'Araujo, Iris Wiley, and Cheri Dunn, my editors, made suggestions that improved the manuscript. Paula Newcomb did a fine job designing the book. And finally, my wife, Ann, prepared the graphics and perhaps contributed more than anyone by making it possible for me to have the time and the freedom to do the work.

WHY YOU NEED THIS BOOK

There are over 120 campgrounds and campsites in Hawai'i. Yet, until this book was written, there has been no single source that a prospective camper could refer to for complete camping information about the Islands. Federal, state, and county authorities all publish fact sheets pertaining to their own jurisdictions, but these contain only limited information, such as a list of campgrounds, where to apply for a permit, length of stay, and so forth. And unless a camper had a knowledgeable friend or other source, there was no way to obtain information about other public lands and private property where camping is allowed. Churches, youth groups, and other nonprofit organizations also have camps and lodges that are open to the public when not being used by their own members.

During my years of leading camping and backpacking trips, I learned that an increasing number of people of all ages want to get away from "Tourist Hawai'i"—Waikīkī Beach, the glitzy hotels of North Kona, the condominiums of the Kā'anapali Coast—and explore the breathtaking *natural* beauty of the Islands. Whether by vehicle or on foot, they seek the less-trodden path, the secret beaches, the hidden valleys, a place to be alone under the stars. It is for them that this book is written.

I have tried to make *Camping Hawai'i* much more than a simple listing of campgrounds and campsites. In Part One you will find important information about Hawai'i and the environment of the Islands. After these introductory chapters, each of the Islands is given a separate chapter in Part Two, in which campgrounds are described in detail. Each chapter begins by setting the stage for your camping trip. You will find useful information about each island and what to see and do while you are there. Next, every campground on that island has its own section, which tells where it is, what facilities are provided, what activities can be enjoyed there, where to apply for permits and how much they cost, how to get there, and describes nearby points of interest. When appropriate, I make special comments about individual campsites and the surrounding area. For each island, at least some mention is made of hiking. Not only are some campsites located at the end of hiking trails, but hiking in Hawai'i is so much a part of the camping experience that it is not always possible to separate them.

MAPS. To help you find your way to the individual campgrounds and points of interest, you will need maps. The University of Hawai'i Press publishes an excellent series of reference maps for each island. They are inexpensive and are available in bookstores, airport newsstands, and many other locations. Individual U.S. Geological Survey topographic map sheets may be purchased at The Hawaii Geographic Society, 49 South Hotel Street, or the Pacific Map Center, 560 N. Nimitz Hwy, Suite 206A, Honolulu, HI 96817.

Please keep in mind that this is a camping guide, written primarily for the use of campers, hikers, and other outdoor enthusiasts. There are many guidebooks available that will tell you about hotels, restaurants, shopping, nightlife, and so forth. There isn't space to do so here. Much of that kind of information is also available in free handouts at the airports and travel agency offices.

To make this book as accurate as possible, I have visited every site mentioned herein and camped at most of them. I have hiked all the trails described. To make the book as complete as possible, I have researched the publications and files of appropriate state and county offices, the Sierra Club Hawai'i Chapter, and the Hawaiian Trail and Mountain Club, and talked to officials, old-timers, naturalists, landowners, and veteran hikers, some of whom I have recognized by name elsewhere in this book. If *Camping Hawai'i* should still prove to be less than complete or contain inaccuracies, the fault is mine alone. Any oversights brought to my attention will be gratefully received and acknowledged.

The University of Hawai'i Press and the author have attempted to make this guide error free. Camping in Hawai'i is generally safe, but, as campers find everywhere, there are hazards. Do not rely entirely on this book; be careful, be alert, and use your own judgment and common sense.

Metric Equivalents of U.S. Units of Measure

U.S. UNIT OF MEASURE	METRIC EQUIVALENT
Capacity (liquid measure)	
gallon	3.785 liters
quart	0.946 liter
pint	0.473 liter
Length	
mile	1,609 kilometers
acre	4,047 square meters
yard	5.029 meters
foot	30.48 centimeters
inch	2.54 centimeters

Part One

HAWAI‘I—

A LAND OF

SUPERLATIVES

AND CONTRASTS

In Hawai'i it is possible to ski down the snow-laden slopes of a 13,000-foot mountain in the morning, and in the afternoon swim in warm, blue waters off a palm-fringed beach. Hiking trails wend their way through dense tropical rain forests and across powder-dry deserts; along hot sandy beaches and cold mountain ridges. Hawai'i contains one of the wettest spots in the world, yet, only a few miles away cactus grows in a parched landscape. Although it is the fourth-smallest state in land area (after Rhode Island, Delaware, and Connecticut), if you include its territorial waters Hawai'i covers an area larger than Alaska. Its magnificent beaches are composed not only of white sand, but also black, gray, brown, red, and even green sand.

Hawai'i is the southernmost state of the United States. It is the only state that was once an independent kingdom, and the only one containing a royal palace. Mauna Kea is the highest mountain in the world when measured from the ocean floor, and its sister peak, Mauna Loa, is the largest mountain in sheer volume. Mauna Kea is also the world's premier astronomical laboratory, housing the largest telescope and the most observatories—nine at last count, with a total of thirteen planned by the year 2000. Kīlauea is the world's most active volcano. In Hawai'i, species of animal and plant life not found anywhere else have evolved. It is the only place in the nation where coffee is grown. Recent surveys have found Hawai'i to be the "healthiest" state of the union, and the state where people live the longest.

Each of the islands of Hawai'i has its own charm and special beauty. The wave-pounded surfing beaches of O'ahu; the dark, brooding volcanoes of Hawai'i; the spectacular Nā Pali sea cliffs of Kaua'i; the lush, green valleys of Maui; and the awesome waterfalls of Moloka'i all combine to afford the visitor an unforgettable experience. It is a paradise for campers.

The Setting

This part of the book is not a history or geography lesson, and at the end of it there is no exam. Its purpose is to provide you with the essentials of the Hawaiian experience and environment, information that will make your camping trip in the Islands more meaningful and enjoyable. Some people find statistics dull. If you are one of them, please scan this chapter anyway. That way, you will know what it contains and will be able to refer to it later, if you need to.

GEOGRAPHY. The Hawaiian Islands are the peaks of a submerged volcanic mountain chain in the North Pacific Ocean, lying at the same latitude as Mexico City and Hong Kong. The Islands stretch across 1,523 miles of ocean, from Hawai'i in the southeast to Kure Island in the northwest. Midway Island, although geographically part of the island chain, is not part of the state, but is administered separately by the U.S. Fish and Wildlife Service. Hawai'i consists of 132 islands, but only seven are inhabited. The eight largest islands contain over 99.9 percent of the state's 6,425 square miles of land area. They are, in order of size, Hawai'i, Maui, O'ahu, Kaua'i, Moloka'i, Lāna'i, Ni'ihau, and Kaho'olawe. The last of these, Kaho'olawe, is uninhabited. Until recently, it had been used as a bombing range by the U.S. military. The island of Hawai'i is larger than all the other Islands combined and contains almost two-thirds of the state's land area. It is the largest island in the United States and is three times the size of the state of Rhode Island. Ni'ihau is privately owned, and visitors are not allowed. It has only about 230 inhabitants, all of Hawaiian ancestry, who work in ranch operations for the owners. It is the only place in the state where Hawaiian is spoken as the everyday language.

CLIMATE. The climate of Hawai'i is one of the most pleasant and agreeable anywhere. All warm-weather sports, including water sports, can be enjoyed year-round. The average temperature at Honolulu airport ranges from 72 degrees (Fahrenheit) in the winter to 81 in the summer. Ocean water temperatures remain between 74 and 80 degrees. Although the Islands are within the tropics—just south of the Tropic of Cancer—the weather is moderated by the effect of the trade winds. Although humidity is relatively high, the trades ensure that Hawai'i escapes the stifling hot summers common along the U.S. East Coast, and it has none of the oppressively high heat of the Southwest. The warmest months are August and September, and the coolest are January and February. Temperatures decrease 3 degrees for every 1,000 feet in elevation gain, an important consideration for hikers and campers, who may often find themselves at the higher altitudes. The longest day in Hawai'i is 13.5 hours, and the shortest is 11 hours. After sunset, darkness falls quickly, usually in about 30 minutes.

Although it does rain more in the winter months than in summer, rainfall in Hawai'i is more a matter of location, rather than time of year, and it varies greatly over the state. The average rainfall in Honolulu is 24 inches; in Lahaina it is 14; in Hāna 69; and in Hilo, a heavy 141. The wettest place in Hawai'i is Mount Wai'ale'ale, on Kaua'i, with an average rainfall of 451 inches, qualifying it as one of the wettest spots on earth. Wai'ale'ale outdid itself in 1982, when it received a record 665 inches. The place with the lowest average rainfall is Kawaihae, on the island of Hawai'i, with 8.7 inches. The lowest recorded rainfall in the state also occurred there in 1953 —0.2 inches.

One of the important things to know about rain in Hawai'i is that if it is raining where you are, it is often clear somewhere else, usually not too far away. Generally speaking, the windward sides of all islands receive considerably more rain than their leeward counterparts. This is because the moisture-laden trade winds blowing from the northeast drop much of their rain when they come up against the windward mountains. Coastal areas receive less rain than inland regions, and lower areas receive less than higher ones. Much of the annual rainfall throughout the state comes at night or in the early morning hours, with the remainder of the day often clear and warm.

HISTORY. Although Captain James Cook is credited with discovering Hawai'i in 1778, it was actually the Polynesians who found the Islands more than a thousand years before Cook's arrival. Setting out in large, double-hulled sailing canoes, they carried not only the standard provisions, but also live animals and plants to establish a food supply in a new homeland. Without navigational instruments of any kind, guided only by stars, winds, currents, and clouds, they crossed over 2,000 miles of ocean and settled the Hawaiian Islands.

The first settlers are believed to have arrived from the Marquesas, sometime before the fifth century A.D. They were followed by subsequent migrations from Tahiti in the eleventh century. For some reason, contact between the two societies then ceased, and Hawai'i became the most isolated inhabited group of islands in the world. Repeated sailing expeditions across the Pacific and regular "Manila Galleon" runs apparently failed to find the Islands until Cook's arrival.

Shortly after Cook's visit, Kamehameha, a young chieftain of a district on the island of Hawai'i, began a campaign of conquest. Assisted by Western advisers and their technology, including cannons and warships, he subdued all the Islands but Kaua'i, which he brought under his control by negotiation. In 1810, for the first time, all the Hawaiian Islands were united under one ruler.

In 1820, a group of New England missionaries arrived in the Islands, just after the Hawaiian people had repudiated their own ancient religion. The missionaries gradually converted most of the Hawaiian people to Christianity, including a large segment of the *ali'i,* or ruling class. Over the years, the influence of the missionaries and their descendants resulted in increasing American social, political, and economic control of the Islands. The Hawaiian Kingdom continued as an independent nation under the successors of Kamehameha until 1893, when it was overthrown by a coup headed primarily by influential American businessmen. The leaders of the coup were interested in bringing Hawai'i under the American flag to avoid customs duties on Hawaiian exports, particularly sugar. At first, the U.S. government did not look favorably upon the overthrow of the Hawaiian monarchy. But the Spanish-American War changed American perspectives in the Pacific. With the Philippines now a U.S. territory, the strategic location of Hawai'i became obvious, and in 1898 the former island kingdom was annexed by the United States. Administered as a territory for 61 years, Hawai'i became the fiftieth state of the union on 21 August 1959.

POPULATION. The population of the Hawaiian Islands in 1990 stood at 1,031,000. Of this total, 840,000, or just over 81 percent, reside on the island of O'ahu, the site of Honolulu, the state capital and its largest city. Hawai'i is the only state in the union in which Caucasians are not a majority of the population. In fact, no racial group can claim that distinction. Hawai'i is a society of minorities. Caucasians are, however, the largest minority, with 33.4 percent of the population. They are followed by persons of Japanese ancestry with 22.3 percent, Filipino 15.2 percent, Hawaiian and mixed Hawaiian 12.5 percent, Chinese 6.2 percent, other Asian-Pacific 5.6 percent, and all others about 5 percent. If you should find these figures at variance with some that you read in another source, it is because Hawai'i is a demographer's nightmare. A woman named Sarah Wong may be more than half Caucasian, and Charles Smith can be half Hawaiian. Bernice Bishop, whose estate funds the Kamehameha Schools, was pure Hawaiian, but many persons with Hawaiian names have more Caucasian, Chinese, or other blood in their veins than Hawaiian.

INDUSTRY. It should come as no surprise that tourism is the number one industry in Hawai'i. The second largest source of income to the state is federal government spending, primarily for defense. Next is agriculture, with sugar leading the way, followed by pineapple, livestock, flowers and nursery products, and macadamia nuts.

COST OF LIVING. Hawai'i has the unenviable distinction of having the highest cost of living of any state in the nation, and as a camper you will feel its sting in the grocery stores and when buying gas. On Kaua'i in 1993, for example, where prices are highest because of its distance from Honolulu, you would spend $5 or more for certain brands of dry cereal, $2.75 for a loaf of bread, and up to $2 for a gallon of gas. Prices on the other Islands aren't much better. Honolulu has the highest housing rents in the country and the highest median cost of a single family home, $360,000 in 1996. Compare that with Saginaw, Michigan, at $52,000! Unfortunately, family incomes are not on a par with the cost of living; Hawai'i places tenth in that category. In many families, both husband and wife must work to make ends meet, and increasing numbers of young couples are forced to live with their parents, frozen out of the high-cost housing market. Hawai'i, touted as a paradise for tourists, is at the other end of the line for many of its permanent residents.

STATE FLAG. The flag of the state of Hawai'i was created during the reign of King Kamehameha I and has flown over the kingdom, the republic, the territory, and now the state. Many visitors are surprised to see the Union Jack holding the place occupied by the field of stars on the American flag. This symbolizes the early ties of Hawai'i with Great Britain, through explorers such as Cook and Vancouver. Beginning at the top, eight alternating stripes of white, red, and blue represent the eight major islands of the chain.

STATE MOTTO. In 1843 a British Consul who had a grievance against the Hawaiian government persuaded the commander of a British warship in port in Honolulu to haul down the Hawaiian flag and proclaim Hawai'i a possession of Great Britain. In contrast to the actions of the American government some 55 years later, the British parliament nullified this illegal action and restored Hawaiian sovereignty. When the Hawaiian flag was once more raised, King Kamehameha III is reported to have said, *"Ua mau ke ea o ka 'āina i ka pono"* (The life of the land is perpetuated in righteousness).

STATE ANTHEM. "Hawai'i Pono'ī," written by King Kalākaua and set to music by the royal bandmaster, Henry Berger, was also the anthem of the kingdom and the territory.

STATE FLOWER. A native yellow hibiscus is the state flower. It grows throughout the Islands, and this particular variety is endemic to Hawai'i.

STATE TREE. The *kukui* tree is also known as the candlenut tree. Ancient Hawaiians impaled its oily nuts on a sharp stick and lit them to furnish light. The nuts also provided relishes and were used for medicinal purposes. Today, they are often made into highly polished leis and necklaces.

STATE MAMMAL. In selecting the humpback whale, the state legislature passed over a native resident in favor of a popular "tourist." Whales only spend a short time in Hawaiian waters every year. Although everybody loves whales, and visitors and residents alike enjoy whale watching, a more deserving candidate for the honor might be the Hawaiian monk seal, a full-time resident and one of only two native mammals.

STATE FISH. If you can't say *humuhumunukunukuāpua'a,* just call it a rectangular triggerfish, although that will mark you as a *malihini* (newcomer).

STATE BIRD. The *nēnē,* a native of the Islands, is a variety of goose that has given up its aquatic environment and has traded its webbed feet for something more useful on dry land. It is the largest land bird in Hawai'i. Driven almost to extinction by hunters and animal predators, the *nēnē* is now protected by law. To restore their numbers, they are being raised in captivity and released in suitable environments. One problem resulting from this program is that they seem to remember who raised them and tend to hang around where people are. At places such as the campgrounds on Haleakalā, you may be followed by *nēnē* looking for a handout, instead of fending for themselves in the wild, which is the way things were intended.

The Outdoor Environment and the Camper

Camping in Hawai'i is a year-round experience. Campgrounds can be found on beautiful sandy beaches or rocky, shoreline cliffs; in low, lush valleys or on high mountain slopes; in dense rain forests or dry, open deserts; in green meadows or black, lava-covered fields; at sea level or well over 13,000 feet. You can pitch your tent at a campground with other campers that contains facilities such as rest rooms, showers, dishwashing facilities, and barbeque grills or opt for a primitive campsite in the backcountry with no facilities, far removed from any other human being. It is also possible to stay in low-cost cabins or lodges, some with their own kitchens and bathrooms, others with centralized, shared facilities. The choice is yours.

In Hawai'i, there is a campground for everyone and for every purpose. From one or more of the over 120 official camping spots, it is possible to swim, snorkel, scuba dive, bodysurf, board surf, windsurf, fish, beachcomb, hike, hunt, or just lie around and enjoy the magnificent scenery. This book will introduce you to all of them, and this chapter will provide you with information that will make your camping experience in the Islands safe and enjoyable.

The comments about plants, wildlife, racial problems, safety, and so forth, are not intended to cover everything you might want to know. There are many good books and other references that deal with these subjects in detail.

THE CLIMATE AND THE CAMPER

The season of the year is not a factor in camping in Hawai'i, except that a bit more rain can be expected during the winter months. Campers in Hawai'i must be prepared for rain at any time of the year, including the possibility of a tropical downpour or even an occasional hurricane. Although there have been more than 100 hurricanes in Hawaiian waters in the last 40 years, only five have caused extensive damage. The latest, however, 'Iniki, devastated Kaua'i in September 1992, and although most of the island has recovered, as of May 1996 four major hotels remain closed due to its effects. Earthquakes, which occur almost exclusively on the island of Hawai'i, are usually related to volcanic activity. Even rarer is the tsunami, erroneously called a tidal wave. The last one occurred in 1975. In the past they have caused heavy damage and loss of life, but a worldwide and local warning system is now in place, which will minimize danger to people. Flash floods can occur in many otherwise gentle streams, particularly after a heavy rain. In 1987 five hikers died in three separate incidents while hiking to Sacred Falls on O'ahu when the normally low-flowing stream flooded, and in October 1993 part of a Boy Scout troop had to be rescued by helicopter from the same trail. A Boy Scout was killed by a flash flood in 1994 that caught his troop as they were hiking out of Koloa Gulch.

But if the season is not a factor in Hawaiian camping, elevation definitely is. Camping on a hot, sandy beach, where the temperature can reach 90 degrees, is a far cry from pitching a tent on the windy slopes of Mauna Kea, where the mercury frequently registers below freezing. If you plan to do both, you must be prepared for both. Listed below are a few of the things you should have for comfortable camping in Hawai'i. I will not bore you with a laundry list of everything you should bring along. I am assuming that you are a reasonably experienced camper and know what items are necessary for your own specific purposes.

CAMPING EQUIPMENT

TENT. Although at first glance the need for a tent at low altitude in Hawai'i might seem optional, it is an important item. It rains often in Hawai'i, and much of that rain falls at night. If you enjoy sleeping out under the stars, by all means do so. But have your tent pitched, so that if the heavens open up, you have someplace to go. A tent will protect you from mosquitoes and other unwelcome sharers of your bed, such as scorpions and centipedes. It will also provide shade from the hot sun on the beach and protection from wind and cold in the mountains.

The type of tent you choose depends on what you plan to do. If you plan a lot of backpacking, you will want the lightest one that will do the job. If you are going to "auto camp," that is, drive from one location to another, you can select a heavier, roomier model. In either event, your tent should include a rain fly or some protective cover that goes over an inner tent. It should also have a built-in floor and complete insect screening. I like a tent that opens at both ends, allowing for maximum ventilation on hot, sunny beaches, and can still be closed at one end or both in colder places.

SLEEPING BAG. If your camping will be limited to beaches and other low-altitude places, you will be able to get away with a light blanket, but if you plan to enjoy some of the beautiful upland forests of Hawai'i, a lightweight sleeping bag will keep you more comfortable. Warm enough to keep you comfortable in the higher regions, on the beach you can leave it unzipped or sleep on top of it.

GROUND PAD. Either a closed- or open-cell ground pad will let you sleep on hard and rocky ground, which exists in many of the campgrounds. It will also keep you dry in case a heavy rain soaks your tent floor. I prefer an open cell, such as a Therm-a-Rest, because it rolls up into a small package and is more comfortable than the closed-cell models. The lightest weight model should do.

STOVE. Firewood at campgrounds is often scarce or wet, and it is unlawful to chop down or take branches from living trees or shrubs. A camp stove will solve this problem and will also allow you to move the cooking operation inside your tent or under a park pavilion in the event of rain. Any good camp stove will work well in Hawai'i, even at the higher, colder altitudes, and white gasoline, propane, and kerosene are easily obtainable in hardware stores and many supermarkets. GAZ, and some other European cylinders, are readily available only at camping supply stores in Honolulu and can sometimes be found in similar stores on Maui, Hawai'i, and Kaua'i.

If you are backpacking, you will probably want a light, single-burner model. If you are auto camping, a larger two- or three-burner model might be your choice. I prefer a propane stove in either of the above situations. I am tired of fiddling with gas stoves that only have two settings—too hot and off. Also, I dislike carrying spillable, highly inflammable gasoline in my pack. Propane solves both problems very nicely. The flame adjusts perfectly, no priming is necessary, and there is nothing to spill. You will have to pack out the spent cylinder, but you have to carry out your empty gasoline container, so what's the difference?

Another reason for considering propane is that ticket agents on interisland airlines frequently refuse to allow a stove with an attached fuel container to go on board the aircraft, even if the container is empty. The same thing applies to your empty fuel bottles, if they find them. A propane stove is not affected, because it does not have a permanently attached fuel source. If you are doing interisland camping, you will need to buy and discard your propane cylinders on each Island, as it is unlawful to transport propane, butane, GAZ, or any other type of pressurized fuel container on a commercial aircraft.

INSECT REPELLENT. I never used to believe that insects favor certain people over others. But after leading hundreds of hikers and campers into the backcountry of Hawai'i, I have changed my mind, at least as far as Hawaiian mosquitoes are concerned. Time and again, while sitting beside a forested pool, I have seen some hikers swat furiously, while others beside them are completely unbothered. Whether it has to do with blood type, body odor, or the kind of shaving lotion or perfume they are wearing, I have no idea. My only advice is to "know thyself" and come prepared.

Mosquitoes are no worse in Hawai'i than in most other places. They are nowhere near as bad as in Alaska or parts of New Jersey. Mosquitoes do not usually bother hikers on the move, they are rarely found in beach campgrounds, and they diminish sharply at altitudes above 4,000 feet. But they are apt to descend on people stopped for lunch in a deep, wet forest or buzz annoyingly around your head at night, unless the campfire is smoky. Unfortunately, I usually find that if it is too smoky for them, it is too smoky for me. Any good repellent of your choice should keep them away, and a tent with a floor and bug screen will assure you of a good night's rest.

WATER PURIFICATION. Most official campgrounds that have facilities provide water that does not need to be treated before drinking. If it does need treatment, you will be told, by signs or notices and sometimes on your camping permit. Water at undeveloped campsites, and in the backcountry, needs to be boiled or treated before use. The streams and waterfalls of Hawai'i, crystal clear and rushing down from uninhabited mountains, may seem perfectly pure. But even without human contamination, there are birds, goats, and pigs upstream, and none of them is particularly concerned about sanitation. Giardia and leptospirosis have both been found in Hawaiian streams (see below for more on leptospirosis).

Boiling is probably the best method of purification, because it does not impart a foreign taste to the water. But it is often impractical and it uses fuel. Ceramic-type water filters are available from camping suppliers, but they are relatively bulky and may not be effective against all organisms. Chemical treatment is easy, but requires a waiting period. Halazone and chlorine, long-time standbys, do not offer complete protection from today's contaminants. Iodine does, but some people cannot stand its bitter taste. Iodine, a necessary nutritional ingredient, is also a poison, which makes some people leery, but after all, that's why it kills the bugs.

I use iodine crystals in solution, because I find the pills too slow to dissolve. Another advantage of the crystal solution is that a 2-ounce bottle seems to last forever. When the solution runs low, you simply refill the bottle with water, the crystals on the bottom dissolve the appropriate amount of iodine, and you have a new batch. Your local druggist may be able to prepare this for you, but REI puts one out called Polar Pure, which is good for 2,000 quarts of water and comes with directions and a particle trap to prevent the crystals from getting into your canteen. The iodine taste can be masked with Tang, iced tea, or lemonade powder.

SUN PROTECTION. Simply said: bring it and use it. Use it on the beach, in the open fields, on the ridge lines, and in the high country. Remember, Hawai'i is in the tropics, at the same latitude as Mexico City. The air over Hawai'i is some of the clearest in the nation. Although that is a definite plus, it also means that there is less haze and smog to filter out the rays that cause sunburn. And even though it may seem cold on the slopes of Mauna Loa, you may be closer to the sun than you have ever been before. Sunscreen lotions should not be relied on exclusively, especially during all-day hikes on a sunny day or at high altitude. A wide-brimmed hat should be part of any outing, and a long-sleeve shirt and long pants afford total protection when it is needed.

WHAT'S DANGEROUS OUT THERE?

Although the natural environment of Hawai'i is more benign and less threatening than most, there are a few things in the wilderness that can cause injury or illness if you are not aware of them.

PLANTS. There are no poisonous contact plants in Hawai'i, such as poison ivy. There are plants that are poisonous if eaten, but I give you credit for having enough sense not to eat something with which you are not familiar. Lots of mushrooms grow in Hawai'i, many sprouting after a rain. Unless you are an expert, leave them alone. It is a good idea to exercise care when cutting a branch for skewering food over a fire. Choose something you know, and avoid plants with milky sap. Later on, in a section about living off the land, I will list fruits that grow wild in Hawai'i that are safe to eat.

A particularly dangerous plant, and one that may cause confusion, is the apple of Sodom, a low, prickly bush with a tomatolike fruit that is highly poisonous. How to tell the apple of Sodom from the wild tomato that grows prolifically in Hawaiian wild places? The apple of Sodom is a bush with small thorns, and the fruit looks like an over-sized cherry tomato. It is green until ripe, when it turns yellow. The wild tomato grows like a vine, it is not prickly, and its fruit is smaller, about as big as a large huckleberry. If you have any doubts, don't eat it.

REPTILES. There are no snakes in Hawai'i, and most mainland hikers and campers breathe a sigh of relief when hearing this information. Although few residents would agree, Hawai'i might have benefited from the introduction of certain species of harmless snakes. The rodent-eating northeastern king snake might have been a better choice than the mongoose, which was brought in to combat rats in the cane fields. The mongoose ignored the rats, but succeeded in virtually wiping out every species of ground-nesting bird on all the Islands except Kaua'i, where it was never introduced. The snakes might have also attacked the birds, but at least they would have gone after the rats too. No reptiles in Hawai'i are dangerous.

ANIMALS. None of the wild animals in Hawai'i is dangerous to humans. Those big enough to cause a problem, such as goats and pigs, will stay away from you if given any chance at all. In some areas, such as Kalalau Valley on Kaua'i, goats are becoming used to people and occasionally will browse close by. They are harmless and can be frightened off easily by sudden movement or shouts. Unless you go hunting or try really hard, you will probably never see a wild pig. The closest you will get is evidence of their rooting and wallowing along some of the trails.

INSECTS AND OTHER ARTHROPODS. Black widow and brown widow spiders have been reported in Hawai'i, but I have never seen one, and no one I know has ever seen one. The black widows are shiny black, about the size of a penny, and have an orange-red hourglass marking on their underside. Their webs are said to be built below knee level. I have hiked hundreds of miles on Hawaiian trails, brushed through hundreds of spider webs, and have never been bitten by any kind of spider. I refuse to worry about it or wear long pants where shorts are more comfortable. Most spiders will run when their webs are destroyed by someone blundering into them.

Hawai'i has the usual insects that can give painful stings (bees, wasps, yellowjackets, etc.), but these are not dangerous except to persons allergic to their toxins. Scorpion stings and centipede bites are more serious (and more painful), but again, they are not usually dangerous. There are ticks in Hawai'i, but they rarely attach themselves to humans and do not carry Lyme disease. By far, the worst outdoor insect pests in the Islands are mosquitoes, which can make life unpleasant not only for the camper, but for residents as well. Many a Hawai'i householder, enjoying a gin and tonic on his lanai, is forced inside or behind screens as soon as the sun goes down.

MICROORGANISMS. Giardia has found its way from the mainland to Hawai'i, although cases have been few. The organism, which causes diarrhea and nausea, is ingested by drinking untreated water from streams, ponds, or other sources. Boiling or iodine treatment prevent infection.

Leptospirosis is a bacterial disease that can be transmitted from animals to humans via fresh water or muddy soil; the organisms can enter the body through an open cut, as well as by drinking. Boiling or treating with iodine renders drinking water safe, but it is still possible to get the disease by swimming in water where the organisms are present if there is a break in the skin. Muddy water is more likely to harbor the disease organisms, but they can be present in clear ponds and running streams. Symptoms occur anywhere from 2 to 20 days after exposure and resemble influenza: chills, fever, headache, diarrhea, weakness, and vomiting. Most cases of the disease are mild, and people usually recover without treatment. However, severe symptoms, such as stiff neck, backache, blood in the urine, or jaundice, require immediate medical treatment.

Ciguatera is a highly toxic organism sometimes found in fish that feed on algae growing on coral reefs. These colorful reef fish are easily identifiable, but it is also possible to get the disease by eating larger fish that have fed on an algae eater carrying the organism. Symptoms are vomiting, weakness, and numbness, and immediate medical treatment is required.

SEA LIFE. Shark attacks do occur in Hawai'i, including some fatal ones. Until recently, they were amazingly few, considering the large number of people in the water, the fair number of sharks, and the year-round nature of water sports activity. Before 1991, there had not been a documented shark fatality in over 30 years. But then, in that year, there were three attacks, including one death—a Maui woman who was killed while snorkeling off her beachfront home near Olowalu.

In 1992, there were five attacks, including two fatalities. In February, a surfer disappeared on the north shore of O'ahu. Later, his body board was found with a large missing section, consistent with a shark bite. In March, a surfer was attacked near Hā'ena, Kaua'i, but escaped with foot injuries. In October, a 14-foot tiger shark tore a large chunk from a surfer's board at Laniākea, O'ahu, but the surfer escaped unharmed. In November, a bodyboarder was killed by a large shark in shallow water close to shore, off Kea'au Beach Park, O'ahu. And, in late December, a shark attacked a surfer at Chun's Reef, on the north shore of O'ahu. Although his board was destroyed, the surfer escaped with only minor injuries. There were three shark attacks in 1993. In March a surfer was attacked and seriously bitten on the legs at Keanae, Maui. In June another surfer suffered leg injuries in an attack off Mālaekahana State Recreation Area on O'ahu. A third surfer received leg injuries at Wailua Beach on Kaua'i in November. As a result of these incidents, the state instituted a program of selective shark hunting in waters off the most popular beaches on O'ahu. Several tiger sharks, some over 12 feet long, were caught. Attacks seem to be on the decline, with two each in 1994 and 1995, and one as of the end of March 1996.

Various reasons have been put forth for this sudden increase in shark encounters. One theory is that heavy offshore fishing, especially by long-lines boats, has depleted the food chain, requiring the large predators to seek prey closer to shore. Another relates to a previous state shark control program, in which the state regularly fished large sharks out of Hawaiian waters. This program was ended in the mid-1970s, and the theory is that since then shark populations have increased, and they are competing aggressively for food.

Shark behavior is not fully understood, but it is suspected that shark attacks on humans in Hawai'i are most likely a case of mistaken identity. A standard surfboard may look like a seal to a shark, and a person on a body board bears a strong resemblance to a turtle when seen from underwater. Both of these animals are eaten regularly by large sharks. If you wish to minimize the chance of an encounter with a shark, do not swim in murky water, stay close to shore, swim with quiet strokes, avoid thrashing activity, and do not spear fish.

Jelly fish, including the Portuguese man-of-war, are frequent visitors to Hawaiian beaches, and they can inflict a painful sting, even when washed up on the shore. The only defense is to avoid them.

Sea urchins can be painful if their spines penetrate the skin, and some varieties can sting if the spines are merely touched. They are usually found along rocky shores and on shallow reefs.

PERSONAL SAFETY

Do not hike alone, and do not swim alone in the ocean, especially at deserted beaches or where there are no lifeguards. Obey beach warning signs. Hawaiian waters can be hazardous, especially during the winter months, but at other times of the year as well. Be particularly alert along shoreline reefs where waves are breaking. Never turn your back on the ocean in such locations. Use caution in crossing streams, especially during or after a heavy rain. Many usually gentle streams are subject to flash floods.

Do not bushwhack or leave established trails. In most places, you will not be able to do this even if you try. The backcountry of Hawai'i is rough, steep, and tangled with dense vegetation. Deep gullies and fissures can be completely hidden from view by heavy growth, revealing themselves only after a serious fall. Do not attempt to rock climb anywhere in Hawai'i. The volcanic rock is soft and crumbly and often gives way even under light pressure from hands or feet.

IF YOU BECOME LOST

How can anyone get lost on a small, populated island? A veteran hiker with many years experience in the Islands gives this answer. "People don't get lost, they get *stuck*. They get into a position where they can't go up, can't go down, and can't move in any direction. In a few days they're pig food." This will probably not happen to you in Hawai'i if you stay on marked trails. It has a good chance of happening if you don't. A hiker disappeared when he left the trail on Mauna Loa to take a shortcut. Two experienced hikers attempting to make their way up Mount Wai'ale'ale on Kaua'i in 1990 have never been found. A hiker disappeared in uninhabited Wailau Valley on Moloka'i in March 1993, and two hikers vanished in the Ko'olau Mountains on O'ahu in 1995. The fire department is frequently called to rescue hikers marooned on steep cliffs or ledges. This will not happen to you if you stay on established trails. However, if in spite of your best efforts, you do get lost, it is probably just a temporary condition. As anywhere, it is important to remain calm and think clearly. If you are in the mountains, try to make your way downhill. If you can see the ocean, head for it. Almost all settlement is along the coast. Try to follow a ridge line, rather than a stream. Most streams in the mountains drop in a series of waterfalls, making them difficult or impossible to follow, and their sides are steep. A compass may not be reliable in certain areas, because of the high iron content of Hawaiian rocks and soils. If your way is blocked by an impassable or dangerous descent, retrace your steps and try to find another route. Stay calm and do not panic. Remember, you are not far from help, and there is nothing out there that can hurt you. No wild animals, poisonous snakes, or cannibals, and the weather is not a problem except at the highest altitudes. If you must spend the night in the woods, it may be uncomfortable, but it won't be life threatening. The environment of Hawai'i is one of the most benign in the world.

LIVING OFF THE LAND

Some people, and some publications, will tell you that it is easy to live off the land in Hawai'i. Do not believe it. If you trudge off into the wilderness without visiting the grocery store first, expecting to find your food by hunting and gathering, you will wind up being one hungry camper. Edible goodies do grow in the wild in Hawai'i, but they are not always where you want them, when you want them, or in the quantity you need.

Huge, old mango trees in Hanakāpī'ai Valley on Kaua'i literally carpet the ground with luscious fruit for a few weeks in June or July, but the rest of the year the ground is bare. Many trails are lined with blackberry and thimbleberry bushes, but few people are content to make a meal of them. Mountain streams contain tasty freshwater prawns, but they don't often jump into your net. Shoreline fishing can provide a feast or hours of casting with nothing to show for it except recreation.

Listed below are most of the edibles that you might find growing wild in Hawai'i. Many of them escaped from somebody's garden, and they are apt to appear anywhere, sometimes in the most unlikely places. The quantity varies. Usually it will be a snack, occasionally a meal, only rarely a steady supply.

Avocado are usually found only near former dwellings or settlements. Only the old trees bear fruit. Although a new tree will grow in the wild from the large avocado seed, the Hawaiian variety will not fruit. Fruit comes only from grafted stock.

Several varieties of bananas grow wild, usually in valleys and gulches, in well-watered areas between 1,500 and 2,000 feet. You will rarely find a ripe, yellow one, but the green ones can be cooked.

Banana poka is not a banana, but a member of the passion fruit family. This tasty, but seed-filled fruit grows on vines, mostly in upland forests, such as Kōke'e, on Kaua'i. The fruit is cucumber shaped, but smaller, and with a much softer skin. It is considered a pest, because it crowds out native growth in many areas. Dispose of seeds where they cannot germinate.

Blackberry is a rampant pest, which is endangering Hawaiian native plants by taking over their habitat and crowding them out. Blackberries grow mostly along trails, where hikers' boots and nibbling habits distribute the seed. (Don't feel too guilty, birds do the same thing.)

Breadfruit are sometimes found in low-elevation forests, but the large, green, clustery fruit of this tree must be baked or otherwise cooked.

Citrus trees (orange, tangerine, lemon, lime, and grapefruit), when found, can usually be relied upon for a fruit or two any time of the year. They grow almost anywhere except at higher elevations.

Coconut palms grow most often near the seashore. Some low-growing varieties bear fruit at reachable levels. For the taller trees, fruit can often be found on the ground. Opening the husk and the inner nut requires a knack I can't help you with.

Guava trees are very prolific. Guava is rapidly taking over in secondary growth areas and is making inroads into low-elevation forests. The ripe fruit is yellow and about the size of a large lemon. Its pink interior is loaded with seeds. Unfortunately, the customary way of eating guava, sucking out the interior and spitting out the seeds, produces more guava trees. We already have more than enough.

Hawaiian raspberries *('akala)* are very rare fruits that deserve mention as one of only two native fruits on this list. They grow at higher elevations, usually at about 4,000 feet. The fruit is dark pink and resembles a standard raspberry, but is much larger, 1 to 2 inches. The only accessible place I have seen these plants in abundance is around the cabin in Palikū Campground on Maui. They also grow in some of the *kīpuka* along the misty Pu'u 'Ō'ō Trail on the island of Hawai'i.

Java plum is a dark purple fruit, about the size of a large cherry. The tree can usually be spotted at lower elevations by the purple splotches made by fallen fruit at the base of the tree. It was also used as a dye by the Hawaiians, and if the juice gets on your hands or clothing, you'll know why.

Mangoes are found almost exclusively in formerly inhabited areas. They are the most delicious item growing out there. Most wild trees are so large that fruit can only be harvested from the ground, and the fruit flies and the ants will probably get there before you. But you should still be able to find some untouched fruit, and if you don't mind sharing, the affected portions can be cut away. Sadly, the mango season is short, 2 or 3 weeks, in June or July.

Mountain apples fruit seasonally. This relatively mild, but juicy fruit resembles a small apple of the Delicious variety. It grows in wooded areas at lower elevations, usually along or near streams, such as in the valley leading to Sacred Falls on O'ahu. Most trees are too high or slender to be climbed, and the fruit usually must be shaken down or harvested from the ground. A strong, vinegary smell in the woods means that mountain apples are rotting on the ground. Look around for some good ones or start shaking the trees.

'Ōhelo berry is the other native plant in this list. The ancient Hawaiians considered this berry sacred to Pele, the fire goddess, because it grows prolifically in the vicinity of Kīlauea Volcano. This 1- to 2-foot shrub is a cool-weather plant; therefore it does not grow at low altitudes in Hawai'i. It is found on Maui, particularly on the upper slopes of Haleakalā, and is seen occasionally on O'ahu and Kaua'i, above 3,000 feet. Related to the huckleberry, it is about the same size, but its color is yellowish orange to pale red. It has a mild, semisweet flavor.

Papayas are easily grown from seed and can often be found near wilderness campsites, up to 1,200 feet, where hikers have eaten the fruit and tossed the seeds. The fruit is ripe when it begins to turn yellow. You will rarely see it in deep forests, because it likes sunny locations.

Passion fruit is not an aphrodisiac, but was named by someone who thought its flower resembled Christ's crown of thorns. The fruit can be either dark purple or yellow when ripe and has a hard rind, which must be cut or cracked to get at the juicy, but seed-filled interior. This fruit is usually eaten in the same manner as the guava (see above), with the same undesirable effect.

Some excellent wild plums grow in Kōke‘e State Park, on the Kaluapuhi Trail and along the road between the Kalalau and Pu‘u o Kila lookouts. Fruiting season is June and July, but get there quickly or the local residents will beat you to them. Plums can also be found in Polipoli Springs State Recreation Area on Maui, along the Plum Trail, particularly where it intersects with the Redwood and the Boundary trails. Here, they ripen a little later.

Strawberry guavas are much tastier than their lowland cousin. This small, red fruit usually grows on a bush, rather than a tree. It is common along higher, mountain trails, where it provides juicy snacks for tired, thirsty hikers. Regrettably, like its cousin, it endangers native plants.

Taro was cultivated as a staple in the Hawaiian diet. Wild taro grows along streams and in marshy areas. Both the root and the leaves are edible, but they must be very well cooked. The plant, especially the leaves, contains oxalic acid, which has a paralyzing effect on the mouth unless broken down by prolonged cooking.

Thimbleberry is a light red berry, resembling a raspberry, that grows on thorny bushes, usually along trails. It has a slightly sweet, bland flavor.

The wild tomato is so small (about the size of a huckleberry) that it takes dozens of them to make the equivalent of a normal sized fruit. Unfortunately, you will rarely find that amount on one plant. You might get enough to lightly garnish a salad. Warning! Beware of the poisonous apple of Sodom (see the section on Plants, above).

Watercress grows along the edges of streams and pools. If you find a supply, it will usually be enough for a good salad.

It is possible to catch both freshwater and salt-water fish to augment your diet and with surprisingly basic equipment. Where the fish are, and how best to catch them, is covered in the sections describing individual camping places. Warning! Do not eat reef fish, which can be infected with ciguatera, a sometimes deadly parasite. Reef fish are generally small, very colorful, and look like they belong in an aquarium.

Prawns (freshwater) are delicious, easy to cook, and almost worth the effort it takes to catch them, particularly if you have lots of time, with nothing better to do. I once hiked past a young woman sitting beside a stream in Kalalau Valley, at a point where the water ran over a wide, flat rock. She was waiting for the prawns to come by. When I returned, about 6 hours later, she had caught eight, or just over one per hour. A better method is to use a face mask, enter the ponded areas of the stream, and search under rocks and in crevices with a gloved hand or small gig. Even then, it can take hours of patient seeking and probing in cold water to provide a meal, if the little critters are around.

There is a story that years ago, a Frenchman living in Hawai'i and homesick for the taste of escargot imported a batch of snails from his native land. Some of these delicacies managed to escape his table, and their descendants now roam free. The story may be true, but the snail you are most likely to encounter in the Islands is the giant African snail, imported from Japan in 1936. Unfortunately, these are too large for the standard escargot platter. Most snails prefer to hang around populated areas, munching happily in suburban gardens. However, you may find them in fields after a rain. But beware of eating them, because they can harbor a dangerous parasite.

The Other Side of Paradise

As much as you might like to believe it, and as much as the tourism brochures might like to convince you, everything in Hawai'i is not sweetness and light. Hawai'i has its problems, some of them similar to those on the mainland, others unique to its own special status. Being aware of the important ones will help you avoid possible unpleasant situations and enhance your vacation with a deeper understanding of where you have been.

THE ALOHA SPIRIT

Hawai'i has long been touted as a place where people of many races live in understanding and harmony with each other. The aloha spirit can perhaps be described as a polite, friendly, helpful attitude in relationships between all classes of people: employer and employee, sales clerk and customer, bus driver and passenger, tourist and resident. It was alive and well when I first came to the Islands in the mid-1960s, and it is still alive today, although maybe not quite as well. It is under strain caused by population pressures, crowded living, gridlock traffic, and a murderously high cost of living. Responsible, also, is the increasing pressure of tourism, which brings almost seven times the state's population to its shores every year. Although residents of Hawai'i are well aware that their economy would collapse without tourism, it was a lot easier to show the aloha spirit to everyone when Hawai'i hosted the thousands of tourists who came by boat, rather than the millions who now come by plane. But it is still out there. You just may have to look a little harder and show some of it yourself.

THE RACIAL ISSUE

As stated earlier, no racial group holds a majority share of the population in Hawai'i. We are all minorities, and the main reason for racial harmony stems from that fact. No majority group can dictate to the rest. People must cooperate and respect each other's views if they are to get anything done, politically, economically, or socially. In general, the races get along quite well in Hawai'i. But there is one group in which dissatisfaction is evident, and it is a dissatisfaction that has become more prevalent in recent years. It has its basis in economic, social, and historic issues.

When foreigners first began arriving in these Islands after Cook's visit, they were welcomed warmly by the Hawaiians and accepted freely into their society. It was to cost them dearly. Western diseases, from which they had no immunity, caused thousands of deaths. American and other foreign businessmen gradually accumulated vast tracts of land, either by purchase or by marrying into Hawaiian royal families. Large numbers of workers from China and Japan were imported to work on the sugar plantations, turning Hawaiians into a minority in their own land. And then, in 1893, a group of influential Caucasians overthrew the Hawaiian monarchy, an act that eventually led to annexation by the United States.

Today, persons of Hawaiian and part-Hawaiian ancestry make up only about 12 percent of the population. On average, they have the lowest incomes, suffer the poorest health and shortest life expectancy, and live in the poorest neighborhoods. Over the years, they have watched helplessly as the land, the money, the businesses, and the political power have been taken over by others. It is hard for them to accept, considering that they used to own the place. If they occasionally strike out with rudeness or violence, at least it is clear where they are coming from.

That said, there is another side to the coin. Pure Hawaiians represent less than 1 percent of the population. Many part-Hawaiians have a very small percentage of Hawaiian blood, but the trend is to identify with that portion, because that is where the action is. Members of other racial groups sometimes find it difficult to feel sympathy for a person who is 95 percent Filipino and who is demanding his or her ancient "Hawaiian" rights. And it is not unknown for persons with no Hawaiian blood at all to get on the bandwagon, based upon racial and color similarity, economic status, or social orientation.

What does all this mean to the camper? If you use state and county campgrounds, you will share them not only with other visiting campers, but with local residents as well. This is particularly true of beach campsites, where local families often come to swim, picnic, and fish. Many of these people will be part-Hawaiian. The average tourist rarely sees a Hawaiian except as an entertainer, a tour guide, or a bus driver. You, on the other hand, will be living with them, sharing rest rooms, showers, and other facilities. If you have read the above paragraphs, you already know more than the average tourist does about the people, and you will be able to interact with them from a position of knowledge and understanding. Most local people are friendly and outgoing. They want you to feel welcome and at home. Common sense, courtesy, and the information furnished above should help you enjoy your relationships with them.

CRIME

Unfortunately, there are still rascals in paradise. Hawai'i suffers from the same ills of civilization that afflict other parts of the world. Although the crime rate here is lower than the national average, crime does occur, as any scanning of the daily newspapers will show. Campers and hikers have been victims in the past and probably will continue to be. But the overall incidence is low, and the individual camper, exercising common sense and following the advice below, need not ruin his vacation worrying about his safety or the security of his belongings.

The closer a campground is to a population center, the higher the risk of an incident. The risk decreases the farther away you get from such areas. It is not a good idea to camp alone. It is especially unwise for a young woman to camp alone—in Hawai'i or anywhere else, for that matter. Do not pitch your tent in the vicinity of a group of noisy, boisterous young people, especially where alcohol is being consumed, unless, of course, you intend to join the party and accept the inherent risks.

Never leave valuables unattended at a campsite or in a vehicle, even if it is locked. A good rule of thumb is never leave anything unprotected that would ruin your vacation if stolen. Money, credit cards, passports, airline tickets, cameras, binoculars, and such should always be carried with you. On the other hand, I have camped with groups for years all over the Islands and have left the campsite for the day with tents pitched and sleeping bags, pads, toilet kits, and so forth inside. They have never been disturbed. But if your camping gear is especially valuable, you may want to bundle it up and put it in a locked vehicle, if you have that option. It will be a little harder to get at that way. Some folks pack up their camping gear in a large plastic "garbage" bag and hide it in a bushy spot in the woods for the day, picking it up upon their return.

MARIJUANA

A lot has been written and said about the growing of marijuana in Hawai'i and the danger it poses to hikers and campers who might stumble upon fields of it accidentally. There are even rumors of hikers being shot at under such circumstances. It is difficult to sort fact from fiction. For years many people accepted the statistic that marijuana was the state's largest cash crop, although it was obviously impossible to verify such a claim, because growers are understandably reluctant to provide figures. If it was ever true, it is no longer so today.

According to some police officials "Green Harvest," an ongoing cooperative effort of several law-enforcement agencies, has done much to end large-scale pot growing in the Islands. At its peak, it was not uncommon for up to 20,000 plants to be uprooted in a single day, and in 1987 alone, almost 2 million plants were destroyed statewide. In 1990, marijuana worth $7.7 billion was destroyed, according to the State of Hawaii Data Book, 1991. Former major marijuana growers pretty much agree that "Green Harvest," especially with its use of the helicopter, has put them out of business. Some of them are now directing their efforts toward making marijuana legal.

Certainly, pot is still grown in the Islands, but it is mostly for personal use—small patches, in out-of-the-way places, safe from discovery by the ubiquitous whirlybird. Big growing operations have been forced indoors, but even these are gradually being discovered and eliminated. A 1-acre warehouse was found in October, 1989, and $1 million worth of marijuana was discovered in a converted lava tube in January, 1992. Obviously, this kind of activity does not pose a threat to the hiker or camper.

I have camped at or visited every site mentioned in this book and hiked most Hawai'i trails, and have only come upon marijuana once. It was in 1983, on the island of Moloka'i, in a valley accessible only by private boat, or over a long, unmaintained trail. You probably will not be going there, and if you do, the pot will almost certainly be long gone. If you should come upon a marijuana patch, the sensible thing to do is make a wide swing around it or, if that is not possible, go back the way you came.

HOMELESS PERSONS

Hawai'i has its share of the homeless, perhaps more than its share, because of its benign weather and equally benign welfare system. Homeless families sometimes can be found at official campgrounds, particularly those on the beach. The attitude of government officials toward this situation swings back and forth from toleration to crackdown. It seems to depend on how many homeless are there and how many complaints there have been. All county and state campgrounds on O'ahu must be vacated on Wednesday and Thursday, for cleanup purposes, but also to get the homeless to move. It doesn't always work out that way.

At some campgrounds it is possible to share use with homeless families, but at others it is decidedly uncomfortable. Some parks are so large that a few homeless families present no more impact than any other group of campers. Others are so crowded with the homeless that camping in their midst would prove to be anything but a vacation. In the description of individual campgrounds I point out which these are. A good way to get updated information is to ask about the situation when applying for your camping permits.

CAMPGROUND MAINTENANCE

The upkeep of campground facilities in Hawai'i runs the gamut from excellent to awful. It is sad, but true, that some of the most beautifully located campgrounds in the state suffer from dirty, graffiti-smeared rest rooms, broken benches and picnic tables, missing shower heads, water faucets without handles, empty light-bulb sockets, barbeque grills without grates, overflowing garbage containers, and other such unpleasantries. The best-maintained facilities are usually those operated by the federal and state authorities, and the worst are those under county administration. This is, of course, a generality, and exceptions will be found. Individual descriptions of each campground will make you aware of such conditions.

A WORD ABOUT RECREATIONAL VEHICLES

Some camping guides, including one by a major publisher, list certain campgrounds in Hawai'i as having hookups for trailers and recreational vehicles. Their authors have obviously never been here. No campground in the state has hookups for RVs. Almost all of them have water, and some have electricity, but none has the type of fixtures that would allow hookup to a vehicle, and none has anything even resembling a dump station.

The typical RV and trailer parks common throughout the mainland are unknown in Hawai'i. Some campgrounds permit vehicle camping; others do not (this guide will tell you which are which). Where permitted, the vehicle is almost always restricted to the regular parking area and not allowed onto the grassy space where tent campers are located. If you are rich enough to bring an RV to Hawai'i, you will have to haul water from a central faucet, and it is illegal to run an extension cord from any outlet to your vehicle, even if the guy who has his boom box plugged in there would let you get away with it.

It is no longer possible to rent campers or trailers in Hawai'i. Some travel guides still say you can, but all of the cited operations have been out of business for years. Initially attractive to some tourists, rental campers eventually proved unable to compete with low-cost room/car packages offered by the hotels. You might be able to rent a camper from a private owner, but that would raise insurance and liability problems. The cost of shipping a large RV to Hawai'i is prohibitive. Most residents settle for a camper shell on a pickup bed or a Volkswagen pop-top.

The Language

Although it may seem obvious, and unnecessary to say so, the language of the Hawaiian Islands is English. There are still some visitors, mostly from Europe and Asia, who are not quite sure. The language you may hear being spoken by local residents is, sadly, not Hawaiian, but probably Japanese or Tagalog (Filipino) or even pidgin, a local patois that can sound foreign until you get used to it. Although Hawaiian has official status as a second language and is taught selectively in schools, it is rarely spoken in public and is understood by very few people. However, Hawaiian is still used in nearly all place names and most street names, and many Hawaiian words are used in daily speech. As in most guide books, I have included a list of those that will be helpful to you, especially as a camper. I have deliberately kept the list short. You can pick up additional words from other references or as you go along. Unlike many guide books, I have not included a list of pidgin words. Pidgin is an "insiders" language, spoken by a local fraternity of people who share certain cultural interests. Your attempt to speak it will not be appreciated, and you will sound foolish. Virtually everyone who speaks pidgin understands conventional English, and most can speak it.

PRONUNCIATION OF HAWAIIAN

On first impression, Hawaiian can look almost impossible to pronounce, but it is really simple, once you know the rules. Pronunciation of Hawaiian is certainly easier and more regular than English. The Hawaiian language has only twelve letters: the vowels a, e, i, o, u, and the consonants h, k, l, m, n, p, w. The consonants are pronounced like they are in English (except that w is sometimes pronounced as v), and the vowels are pronounced as they are in Spanish, rather than English. Thus,

a is pronounced as in f*a*ther
e is pronounced as in th*ey*
i is pronounced as in mach*i*ne
o is pronounced as in aut*o*
u is pronounced as in Z*u*lu

In addition, Hawaiian has four diphthongs:

au is pronounced as the *ow* in c*ow*
ae and ai are both pronounced like *eye*
ei is pronounced like the *ay* in d*ay*.

In general, all letters in Hawaiian are pronounced, and the accent falls on the next to the last syllable of a word. Vowels marked with macrons, such as in *nēnē* are somewhat longer than other vowels, and are always stressed. A glottal stop occurs in many Hawaiian words and is indicated by a reverse apostrophe (‘). The word *a‘ā* is thus pronounced in the manner of the English *oh-oh.*

The above rules are not infallible; exceptions do occur. But they will get you by. To learn more, you will need to consult a more detailed reference.

SOME USEFUL HAWAIIAN WORDS

‘a‘ā One of the two types of lava flows, *‘a‘ā* has a rough, clinkerlike appearance.

‘āina Land, earth.

ali‘i Chief, noble, member of the ruling class.

aloha The most used and abused word in the language. Its meanings are many. It is used as a greeting (hello, goodbye), and it can mean love, affection, compassion, mercy, pity. It is pronounced with the accent on the second syllable, never on the third. The worst abuse of the word, and its pronunciation, is the habit of tour guides and many entertainers of greeting a large group by shouting ah-lo-HA, drawing out the second syllable and barking the third. The group, or audience, then dutifully responds in unison, ah-lo-HA. This is garbage. Don't do it, and maybe the practice will die out, as it deserves to.

hala Also known as the pandanus in other parts of Polynesia, it was an important plant in Hawaiian culture. The leaf, or *lauhala,* had many uses, including weaving of hats and bowls.

hale House, structure.

haole Originally a foreigner, now a Caucasian, whether foreign or not.

heiau A temple or place of worship of the old Hawaiian religion. Nothing remains of most *heiau* today except their stone foundations, although some are being restored.

hukilau A community-effort net fishing party.

iki Little, such as Kīlauea Iki (Little Kīlauea).

imu A pit dug in the ground and lined with hot rocks to cook food, primarily *kālua* pig.

kahuna Priest, expert.

kai Sea, sea water.

kama'āina A native-born person or long-time resident.

kāne Male (Kāne, when capitalized, is the god of creation).

kapu Taboo, forbidden. When seen on a sign, it means keep out or do not touch.

kiawe A dry-area tree and a relative of mesquite. Used as fodder, for charcoal, for fuel, and to reforest dry, lowland areas.

kīpuka An island of vegetation surrounded by a lava flow.

koa An important native tree, used for making canoes in ancient Hawai'i and still used for bowls, furniture, and floors.

kokua Help, assistance.

Kona Leeward, particularly the leeward side of an island. Thus, Kona winds blow toward the leeward side, as opposed to the customary trade winds, which blow toward the windward side of the islands.

Ko'olau Windward; the windward side of an island.

kukui The state tree of Hawai'i; also called the candlenut tree.

lānai Porch, deck, veranda. Lāna'i, when capitalized, is the sixth largest of the Hawaiian Islands.

laulau Wrapping; food wrapped in ti leaves and baked.

lei Garland, necklace, or wreath, made of flowers, leaves, or shells.

local Obviously not a Hawaiian word, but it has such a specialized meaning in the Islands that you should be aware of it. A "local" person in Hawai'i is not simply a resident, but one who is a mixture of the races that have come to the Islands. Otherwise, the term is used as a modifier, as in "local *haole*."

lua Toilet, outhouse.

lū'au Feast.

mahalo Thank you.

makai Toward the sea. In Hawai'i, directions are frequently given in relation to a geographic reference. You may be told that where you want to go is "makai three blocks, then go Diamond Head two more blocks."

malihini Newcomer.

mauka Toward the mountains (see *makai* above).

mauna Mountain, as in Mauna Kea (white mountain).

moana Ocean.

'ohana Family.

'ōhi'a The most common tree in Hawai'i; thousands of acres of native *'ōhi'a* forest still exist, particularly on the island of Hawai'i. It grows at elevations from 1,000 to 9,000 feet and, depending on growing conditions, can appear as anything from a bush to a forest giant.

'ono Tasty, delicious. *Ono* is also the name of a fish (wahoo), which tastes *'ono*.
pāhoehoe The other type of lava flow, with a smooth, rope-like surface. *Pāhoehoe* is the Hawaiian word for rope.
pali Cliff, precipice.
paniolo Cowboy on the ranches of the Big Island, Maui, and Moloka'i. A corruption of Español, from the Mexican derivation of the first cowboys to arrive in the Islands.
pau End, finished.
pau hana Quitting time.
Pele Goddess of fire, of the volcano.
puka Hole, depression.
pūpū Appetizer.
pu'u Hill, rise.
ti (*kī* in Hawaiian). An important plant; its leaves are used to make hula skirts and to wrap food for cooking.
wahine Female, often found on the door of a rest room.
wai Fresh water, liquid.

Throughout *Camping Hawai'i* I have tried to explain the meaning of certain Hawaiian names, particularly places where you will be camping, hiking, or visiting. If some of these translations sound silly or confusing, it's because there may be uncertainty about the word or phrase being used. Like other languages, Hawaiian has many words that are spelled the same, but have different meanings. Although these differences may be made clear by different pronunciation or syllable stress, there are few people left with an ear for the language as it was originally spoken. The translations I have used are from *Place Names of Hawaii* by Pukui, Elbert, and Mookini.

HAWAIIAN FISH NAMES

Most fish in Hawaiian waters are found elsewhere around the world. Ocean fish are usually far ranging, and most of the freshwater fish have been introduced. Therefore, the strange-sounding names that you hear fishermen using here probably describe a fish you already know. If you plan to fish in Hawai'i, it will be helpful to be able to put the Hawaiian name with its English counterpart. That way, at least you will know what you are fishing for, even if you don't catch anything. Listed below are the most common fish caught *from the shoreline* in Hawaiian ocean waters. There are plenty more fish out there. If you plan to do any deep-sea fishing, there's a whole new list to learn. I have also left out the reef fish, those colorful little guys that look like they belong in an aquarium. Although some residents eat them, most of them are algae eaters and can harbor ciguatera (see section on Microorganisms above).

āhole Mountain bass.
akule Big-eyed scad.
'ala'ihi Striped squirrelfish.
'ama'ama Striped mullet.
awa Milkfish.
'āweoweo Red bigeye.
kūmū White-saddle goatfish.
moano Goatfish.
moi Threadfin.
nenue Rudderfish.
'ō'io Bonefish.
'ōmaka Yellow-tailed scad.
'ōpelu Mackerel scad.
pāpio Crevalle (juvenile).
uhu Parrotfish.
ulua Crevalle (mature).
'ū'ū Red squirrel fish, menpachi.
weke Yellow-striped goatfish.

The Thirteen Best Campsites

At the risk of being called wrong, biased, blind, stupid, and several other things by my friends who read this, I am going to tell you which campsites I think are the best in Hawai'i. My main reason for doing this is to assist campers with only a limited amount of time in the Islands to find the best places without a lot of trial and error. Another reason is that I have been to all of them and know how they compare with each other. Of course, my views may not be yours, and it is possible that what I think makes a great campsite might not impress someone else.

Why thirteen? No reason. I just made a list of the ones that I thought were the best, and it came to thirteen. What criteria did I use? Scenery, ambiance, activities, facilities, and access all played a role. Many people put first priority on facilities. Although they have some importance for me, I am more impressed by the natural beauty of the surroundings and the type of activity that can be enjoyed at or near the campsite. My very favorite campsite in the Islands is Kalalau Valley on Kaua'i, which has no facilities at all except pit toilets. Yet, Kalalau is such a wonderful place that not going there because of lack of facilities would be like skipping the Grand Canyon because it doesn't have an escalator.

Anyway, here are my thirteen. They are not in any order of preference.

HAWAI'I

Nāmakani Paio Campground High in a eucalpytus forest in Hawai'i Volcanoes National Park, this excellent campground is an ideal base for hiking and visiting the attractions of the park.

Halapē Shelter A tiny white sand beach surrounded by barren lava fields, Halapē is an isolated oasis on a coast otherwise marked by miles of hostile sea cliffs and crashing waves.

Kalōpā State Recreation Area This immaculately maintained park on the Hāmākua Coast sits in a beautiful native *'ōhi'a* forest, with nature walks and interpretive trails.

MAUI

Hosmer Grove A small but attractive campsite high on the slopes of Haleakalā, Hosmer is the gateway to the national park and the start of a self-guided nature trail.

Palikū Cabin and Campground Inside Haleakalā Crater, just before the Kaupō Gap, the lush, green fields of Palikū contrast sharply with the volcanic cinder and ash of the rest of the crater.

Wai'ānapanapa State Park A remote black sand beach, water-filled cave, and ancient Hawaiian trails are some of the features of this beautiful park on the rugged coastline near Hāna.

O'AHU

Waimānalo Bay Beach Park The campground sits in the shade of an ironwood grove on one of O'ahu's longest and loveliest beaches.

Ho'omaluhia Botanical Garden Right at the base of the dramatic Ko'olau cliffs, this quiet, lovely park, with its beautiful plantings, sweeping views, and excellent facilities, is a tent camper's dream.

Kualoa Beach Park Two large campgrounds, each with its own charm, on a scenic peninsula in peaceful Kāne'ohe Bay, make this park a special place to stay.

Mālaekahana State Recreation Area Another great beach, isolated and far from the crowds, with the campground located in a spacious ironwood grove.

KAUA'I

Kōke'e State Park Over 4,000 acres of forest with miles of trails and breathtaking views, Kōke'e offers a campground, cabins, and lodges at an elevation of 4,000 feet.

Kalalau Valley At the end of the 11-mile Nā Pali Coast Trail, Kalalau gives the definition to "tropical paradise." Magnificent beach, awesome cliffs, lush green valley, waterfalls, pools, streams, spectacular sunsets—what else is there?

Polihale State Park At the end of the road on the leeward shore, Polihale offers campsites overlooking the ocean on Kaua'i's longest and widest beach, with a dramatic cliff backdrop and great sunsets.

Part Two

ISLAND CAMPGROUNDS

Hawai'i

Where is the only place in the United States that you can watch the eruption of an active volcano? Where is the only place in the country that you can snow ski in the morning and swim at a palm-lined tropical beach in the afternoon? Where is the largest privately owned cattle ranch in the United States? No, it's not in Texas. We are talking, of course, about the island of Hawai'i. If you could put together the rain forests of Kaua'i, the valleys of Maui, the ranches of Moloka'i, and O'ahu's Waikīkī Beach without the crowds and with nicer hotels, then add a full-fledged desert and the world's only drive-in volcano—you've got Hawai'i. The Big Island has it all.

Hawai'i was the first island reached and settled by the Polynesians. Kamehameha, who unified all the Islands, was born here and died here. Captain James Cook was killed here, at Kealakekua Bay, in 1779. The first American missionaries also landed here. More petroglyphs (ancient rock carvings) have been found here than on all the other Islands combined. Hawai'i looms large in the history of the Islands.

Largest by far of the Islands, at 4,034 square miles, Hawai'i is almost twice the size of all the others combined. It is also the largest island under the jurisdiction of the United States. Ninety-three miles long and 76 miles wide, it has the state's highest elevation; Mauna Kea, 13,796 feet. Geologically, Hawai'i is the youngest island in the chain, somewhere between 650,000 and a million years old, and still growing. Formed by five volcanoes, the island was originally over 18,000 feet high. Even today, Mauna Kea and Mauna Loa are the highest peaks in the Pacific, both more than a thousand feet higher than Japan's Mount Fuji. Of the five volcanoes, two, Kīlauea and Mauna Loa, are still active. Two more, Hualālai and Mauna Kea, are considered dormant. Only the northernmost, Kohala, has apparently spewed its last eruption.

The population of the Big Island is about 121,000, placing it second to O'ahu. About 50 percent of its residents are of Japanese ancestry, a higher percentage than on any other island. The main industry, as everywhere else in the state, is tourism. Next in line is agriculture, with livestock taking first place, followed by macadamia nuts, orchids, and other ornamental flowers. Sugar, the mainstay of the island's industry for over 100 years, saw its last crop in 1996. The Kona district of Hawai'i was, until recently, the only place in the United States producing coffee, but crops are now being

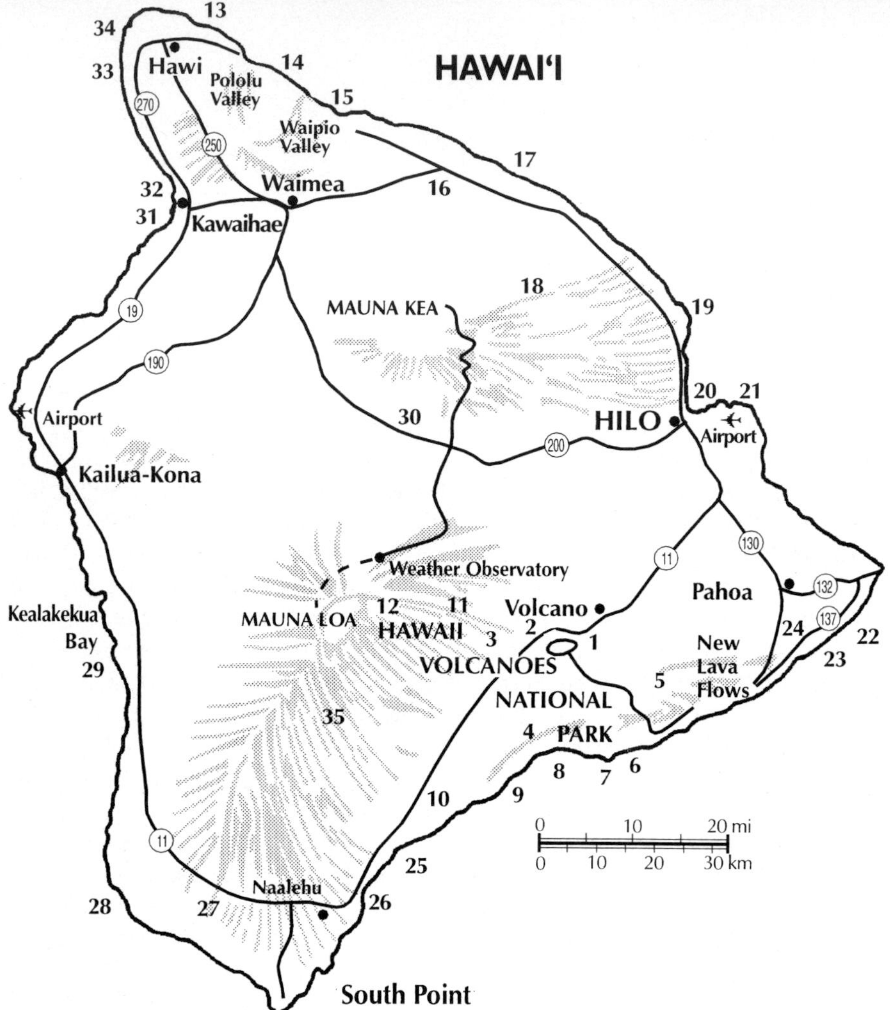

Hawai'i Campgrounds

1. Kīlauea State Recreation Area
2. Kīlauea Military Camp (KMC)
3. Nāmakani Paio Campground
4. Kīpuka Nēnē Campground
5. Nāpau Crater Campsite
6. 'Āpua Point Campsite
7. Keauhou Shelter
8. Halapē Shelter
9. Ka'aha Shelter
10. Pepeiao Cabin
11. Mauna Loa—Red Hill Cabin
12. Mauna Loa—Summit Cabin
13. Kēōkea Beach Park
14. Waimanu Valley
15. Waipi'o Valley
16. Kalōpā State Recreation Area
17. Laupāhoehoe Beach Park
18. Keanakolu Cabin
19. Kolekole Beach Park
20. Onekahakaha Beach Park
21. James Kealoha Beach Park
22. Isaac Hale Beach Park
23. MacKenzie State Recreation Area
24. Kalani Honua Conference and Retreat Center
25. Punalu'u Beach Park
26. Whittington Beach Park
27. Manukā State Park
28. Miloli'i Beach Park
29. Ho'okena Beach Park
30. Mauna Kea State Recreation Area
31. Hāpuna Beach State Recreation Area
32. Spencer Beach Park
33. Māhukona Beach Park
34. Kapa'a Beach Park
35. 'Ainapō Trail Shelter

grown in Kaua'i, Maui, Moloka'i, and O'ahu. After toying with tourist nicknames such as "The Orchid Isle" and "The Volcano Island," the name "Big Island" stuck. It is the only nickname for any of the Islands that you will normally hear residents use.

The geography of Hawai'i conforms to that of the other Islands, in that it has a windward (wet) side and a leeward (dry) side. Despite its size, Hawai'i has fewer beaches than the other islands, and most of these are on the leeward side. With the demise of sugar, windward interests have tried desperately to promote tourism, attempting to divert some of the heavy flow from the Kona coast. A new air terminal facility, which can handle the latest aircraft, was constructed for that purpose. But although Hilo has the terminal, Kona has the weather. After a short tryout period, mainland jets stopped coming to Hilo, and the windward coast languished.

Kona, on the other hand, with the weather and the beaches that tourists come for, thrives. Luxury hotels have proliferated, especially along the "Gold Coast" of North Kona and South Kohala. Proliferating and prospering, however, are two different matters. In many cases, occupancy rates are not high enough to achieve profitability. For reasons difficult to fathom, the industry's answer to this problem seems to be to build more and bigger hotels.

But the camper need not be concerned with these problems. You can go almost all the places that the well-heeled tourists can, and many places that they can't. In fact, only a camper can see all the magnificent facets that the Big Island has to offer.

Hawai'i does have public transportation, of sorts. The Hele-On service has five buses arriving in Hilo in the morning from Pāhoa, Ka'ū, Laupāhoehoe, Kona, and South Kohala. These buses return the same afternoon. They currently run Monday through Saturday for the first three locations, Monday through Friday to Kona, and 7 days a week to South Kohala. It is best to call for the latest schedule, 935–8241. Hitchhiking is permitted on Hawai'i.

THINGS TO SEE AND DO. Unlike the other Islands, distances can be significant on Hawai'i. Campgrounds are especially far apart on the Kona coast south of Hāpuna Beach. You may want to keep that in mind when planning your stops in relation to the points of interest shown below.

Point of Interest	**Nearest Campground**
'Akaka Falls	Kolekole Beach Park
Green Sand Beach	Whittington Beach Park
Hawai'i Volcanoes National Park	Within the park
Lapakahi State Historical Park	Māhukona Beach Park

Lava Tree State Monument	Isaac Hale Beach Park
Mauna Kea Summit	Mauna Kea State Recreation Area
Mo'okini Heiau	Kapa'a Beach Park
Place of Refuge	Ho'okena Beach Park
Pololū Valley Lookout	Kēōkea Beach Park
Punalu'u Black Sand Beach	Punalu'u Beach Park
Pu'ukoholā Heiau	Spencer Beach Park
Rainbow Falls	Onekahakaha Beach Park
South Point	Whittington Beach Park
Wai'ōpae Tide Pools	Isaac Hale Beach Park
Waipi'o Valley Lookout	Kalōpā State Recreation Area

HAWAI'I VOLCANOES NATIONAL PARK

When a volcano erupts anywhere else in the world, people go running. In Hawai'i Volcanoes National Park they *come* running—to see the show. That they can do so safely is due to the unique nature of Hawaiian volcanoes, which, although they are the most active in the world, are also the most gentle.

Established in 1916, the park encompasses 344 square miles, stretching from the summit of Mauna Loa at 13,677 feet to sea level almost 20 miles away. Mauna Loa last erupted in 1984, but Kīlauea, the centerpiece of the park, has been in continuous eruption since 1983. Although the source of the lava has moved eastward from Kīlauea Crater itself and cannot be reached on foot because of constant eruptive activity, helicopter trips over the area are an awesome experience. The flows moving downslope can often be viewed close up as they make a spectacular plunge into the sea.

The park is a paradise for hikers and campers. Starting from a campground in a tall eucalyptus grove, you can circle Kīlauea's caldera, 2.5 miles long, 2 miles across, and 400 feet deep. You may also descend into the crater, hiking across it and its neighbor, Kīlauea Iki. From the park's elevation at 4,000 feet, you can hike down to the ocean, camping at lovely, isolated beaches rarely visited by anyone. Or, winter clothing in hand, you can trudge to the summit of Mauna Loa, staying in cabins along the way. Why not do it all? This section will show you how.

Space is not available here to cover all things you should know about the park or all the things you can do there. For that reason, your first stop should be the Visitor Center. There you will find a free movie, brochures, books, and maps. It's also the place to get the latest information on hiking trails and campgrounds, and to apply for backcountry camping permits. Finally, keep in mind that Hawai'i Volcanoes National Park is not all lava. Although that is certainly the predominant commodity, you will also find deserts, rain forests, beaches, and, at the right time of the year, even snow.

Sad to say, Kamoamoa Campground, one of the prettiest in the park, was overrun by lava late in 1992. Kamoamoa, a welcome oasis of green lawns and palm trees at the end of the Chain of Craters Road, had gained a new black-sand beach in 1986. Lava entering the sea to the northeast fractured into tiny particles as it met the cold ocean water, and currents carried the sand to Kamoamoa. But in October, 1992, the lava flows began a slow, steady assault on the campground itself. Crossing the road, the flows first circled the campground and reclaimed the black-sand beach. By mid-November, the lava had covered nearby petroglyphs and an ancient *heiau*. By the end of the month the campground was gone, suffering the same fate as its former neighbors, the famous Queen's Bath, and the park's Waha'ula Visitor Center, which had disappeared beneath the relentless lava flows a few years earlier. What Madame Pele giveth, she also taketh away.

Kīlauea State Recreation Area

LOCATION: This lone state park cabin is located on Kalanikoa Road in the town of Volcano, just off Highway 11.

DESCRIPTION: Attractively located in a native *'ōhi'a-hāpu'u* forest at 3,700 feet, the cabin is on the border of the town. Kīlauea means "spewing," as a volcano spews lava and ash.

FACILITIES: Cabin only, no tent or vehicle camping. One housekeeping cabin, sleeping up to six people, consists of a kitchen, dining-living room, two bedrooms, and a bathroom with hot shower. The kitchen is equipped with a sink, refrigerator, electric range, and cooking and eating utensils. Blankets, bedding linen, and towels are furnished. Gas and limited groceries are available in town. More extensive shopping is also available in Hilo.

PERMIT/RESERVATIONS: A permit may be obtained from a state parks office on any island. The following address is for the state office on Hawai'i: Division of State Parks, P.O. Box 936, Hilo, HI 96720; phone, (808) 974-6200.

TIME LIMIT: Five nights in any consecutive 30-day period.

COST: Cabin rents for $45 per night for one to four persons, $5 for each additional person.

SPECIAL COMMENTS: Reservations for this cabin should be made well in advance, because it is in demand all during the year.

HOW TO GET THERE: From Hilo (29 miles), take Highway 11 south to Volcano exit (Wright Road, Hwy 148), then turn left on Old Volcano Road and right on Kalanikoa Road to the cabin. From Kailua (Kona) (97 miles), take Highway 11 south to Volcano exit (Old Volcano Road), then turn left on Kalanikoa Road to the cabin.

NEARBY POINTS OF INTEREST: The cabin is an ideal base to explore Hawai'i Volcanoes National Park, only half a mile away.

Kīlauea Military Camp (KMC)

LOCATION: KMC is situated on Crater Rim Drive, about halfway between the Visitor Center and the Volcano Observatory.

DESCRIPTION: KMC is a full-service recreational facility for the use of members of the armed forces, active and retired, Department of Defense (DOD) civilian employees, and certain other authorized personnel, and their guests.

FACILITIES: Tent and vehicle camping is not permitted. Accommodations are in cabins, apartments, and dormitories. There are forty-one cabins of various sizes (some with kitchens), six apartments, and a large dormitory. A cafeteria serves three meals per day, and there is a small general store.

CAMPGROUND ACTIVITIES: Recreational services include tennis and basketball courts, a bowling alley, recreation lodge (pool, table tennis, video games), library, weight room, playground, and picnic areas. Daily bus tours operate to points of interest in the park and other tourist attractions on the island.

PERMIT/RESERVATIONS: Department of Defense (DOD) ID card or other authorized identification is required. Reservations should be made by writing or by calling: Reservations Office, Armed Forces Recreation Center, KMC, Hawai'i Volcanoes National Park, HI 96718; phone, (808) 967–8333.

Residents on O'ahu may make reservations by calling toll free: 438–6707. Reservations are accepted on a first-come, first-served basis, according to the following priorities: (1) active-duty personnel, 60 days in advance; (2) retired personnel, 40 days in advance (except September, October, November, January, February, 60 days); (3) DOD civilians and other authorized personnel, 20 days in advance.

TIME LIMIT: Seven days. Extensions may be permitted on a space-available basis.

COST: Fees are based on both rank and type of unit, beginning with $25 per night (single or double) for pay grades E-1 through E-5, up to $73 for pay grades O-4 through O-10 (4 person occupancy). Additional persons cost $5 each, except that children 5 years and under are free. Dormitory fees range from $5 to $10 per night, per person, depending upon type.

SPECIAL COMMENTS: KMC is an excellent facility and is by far the best place to stay if you are eligible. IDs are checked when making purchases, such as in the general store or cafeteria. The camp is at 4,000 feet, so nights are chilly, and even days can be cool, especially in inclement weather. Warm clothing and rain gear are recommended. Because KMC is within the national park, the park entry fee must be paid to stay there. The fee is good for 7 days, so the receipt should be retained for multiple entries during that period.

HOW TO GET THERE: From the Visitor Center (2 miles), turn right leaving the parking lot and proceed on Crater Rim Drive to the camp, on the right.

NEARBY POINTS OF INTEREST: KMC is centrally located and convenient to most of the park attractions. It is just across the road from Kīlauea Crater and the Crater Rim Trail. From this trail you may hike 2 miles west to the Volcano Observatory, 2 miles east to the Visitor Center and the Volcano Art Center, or make a great all-day loop hike on the Crater Rim Trail itself. By driving to places like Kīpuka Nēnē and Hilina Pali the park's entire coastal trail system is within reach, either for day hikes or backpacking adventures.

By car you can easily reach all sections of the park accessible by road. If you don't want to hike, Crater Rim Drive will take you through much of the same scenery as the Crater Rim Trail. Be sure to take the Chain of Craters Road to Mauna Ulu and the new lava flows. Stop along the way to take the mile-long trail to Pu'uloa, where you will see an excellent petroglyph field easily viewed from a boardwalk—providing you get there before Madame Pele, who has been rampaging uninterupted nearby since 1983. Check at the Visitor Center for maps, brochures, and permits.

Nāmakani Paio Campground

LOCATION: The campground is within Hawai'i Volcanoes National Park, 5 miles west of the park entrance on Route 11.

DESCRIPTION: Nāmakani Paio is a large, excellent campground 4,000 feet high, in a tall eucalyptus forest. Its name, which means "conflicting winds," is a misnomer, because although you can hear the wind, the site is relatively protected. Tents can be pitched in an open grassy field, in partial shade from small trees, or in the full shade of the eucalyptus. A trail leads to Kīlauea Crater, half a mile away, across the highway.

FACILITIES: Tent, cabin, and vehicle camping. The tent and vehicle portion of the campground contains a large pavilion (eight tables) with two barbecues and a fireplace. A smaller pavilion with two tables is also available, as are three open picnic tables. An outdoor dishwashing area is located near the enclosed toilets, which have sinks but no showers. Water is drinkable. There is no electricity, except in the rest rooms.

The cabin area is adjacent to the campground and consists of ten cabins that sleep four in two single bunk beds and one double bed. Two shelves for storage complete the furnishings, and there is very little room to move around. However, each cabin has a covered picnic table at the entrance and a fireplace with a grill. Toilets, sinks, and hot showers are in a separate building, with a drinking fountain and a pay phone outside. Groceries and gasoline can be obtained in the town of Volcano, about 1 mile north of the park entrance, just off Highway 11, toward Hilo.

Nāmakani Paio Campground is the most accessible in Hawai'i Volcanoes National Park and is convenient to most of its attractions.

PERMIT/RESERVATIONS: For tent and vehicle camping, none is needed. Reservations for the cabins are made through the concessionaire: Volcano House, P.O. Box 53, Volcano, HI 96718; phone, (808) 967–7321. Keys are picked up at the Volcano House reception desk, where bedding (sheets, blankets, pillowcases) can be obtained without additional cost. Nights can be cold, so users may want to augment this bedding with their own or simply forego the bedding and use sleeping bags. Reservations should be made well in advance for the summer months and holiday periods.

TIME LIMIT: Seven days.

COST: Tents and vehicles are free; cabins cost $32 per night, for one to four persons.

SPECIAL COMMENTS: Warm clothing is advisable at all times of the year, because the nights are chilly, especially during rainy weather. Campers should not expect to use the showers in the cabin portion of the campground, because these are locked, with keys going only to those who have rented cabins.

Cabins at Nāmakani Paio, Hawai'i Volcanoes National Park, provide beds for four persons. Tables and grills are outside each cabin, and toilets and showers are in a separate building.

HOW TO GET THERE: From Hilo (33 miles), proceed southwest on Highway 11 to the sign for the national park entrance turnoff. Do not turn into the park, but continue on Route 11 another 5 miles to the campground sign on the right side of the road. From Kailua (Kona) (91 miles), proceed south on Route 11, past Nā'ālehu and Pāhala. Watch for a sign on the right for Footprints Trail (about 82 miles from Kailua). Continue another 6.7 miles to the campground sign on the left.

NEARBY POINTS OF INTEREST: A 1-mile hike on a marked trail leads to the Volcano Observatory, the Crater Rim, and other connecting trails. A short drive (5.5 miles) reaches the Visitor Center, Volcano Art Center, and Volcano House. The campground is a good starting point for hikes on the Crater Rim Trail and the Halema'uma'u Trail and is a convenient jumping-off place for the climb up Mauna Loa. It is the closest campground to Kīlauea Caldera, Kīlauea Iki, Devastation Trail, and Thurston Lava Tube.

Kīpuka Nēnē Campground

LOCATION: The campground is located in about the center of Hawai'i Volcanoes National Park on the Hilina Pali Road, at an elevation of 2,900 feet.

DESCRIPTION: Kīpuka Nēnē is a medium-sized campground in an open grove of mature *'ōhi'a* trees and other vegetation. The ground is part grassy and part bare, with frequent lava outcroppings. Some partial shade is provided by large *'ōhi'a* trees. The site can be windy. Kīpuka Nēnē gets its name from *kīpuka,* which is an "island" of land and vegetation spared by lava that flowed around it, and the *nēnē,* which is the Hawai'i state bird. It is usually not as crowded as Nāmakani Paio.

FACILITIES: Tent and vehicle camping. A large pavilion contains three tables, a fireplace, and a barbecue. A water tank at the pavilion is fed by catchment. A separate building houses pit toilets, but there are no sinks or showers. Groceries and gas are available at Volcano, 1 mile northeast of the park entrance.

PERMIT/RESERVATIONS: None.

TIME LIMIT: Seven days.

COST: Free.

SPECIAL COMMENTS: From mid-November 1993 to 1 March 1994 Kīpuka Nēnē Campground was closed to allow *nēnē* in the area to nest and breed undisturbed. As this is the normal breeding season for the birds, the campground may be closed during this period annually. Check at park headquarters.

HOW TO GET THERE: From the Visitor Center (20 miles), turn left exiting the Visitor Center parking lot, then right on Crater Rim Drive, just before the toll booths. Proceed to the intersection of Chain of Craters Road and turn left, following the road for about 3.2 miles to the Hilina Pali Road on the right. Follow this road 5.1 miles to Kīpuka Nēnē on the left.

NEARBY POINTS OF INTEREST: Kīpuka Nēnē is a good base for day hikes to the coast and the Ka'ū Desert. The Halapē Trail begins here, leading to one of the prettiest pocket beaches on the Puna Coast (7 miles).

Nāpau Crater Campsite

LOCATION: The campsite is located in Kīlauea's east rift zone, near the end of the Nāpau Crater Trail.

DESCRIPTION: Nāpau is a primitive site, in a stark, volcanic landscape. Situated in a rocky clearing with recent lava flows on two sides, it is only about half a mile from Nāpau Crater, with its excellent view of Pu'u 'Ō'ō. This volcanic cone is the latest one created on Hawai'i and is still active. Nāpau, which means "the endings," is a "dead end" campsite, in that there is no place to go except Nāpau Crater. Hiking off the trail is dangerous, because of the unstable condition of new lava. The ground is extremely rocky, with sharp protrusions guaranteed to cut tent floors. Live steam sometimes rises from many cracks and fissures throughout the campsite. Only minimal shade can be found in some places from medium-sized *'ōhi'a* trees and *hāpu'u* ferns. There are five or six reasonably good tent sites, but you will have to look for them.

FACILITIES: Pit toilets are the only facilities. There is no water anywhere on the Nāpau Crater Trail.

PERMIT/RESERVATIONS: A backcountry camping permit is needed. It can be obtained in person at the Visitor Center on a first-come basis no earlier than noon on the day before your trip and is limited to twelve persons per night. For further information write or call: Hawai'i Volcanoes National Park, Volcano, HI 96718; phone, (808) 967–7331.

TIME LIMIT: Three nights.

COST: Free.

SPECIAL COMMENTS: There is little reason to overnight at Nāpau unless volcanic activity is taking place at Pu'u 'Ō'ō. Hikes to Nāpau Crater and back can usually be completed in a day, either from the Nāpau Crater or Nāulu trails. More than one hiker has awakened in the middle of the night in his own private steam bath, as steam suddenly started rising from beneath his tent or bedroll, but this activity has diminished sharply.

HOW TO GET THERE: From the Visitor Center (15 miles), turn left exiting the Visitor Center parking lot, then right on Crater Rim Drive, just before the toll booths. Proceed to the intersection of Chain of Craters Road and turn left, following the road for about 5.2 miles to the Mauna Ulu turnoff on the left. The Nāpau Crater Trail begins at the end of the parking lot, about 50 yards down the old paved surface, on the left. Follow the trail about 6 miles, to just before Nāpau Crater, where the trail forks. A wooden sign points to the campsite, bearing left.

NEARBY POINTS OF INTEREST: The ruins of a former "pulu" factory can be seen on the trail about 5 miles from the beginning of the Nāpau Crater Trail. Here, *pulu,* the soft, downy product of the *hāpu'u* (tree) fern, was collected and used to stuff mattresses and pillows. Fortunately for the *hāpu'u,* better and cheaper materials came along, and the fern was saved from going the way of the sandalwood tree.

'Āpua Point Campsite

LOCATION: The campsite is located on the coast, 6.6 miles west of the Pu'uloa parking area, on the Chain of Craters Road.

DESCRIPTION: 'Āpua, which means "fish trap," is a windswept point with a small black-sand beach on its western side. Young coconut trees, *naupaka,* and *pōhuehue*—considerably more vegetation than found elsewhere in this barren landscape—back the beach.

FACILITIES: Pit toilets are the only facilities. There is no water, although a small brackish supply can sometimes be found in lava cracks. Don't rely on it. There are enough patches of soft ground to pitch several tents.

CAMPGROUND ACTIVITIES: Swimming should be done with caution, as the backwash is strong, and the bottom turns deep quickly. Swimming is dangerous further offshore, because of strong currents and winds. *Fishing is prohibited except for native Hawaiian residents of the Kalapana area and their guests.*

PERMIT/RESERVATIONS: Back country camping permits are required, limited to twelve people per night, and are issued at the Visitor Center on a first-come basis no earlier than noon on the day before your trip. For further information write or call: Hawai'i Volcanoes National Park, Volcano, HI 96718; phone, (808) 967–7311.

TIME LIMIT: Three nights.

COST: Free.

SPECIAL COMMENTS: 'Āpua is a nesting ground for endangered hawksbill and threatened green sea turtles. To protect them, you will see signs telling you not to camp in certain specific areas. Please obey them. A fishing village located here was destroyed by an earthquake and tsunami on 2 April 1868 and never rebuilt.

HOW TO GET THERE: From the Visitor Center (28 miles), turn left exiting the Visitor Center parking lot, then right on Crater Rim Drive, just before the toll booths. Proceed to the intersection of Chain of Craters Road and turn left, following the road for about 18 miles to the Pu'uloa Parking Area. The Puna Coast Trail begins on the southwest (ocean) side of the parking lot and reaches the campsite after 6.6 miles.

'Āpua can also be reached via the Keauhou Trail (9.9 miles), descending over the Poliokeawe Pali. If you can arrange the transportation, hiking in via one trail and out the other makes a nice loop.

NEARBY POINTS OF INTEREST: Keauhou and Halapē are both worth a visit if you have time, even if you don't plan to camp there. See the sections pertaining to these campgrounds for more information.

Keauhou Shelter

LOCATION: The campsite is situated on the coast, about 7 miles by trail south of Mau Loa o Mauna Ulu Parking Area, on the Chain of Craters Road.

DESCRIPTION: Keauhou is a scenic campsite, on an isolated lava coast. A rocky point divides two small inlets, with small pockets of sand, which make several very small, but pretty beaches, ideal for privacy. Rocky lava outcroppings make tenting difficult anywhere except on the sandy beach pockets described above. Partial shade can be found at some of these, but the rest of the area is completely exposed to the sun and to frequent stiff winds. Keauhou means "new era," or "new current" in Hawaiian.

FACILITIES: A small, three-sided stone shelter, with a roof but no floor, is located at the end of the Keauhou Trail, about 100 yards from the shore. Two persons can fit inside comfortably, but it could take up to four. The floor is gravel and flat. A water tank, with its spigot inside the shelter, is fed by catchment. The water should be treated before use. A small grill, and an outdoor pit toilet complete the facilities. Use of the shelter is on a first-come, first-served basis.

CAMPGROUND ACTIVITIES: The shallow, rocky inlets do not provide very good swimming, but they are a good place to get wet and cool off. Swimming is dangerous further offshore, because of strong currents and winds. Snorkeling is fairly good in the inlets, but hazardous in the deeper water. *Shoreline fishing is prohibited except for native Hawaiian residents of the Kalapana area and their guests.*

PERMIT/RESERVATIONS: Backcountry camping permits are required and can be obtained at the Visitor Center on a first-come basis no earlier than noon on the day before your trip, with a limit of twelve persons per night. For more information write or call: Hawai'i Volcanoes National Park, Volcano, HI 96718; phone, (808) 967–7311.

TIME LIMIT: Three nights.

COST: Free.

SPECIAL COMMENTS: Keauhou was once the terminal of a cattle trail leading from ranches north of Volcano and was formerly known as Keauhou Landing. From here, cattle were swum out to small coastal steamers for delivery to Hilo and other ports. Remains of stone buildings and foundations can still be seen near the shoreline. It is an ideal campsite for those wanting to get away, because it is infrequently visited, except on weekends. Halapē, only 1.6 miles west, is even prettier. If you have time, camp at both; if not, head for Halapē. Be sure to check the status of the water tank before leaving the Visitor Center and bring an emergency water supply, because this information is not always accurate.

The shelter is often overrun with red ants during the daytime and by large cockroaches at night. We spread our mats anyway, and, surprisingly, they did not bother us. For peace of mind, however, you might want to pitch a tent inside the shelter or at least apply liberal doses of insect repellent. Better yet, pitch your tent in one of the pretty sandy coves at the water's edge.

HOW TO GET THERE: From the Visitor Center (15 miles): Turn left exiting the Visitor Center parking lot, then right on Crater Rim Drive, just before the toll booths. Proceed to the intersection of Chain of Craters Road and turn left, following the road for about 5 miles to Mau Loa o Mauna Ulu Parking Area on the right. Look for the Keauhou Trail sign and follow the trail 6.8 miles to the coast. You may also take the Halapē Trail from Kīpuka Nēnē, which is slightly longer, 7.2 miles. This makes a good loop hike, if you can arrange a pickup. For those seeking a more level approach, Keauhou may also be reached via the Puna Coast Trail, which begins at the Pu'uloa petroglyph parking area on the Chain of Craters Road. This is the longest approach of the three, almost 10 miles.

NEARBY POINTS OF INTEREST: See 'Āpua Point Campsite.

Halapē Shelter

LOCATION: The campsite is situated on the coast, about 7 miles by trail south of Kīpuka Nēnē.

DESCRIPTION: Halapē is a delightful campsite, on an isolated lava coast. A small, white-sand beach, lined with young palm trees, curves around a shallow, protected cove. It is the only white-sand beach for miles. The bottom off the beach is sandy, and the cove is protected from all but the worst storms. The dead palm trunks offshore are a reminder of an earthquake that struck Halapē in 1975, collapsing the shoreline and generating a local tsunami that killed two campers. The rocky lava outcropping makes tenting difficult anywhere except on or behind the sandy beach, but that is where you will want to be anyway. Partial shade can be found under the palms and in the shrubbery at the eastern edge of the beach, but the rest of the area is completely exposed to the sun and to frequent stiff winds.

FACILITIES: A small, three-sided stone shelter, with a roof but no floor, is located at the end of the Halapē Trail, about 200 yards from the water. It can accommodate up to four persons, but two is more comfortable. A tent may also be pitched inside. The floor is gravel and flat. A water tank, with its spigot inside the shelter, is fed by catchment. Treat the water before drinking. A small grill and an outdoor pit toilet complete the facilities. Use of the shelter is on a first-come, first-served basis.

CAMPGROUND ACTIVITIES: Safe swimming can be enjoyed inside the cove almost any time of the year. Strong currents require caution in the deeper waters outside the cove. There is not much to see in the cove. Snorkeling is more interesting around the rocks offshore, but note the caution above. The Halapē shoreline is reputed to be an excellent place to catch *pāpio* and *ulua*.

PERMIT/RESERVATIONS: Backcountry camping permits are required, and can be obtained at the Visitor Center on a first-come basis no earlier than noon on the day before your trip, with a limit of twelve persons per night. For more information write or call: Hawai'i Volcanoes National Park, Volcano, HI 96718; phone, (808) 967–7311.

TIME LIMIT: Three nights.

COST: Free.

SPECIAL COMMENTS: Halapē is an ideal campsite for those wanting to get away, because it is infrequently visited, except on weekends. It is worth every ounce of energy it takes to hike there. The area has come back nicely from the earthquake and is one of the prettiest spots on this entire coast. Be sure to check the status of the water tank before leaving the Visitor Center. You may want to bring an emergency water supply, because this information is not always accurate. The shelter is often overrun with red ants during the daytime and by large cockroaches at night.

Halapē means "crushed missing" in Hawaiian. The explanation for this rather unusual phrase is that gourds used to grow here, and they would fall off the trees and become buried in the sand. Not knowing they were there, people would walk over them and thus crush the missing gourds. If you think this is a long reach for a definition, I agree with you. But it is better than some others.

HOW TO GET THERE: From the Visitor Center (11.3 miles), turn left exiting the Visitor Center parking lot, then right on Crater Rim Drive, just before the toll booths. Proceed to the intersection of Chain of Craters Road and turn left, following the road for about 3.2 miles to the Hilina Pali Road on the right. Follow this road 5 miles to Kīpuka Nēnē Campground, where the trailhead is located. Look for the Halapē Trail sign, which follows a jeep road before turning right and descending to the coast (7.2 miles). The campground can also be reached by taking the Keauhou Trail (see Keauhou Shelter), which is slightly longer, 8.4 miles, and via the Hilina Pali Trail, 8 miles. A level approach is by way of the Puna Coast Trail, 11.3 miles (see Keauhou Shelter).

NEARBY POINTS OF INTEREST: Keauhou Landing, 1.6 miles east, and 'Āpua Point, 3 miles farther, are well worth exploring. There is a black-sand beach at 'Āpua, but care should be taken in swimming there. Backwash is usually strong, and the bottom deepens quickly. Turtles nest in this area, so please tread lightly.

Ka'aha Shelter

LOCATION: The campsite is situated on the coast, about 4 miles by trail south of Hilina Pali.

DESCRIPTION: Ka'aha is a small campsite, on an isolated lava coast. Vegetation is limited to small shrubs and dry grass. Rocky lava outcroppings make tenting difficult anywhere except on the floor of the shelter. There is no shade anywhere, and the area is completely exposed to the sun and to frequent strong winds. All of this may sound grim, but the place has a certain isolated attractiveness. Ka'aha means "the assembly" in Hawaiian.

FACILITIES: A small, three-sided stone shelter, with a roof, but no floor, is located at the end of the trail, about 200 yards from the shore. It can house two persons comfortably, three or four less comfortably. The floor is gravel and flat. A water tank, with its spigot inside the shelter, is fed by catchment. The water should be treated before use. A small grill and an outdoor pit toilet complete the facilities. Use of the shelter is on a first-come, first-served basis.

CAMPGROUND ACTIVITIES: Swimming is not recommended in the open ocean, because of the rocky entry and strong currents. You can get wet in a shallow depression about 200 yards in front of the shelter. Fishing may produce *pāpio* and *ulua*.

PERMIT/RESERVATIONS: Backcountry camping permits are required and can be obtained at the Visitor Center on a first-come basis no earlier than noon on the day before your trip, with a limit of twelve persons per night. For more information write or call: Hawai'i Volcanoes National Park, Volcano, HI 96718; phone, (808) 967–7331.

TIME LIMIT: Three nights.

COST: Free.

SPECIAL COMMENTS: Ka'aha is infrequently visited overnight, mostly because of its lack of tent sites and no ocean access. Halapē, 6 miles to the east, is much nicer and has a pretty, white-sand beach. Be sure to check the status of the water tank at Ka'aha before leaving the Visitor Center, and you may want to bring an emergency water supply just in case. Although the chart at the Visitor Center reported it full, we arrived at Ka'aha one time to find the water tank empty! We did not see the ants common to Halapē and Keauhou, but plenty of cockroaches made up for their absence.

HOW TO GET THERE: From the Visitor Center (20 miles), turn left exiting the Visitor Center parking lot, then right on Crater Rim Drive, just before the toll booths. Proceed to the intersection of Chain of Craters Road and turn left, following the road for about 3.2 miles to the Hilina Pali Road. Turn right and drive to the end of the road at the Hilina Pali Lookout. Be sure to take the Hilina Pali Trail, because another trail begins here, leading to Pepeiao Cabin and the Ka'ū Desert. Follow the trail 2.2 miles to a fork. Bear right, leaving the Hilina Pali Trail, and follow the signs to Ka'aha shelter, another 1.6 miles.

Pepeiao Cabin

LOCATION: The cabin lies 4.8 miles southwest by trail from Hilina Pali Overlook.

DESCRIPTION: Situated in a pretty, partly forested portion of the Ka'ū Desert, the cabin is isolated and peaceful. Old lava flow outcroppings make it difficult for anything but scrub and dry grasses to grow, although a few medium-sized trees are close to the cabin.

FACILITIES: Tent and cabin camping. The cabin is small, containing three single beds and three extra foam mattresses, some shelving, a table, and a fair amount of counter space. Water is available from a catchment tank in the rear of the cabin and should be boiled or treated before use. An enclosed pit toilet is located a short distance away. No more than three or four tent sites exist outside the cabin. A small amount of shade is provided by the few trees.

PERMIT/RESERVATIONS: A backcountry camping permit is needed. It may be obtained in person at the Visitor Center on a first-come basis no earlier than noon on the day before your trip, with a limit of twelve persons per night. For more information write or call: Hawai'i Volcanoes National Park, Volcano, HI 96718; phone, (808) 967–7311.

TIME LIMIT: Three nights.

COST: Free.

SPECIAL COMMENTS: The cabin and its surrounding camping space is on a first-come, first-served basis, and facilities must be shared. Your permit will not automatically entitle you to the three beds inside the cabin. There may be others with permits, and the first to arrive get the goodies. Be sure to check the status of the water tank before you leave the Visitor Center. It is a good idea to carry an emergency water supply, because the information at the Center is not always accurate. You may find lots of ants and some roaches outside the cabin, but they do not seem to get inside—providing, of course, that you keep the door closed.

HOW TO GET THERE: From the Visitor Center (21 miles), turn left as if exiting the park gate. Just before the toll booths, turn right on Crater Rim Drive, passing Thurston Lava Tube, to the intersection of Chain of Craters Road, about 4 miles. Turn left, proceed another 3.2 miles to Hilina Pali Road, turn right and drive to the end of the road at the Hilina Pali Lookout. Two trails start here; make sure to take the Ka'ū Desert Trail, not the Hilina Pali Trail. The trail distance to the cabin is 4.8 miles.

NEARBY POINTS OF INTEREST: Pepeiao, which means "ear," is used mainly by backpackers hiking the Ka'ū Desert or making a loop through the park's coastal district. If you have the time, make a loop and return via the Kālu'e Trail and Ka'aha back to Hilina Pali overlook or, even better, push on to the lovely beach at Halapē, perhaps arranging a pickup at Kīpuka Nēnē.

Mauna Loa—Red Hill Cabin

LOCATION: The cabin (campground) is located on the eastern slope of Mauna Loa at 10,035 feet.

DESCRIPTION: Red Hill is used mostly as a way station on the climb to Mauna Loa summit, although an overnight hike here, returning the next day, provides a good introduction to the mountain's fantastic lava landscape. The cabin sits in a small open clearing just below Pu'u 'Ula'ula (Red Hill). The short climb to its top affords excellent views of Mauna Kea to the north and Haleakalā on Maui. The area surrounding the cabin is relatively flat hard-packed red cinder, with some lava outcroppings. Tent sites are limited. As the site is above the vegetation line, there are no trees for shade or wind protection.

FACILITIES: Cabin and tent camping. The cabin has eight bunks, with some extra mattresses, so people can sleep on the floor. At this altitude, you may find that is a better option than a tent. A water tank is fed by catchment from the cabin roof and usually has water. Check this before you leave the Visitor Center. The water should be boiled or treated before use. There is no stove, so bring your own. An enclosed pit toilet is located behind the cabin. The use of the cabin and the surrounding camping area is on a first-come, first-served, sharing basis.

PERMIT/RESERVATIONS: A backcountry permit is required and can be obtained at the Visitor Center on a first-come basis no earlier than noon on the day before your trip, with a limit of eight persons per night per group. For more information write or call: Hawai'i Volcanoes National Park, Volcano, HI 96718; phone, (808) 967–7311.

TIME LIMIT: Three nights.

COST: Free.

SPECIAL COMMENTS: Because the cabin must be shared first-come, first-served, it pays to reach Red Hill early so you can lay claim to the bunks or at least to space inside the cabin. A record is maintained at the Visitor Center of hikers at or en route to Red Hill, but this is not always accurate, because sometimes people use the cabin without getting the required permit. Technically, a party with a permit has priority over those without one. However, if you are going to assert your rights over a group already at the cabin, it would help to have big people with you. Take warm clothes and sleeping bags, as well as wind and rain protection. Snow, rain, and strong winds are possible any time of the year. In addition to their recreational function, the Red Hill and Summit cabins are designated as emergency wilderness shelters. That means that during extreme weather conditions the cabin must be shared with any and all comers, permits or not. Also, injured or seriously ill persons must be allowed in the cabins.

HOW TO GET THERE: From the Visitor Center (22 miles), turn left leaving the parking lot and exit the park to Highway 11. Turn left, in the direction of Kona, and proceed to the intersection of Mauna Loa Road, about 3.8 miles. Turn right, passing Kīpuka Puaulu, up a narrow winding road. Proceed with caution, because the road becomes one lane in many places, with many blind turns. The trailhead begins at the end of the road, at a small parking lot, about 13.5 miles from Highway 11. Follow the Mauna Loa Trail 7.5 miles to Red Hill.

Mauna Loa Cabin

LOCATION: This cabin (campground) is situated on the eastern rim of the Mauna Loa summit crater, at an elevation of 13,250 feet.

DESCRIPTION: The cabin is used primarily by hikers climbing Mauna Loa and exploring the summit area and crater. It sits close to the edge of Moku-'āweoweo, the massive Mauna Loa caldera, more than 1.5 miles across, over 3 miles long, and 600 feet deep. It lies on the opposite side of the crater from the true summit of the mountain, which is accessible by trail and is 4.7 miles from the cabin. Lava and hard-packed cinder surround the cabin, making it difficult to stake tents. Lava stones can be used to hold them down, but the supply is limited. Winds can be fierce and the temperature below freezing at night. If at all possible, use the cabin.

FACILITIES: Cabin and tent camping. The cabin has twelve bunks, with some extra mattresses, so people can sleep on the floor. At this altitude, you may find that a much better option than a tent. A water tank is fed by catchment from the cabin roof and usually has water. Check this before you leave the Visitor Center. Another source of water, if the tank is dry, is a water hole about a quarter of a mile south of the cabin, which is marked by rock cairns that can be seen from the kitchen window of the cabin. Water from either source should be boiled or treated before use. There is no stove. You will need to bring your own if you want hot food. An enclosed pit toilet is located over a deep fissure behind the cabin. The use of the cabin and the surrounding camping area is on a first-come, first-served, sharing basis, and the same rules apply as for Red Hill.

PERMIT/RESERVATIONS: A backcountry camping permit is required and can be obtained in person at the Visitor Center on a first-come basis no earlier than noon on the day before your trip, with a limit of eight persons per night per group. For more information write or call: Hawai'i Volcanoes National Park, Volcano, HI 96718; phone, (808) 967–7311.

TIME LIMIT: Three nights.

COST: Free.

SPECIAL COMMENTS: For information on cabin sharing, clothing, and bedding, see comments in preceding section on Red Hill.

Mauna Loa is the world's largest active volcano and the largest mountain in the world by sheer mass. Its volume is about 10,000 cubic miles (compared with 80 cubic miles for California's Mount Shasta). Altitude sickness can be a problem in the rarified air of the summit. Simple headache and nausea can be treated with conventional remedies, but more serious symptoms, such as disorientation, chest pain, or a rattle when breathing, require immediate descent to lower altitude and treatment.

Mauna Loa is one of the world's most unusual hikes. After leaving the Red Hill Cabin, the hiker enters a moonwalk world without vegetation or sign of life. The only noise is made by the walker; if you stop moving, the silence is total. Grotesque lava forms are everywhere. Cinder cones loom on the horizon; crevices and open pits yawn beside the trail. Surprisingly, there is no lack of color. Black predominates, of course, but you will see that lavas also come in shades of blue, green, brown, and red. The landscape is stark, barren, even grim, but it is never boring.

HOW TO GET THERE: There are two approaches to the Mauna Loa Cabin. From Hawai'i Volcanoes National Park Visitor Center (33 miles), turn left leaving the parking lot and exit the park to Highway 11. Turn left again, in the direction of Kona, and proceed to the intersection of Mauna Loa Road, about 3.8 miles. Turn right, passing Kīpuka Puaulu, up a narrow winding road. Proceed with caution, because the road becomes one lane in many places, with many blind turns. The trailhead begins at the end of the road, at a small parking lot, about 13.5 miles from Highway 11. Follow the trail 7.5 miles to Red Hill Cabin, where you will most likely overnight. From Red Hill, the trail continues for another 11.6 miles to Mauna Loa Cabin.

Another approach is via the 'Ainapō Trail. The trailhead is located halfway between mileposts 40 and 41 on Highway 11, southeast of the national park. From here, it is 18.2 miles to the Mauna Loa Cabin, but a four-wheel-drive vehicle can take you the first 8 miles. A new cabin, the 'Ainapō Trail Shelter, is located 10.7 miles from the highway (see following entry). From there, it is an additional 7.5 miles to the Mauna Loa Cabin.

The shortest way to the Mauna Loa Cabin is from the Mauna Loa Weather Observatory on the northwestern slope of the mountain (6 miles). However, this route is difficult for the visitor unfamiliar with Hawai'i roads. The observatory is located at 11,150 feet at the end of an unmarked road branching off from Route 200 (Saddle Road). This presents an additional problem because most rental car companies prohibit driving on the Saddle Road. The road, however, is a fully paved, two-lane highway. There are far worse roads that the car companies do not restrict, but I have given up trying to argue with them. One firm, Harper's Car Rental in Hilo, permits travel on the Saddle Road for its four-wheel-drive vehicles, which cost about twice the price of a regular sedan. Call 969–1478. If you are able to surmount these problems and are coming from Hilo, take Highway 200 west about 25 miles, watching carefully for a reddish brown dirt road leading off at a right angle to the left. The turn is located at the base of a prominent hill on the left side of the road. If you reach a paved road leading off at a right angle to the right, you have gone too far. At this point, you should also be able to see a small hunter check-in shack on the left side of the road. Turn around, proceed slowly for about half a mile. Turn on the first road to the right. This narrow, one-lane road winds its way uphill for about 8.2 miles to several instrument towers and dishes. At this point turn sharply right and proceed for another 9 miles to the parking lot below the observatory. Signposts will then guide you to the trailhead.

The trail is steep and rough in places and is entirely over *'a'ā* and *pāhoehoe* lava. The grade and the altitude make this a strenuous hike, but the vistas and the view into the massive 3.5-mile-long summit crater are spectacular. It is 6.4 miles to the 13,679-foot peak, but you should allow 10 to 12 hours for the round-trip. It is dangerous to be on the mountain after nightfall. The lower sections of the trail are marked only by rock cairns, which are impossible to pick out in the dark against the black lava background.

If you are taking the Observatory route from Kailua (Kona) (56 miles), take Highway 190 about 35 miles to the junction of Highway 200 (Saddle Road). Turn right on Highway 200, proceed about 26 miles, watching carefully for a hunter check-in shack on the right and a paved road turning off the highway to the left. Make the next right turn, just after a prominent hill on the right side of the road. Follow the directions above.

'Ainapō Trail Shelter

LOCATION: This relatively new (1994) small cabin is located on the 'Ainapō Trail, on the south slope of Mauna Loa at an elevation of 7,750 feet.

DESCRIPTION: 'Ainapō, which means "darkened land (by fog)," is used mainly by hikers climbing or descending from Mauna Loa. It is situated in a small clearing within the Kapāpala Forest Reserve, a mixed mesic *koa/'ōhi'a* forest. It is located about midway along the trail to the summit of the mountain, 10.7 miles from Highway 11, and 7.5 miles from the Mauna Loa Cabin.

FACILITIES: The cabin has six bunks and mattresses (three double bunks), a table, and six stools. A covered porch also houses a composting toilet under the same roof. There is no stove for heating or cooking. A 400-gallon catchment tank provides water, which should be treated before drinking. A separate structure, about 50 feet from the cabin, contains a dishwashing

'Ainapō Trail Shelter, on the slopes of Mauna Loa, is the newest cabin on the mountain.

area and a shower(!), fed by the water tank. Tent camping is permitted by members of the same party, if they exceed the space in the cabin, but tent sites are limited.

PERMIT/RESERVATIONS: Permits are required and may be obtained not earlier than one month in advance from the Division of Forestry and Wildlife, 1648 Kīlauea Avenue, Hilo, HI 96720; phone, (808) 933–4221.

TIME LIMIT: Two nights.

COST: Free.

SPECIAL COMMENTS: No open fires are permitted. No burying or burning of trash is allowed; pack it all out. The four-wheel-drive road from Highway 11 passes through Kapāpala Ranch land for 5.7 miles, and hikers are restricted to the road corridor. Also, access over this road is during daylight hours only. Do not attempt this road in a conventional-drive car! If you are planning to use the Mauna Loa Trail as part of your trip, it will be necessary to obtain a separate permit from the park visitors center.

The 'Ainapō Trail was the original route to the summit of Mauna Loa, pioneered by the ancient Hawaiians. The first European known to have climbed the mountain was Archibald Menzies, the surgeon of Vancouver's 1794 expedition. After 1915, when the Mauna Loa Trail was built, the 'Ainapō fell into disuse, and parts of it disappeared, until it was restored by the Division of Forestry and Wildlife, under the auspices of the Na Ala Hele program in 1993.

HOW TO GET THERE: From Hilo, drive south on Highway 11 to a point halfway between mile markers 40 and 41. A gate, cattle guard, and sign on the right, mark the beginning of an 8-mile long four-wheel-drive road leading to the trailhead at 5,650 feet. It is another 2.7 miles, with an elevation gain of 2,100 feet to the cabin.

WINDWARD SIDE

Kēōkea Beach Park

LOCATION: This park is on the northern end of the windward coast, on a rocky shoreline, between the town of Hāwī and the Pololū Valley Lookout.

DESCRIPTION: Kēōkea is a large, attractive, well-maintained park, protected from the gusty trade winds common to this coastline. A large grassy area and a pretty knoll are set off by *hala* and palm trees. The shoreline is black rock, and there is a small boulder beach. Tents can be pitched either in the open grassy field or in the partial shade of the scattered trees. Kēōkea means "the sound of white[caps]" in Hawaiian.

FACILITIES: Tent and vehicle camping. A very large pavilion contains twelve tables, rest rooms, a dishwashing area, and electric lighting. A smaller pavilion, with one table, sits on a knoll near the water's edge, and five open picnic tables are scattered throughout the park. The showers are outdoors, and the water is drinkable. Groceries and gas are available in Hāwī, about 7 miles to the west.

CAMPGROUND ACTIVITIES: Mediocre at best, swimming is only safe during calm days in the summer and early fall. At other times, high surf, strong currents, and the rocky shoreline make for dangerous conditions. Most frequent catches here are *pāpio,* mullet, and threadfin. You may hook an occasional *ulua*.

PERMIT/RESERVATIONS: Write or call the following: Department of Parks and Recreation, County of Hawai'i, 25 Aupuni Street, Hilo, HI 96720; phone, (808) 961–8311.

TIME LIMIT: Summer months, 1 week; other months, 2 weeks.

COST: Adults, $1 per day; juniors (13 to 17), 50 cents per day; children (12 and under), no charge.

SPECIAL COMMENTS: Kēōkea is an excellent place for those seeking a quiet campground. Because of its isolation, it is frequented mostly by fishermen, who do not usually camp. Even when a local family does have a big beach party, there is plenty of room for all.

HOW TO GET THERE: Although Kēōkea is on the windward side, you will have to go to the leeward side of the island to get there. From Hilo (78 miles), take Highway 19 north to Waimea. Turn right on Highway 250 to Hāwī, then right on Highway 270. Watch for a sign about 5 miles from Hāwī. Turn left and proceed about 2 miles to the park.

From Kailua (Kona) (57 miles), take Highway 19 north to Kawaihae. Bear left on Highway 270, through Hāwī, watching for a sign about 5 miles from Hāwī. Turn left and proceed about 2 miles to the park.

NEARBY POINTS OF INTEREST: Pololū is a beautiful, uninhabited valley, very similar in appearance to Waipi'o and Waimanu Valleys, with which it shares this dramatic coast. A dirt trail leading down from the parking lot of

Kēōkea Beach Park campground, in North Kohala, is frequented mostly by fishermen. It is a good base for exploring Pololū Valley beach.

Pololū Valley beach, North Kohala, as seen from the lookout.

the Pololū Valley Lookout is shorter and much less strenuous than the road into Waipi'o, requiring no more than 10 to 15 minutes. Although the valley is privately owned, you may stroll and picnic on the black-sand beach and swim with caution. A trail leads from Pololū to the next two valleys, Honokānenui, and Honokāneiki. You may hike to the top of the trail leading down to Honokāneiki, but the rest of the trail, and the valley below, is private property. To get there from the campground, return to the highway, turn left, and follow the road to its end, about 1.5 miles.

The statue of Kamehameha in the center of the town of Hāwī has an interesting background. In 1879 the city of Honolulu commissioned a sculptor in Florence, Italy, to make a statue of the first king of Hawai'i. The statue was lost when the ship carrying it was sunk on a reef. A copy was ordered, which now stands in front of the Judiciary Building in Honolulu. Subsequently, the original statue was salvaged and it was placed in Hāwī, to commemorate Kamehameha's birthplace nearby.

For information on the Mo'okini Heiau and the Kamehameha Birth Stones, see Kapa'a Beach Park.

Waimanu Valley

LOCATION: This valley is northeast of Waipi'o Valley on the northern Hāmākua Coast.

DESCRIPTION: This beautiful, isolated valley is accessible only by trail. Waimanu, meaning "bird water," is the destination of hardy backpackers seeking the privacy and beauty of an uninhabited valley on the rugged windward coast of the Island. It is a smaller copy of Waipi'o Valley, with similar waterfalls, sheer valley walls, and black-sand beach backed by large stones. The beach usually erodes during the winter months, leaving the stones. Except for a narrow strip along the beach and the western wall, the valley is mostly swamp. Camping is restricted to this narrow strip, bordered by the beach on one side and the swamp on the other. Nine campsites have been marked in this area. The first and largest is a flat, shaded site, located on the water's edge in a grove of *kamani* trees, just before crossing Waimanu Stream. The best campsites, however, are those found in the tree-line along the beach after crossing the stream and before reaching the western wall. Some of these have been "improved" by previous campers by clearing tent sites, erecting rock walls for wind protection, and creating platforms for cooking and eating. A last, less-desirable site can be found near the far end of the beach, again in a grove of trees. Although this area is sloping, heavy shade keeps the ground damp most of the time

FACILITIES: Two composting pit toilets are the only facilities in the valley. The best source of water is a fast, narrow stream flowing down from the valley's western wall, which can be reached in 15 minutes via a trail from the beach. Because this is a long haul for those camped at the east end of the valley, water may also be taken from Waimanu Stream, which is less attractive, because it drains from the swamp. From whatever source, water should be boiled or treated before use.

CAMPGROUND ACTIVITIES: Caution should be taken when swimming, especially during periods of high surf. Swimming should not be attempted in winter months if the sand beach is gone. Waves pounding on the rocky shore can cause injury to persons trying to enter or leave the water. I have no specific information about fishing and have never fished here, but conditions should be the same as for Waipi'o, meaning *moi, pāpio,* and *ulua* are the best bets.

The valley is best explored from its western side, where several faint trails lead inland. Also from this side, you can hike to Wai'ilikahi Falls, a lovely bridal veil, cascading 320 feet into a magnificent pool. A dip in its brisk waters makes the rough, 1-hour hike worthwhile.

PERMIT/RESERVATIONS: Permits are required to camp in Waimanu, and the nine designated campsites are assigned individually, by number, at the time of application. For permits or information, call or write the following: Division of Forestry and Wildlife, 1648 Kīlauea Avenue, Hilo, HI 96720; phone, (808) 933–4221.

TIME LIMIT: Seven days.

COST: Free.

SPECIAL COMMENTS: During periods of heavy rain, Waimanu Stream can become dangerous and even impassible. Caution should be observed at such times. If you have trouble crossing the Waipi'o Stream en route, you can expect more of the same at Waimanu, especially if the wet weather continues. You are allowed to camp at the large campsite east of the stream until the water subsides. As anywhere, pack out all trash and everything you pack in.

HOW TO GET THERE: From Hilo (59 miles), take Highway 19 north to Honoka'a, then Highway 240 to Waipi'o Valley Lookout. Park at the parking lot, because the road into Waipi'o Valley can only be negotiated by four-wheel-drive vehicles. From the Lookout, you will be able to see a zigzag trail ascending the far wall of Waipi'o Valley. That is the beginning of the Muliwai (Waimanu) Trail, which is your destination. Descend on the paved road to the valley floor, turning right on the dirt road to the beach. Proceed left along the beach, ford the stream, and continue along a path at the edge of the trees. A metal post marks a fork in the trail at the end of the valley. Be sure to take the right fork, as the other leads to the back of Waipi'o. At the top of the strenuous switchback, the trail enters a beautiful coastal forest, which continues for 7 more miles to Waimanu. Some of the largest trees in the state are found here, including very tall Norfolk pines. A delightful small pool and waterfall lie at the second stream crossing, immediately beside the trail. It makes a great lunch spot and provides a welcome dip after the hot hike up the switchback. A trail shelter is located about two-thirds of the way to Waimanu. Consisting of a roof over a wooden floor with a rough wooden counter along one side, it may be used as a campsite en route, if desired.

From Kailua (Kona) (64 miles), take Highway 190 north to Waimea, then Highway 19 to Honoka'a. Turn left on Highway 240 to Waipi'o Valley Lookout and follow directions above.

Waipi'o Valley

LOCATION: This valley is on the Hāmākua Coast, 9 miles north of Honoka'a.

DESCRIPTION: Waipi'o, which means "curved water," is a lovely, verdant valley, hosting waterfalls, streams, and a mile-long gray-sand beach. Taro fields and a few homes dot the sparsely inhabited valley floor. Steep green cliffs border both sides of the valley, with waterfalls cascading down their sides. Groves of ironwood trees line the shore, providing excellent campsites. Behind the beach is a large marshy area, formerly in taro but now lying fallow. Waipi'o Stream forms a large pool just before entering the ocean, on the eastern side of the valley. It is a refreshing place to rinse off after a salt-water swim. Camping is permitted only in the area east of the Waipi'o Stream.

FACILITIES: There are no facilities of any kind. Sanitation is important, because the valley is occupied and many tourists visit the beach daily. Group or individual latrines are easy to dig in the soft soil and should be covered or partially filled after each use. The only water available at the campsite is from Waipi'o Stream and should be boiled or treated before use.

CAMPGROUND ACTIVITIES: Caution should be used when swimming off the beach, because rip currents can occur. Freshwater swimming can be enjoyed in the pond just behind where Waipi'o Stream enters the ocean. Avoid swimming here if the water is muddy. Leptospirosis is a threat in the valley. Local surfers come down when the waves are up (wave height: 2 to 8 feet). Short and long board, body board, and bodysurfing are all possible at such times, usually in winter and spring. Surfing is restricted by the difficulty of getting to the beach. *Pāpio, moi,* and sometimes *ulua* can be hooked here.

The road back into the valley makes an interesting walk. It branches into two routes, both of which eventually dead end, requiring a return via the way you came.

Kaluahine Falls, about half a mile from the east end of the beach, can be reached by scrambling along the coast over a formidable rock slide. Parts of this area are unstable and dangerous, and the hike should only be attempted at low tide. Standing in the spray behind the falls as it drops into the ocean is an exhilarating experience.

Hi'ilawe is a dramatic twin falls, cascading from the headwall of a perfect amphitheater valley branching off from Waipi'o. Unfortunately, one of the falls is often diverted at the top for irrigation, destroying its symmetrical beauty. The trail to the falls was washed out several years ago, so it can now only be reached by rock hopping up the stream.

Na'alapa Falls, on the western wall of the valley, is the easiest to reach. Although there is no trail, by following the road back into the valley and fording the stream near the west end, you can pick your way to the falls and several pools. Caution should be observed crossing Waipi'o Stream, especially in rainy weather. The stream floods easily and is sometimes impassable.

PERMIT/RESERVATIONS: No permit is required for camping in the area along the beach east of the stream, which is owned by Bishop Estate. The land on the western side of the stream belongs to several private owners, including the Bishop Museum. Permits to camp are not given by any of these owners, although you may see people camping across the stream without permits. They do this seeking privacy from the tourists who descend in four-wheel-drive shuttle tours to the east side of the beach. If your stay is short, you may not be disturbed if you camp on the west side, but camping there is nevertheless illegal.

TIME LIMIT: Seven days.

COST: Free.

SPECIAL COMMENTS: Waipi'o is the largest valley on Hawai'i and is famous in Hawaiian history. Several of the chiefs of Hawai'i made their homes here, and in 1780 Kamehameha received custody of the war god Kūkā'ilimoku here, foreshadowing his rule over all the Islands. At one time more than 1,500 people lived here, and the settlement boasted four schools, five churches, five stores, restaurants, a post office, and a hotel. Valley farms were an important source of rice and taro. Two devastating tsunamis, in 1946 and 1961, wiped out the settlement and the agriculture, and it is only in recent years that people have begun to return to the valley.

The road from Waipi'o Valley Lookout to the valley floor is for four-wheel-drive vehicles only; the 25 percent grade cannot be managed by a standard car. A parking lot at the Lookout can accommodate a limited number of cars, and parking is also available along the road at the top. On foot, the trip to the valley floor takes from 20 to 30 minutes. Several tour companies operate four-wheel-drive shuttles into the valley. Most of them can be contacted in the parking lot.

HOW TO GET THERE: From Hilo (47 miles), take Highway 19 north to Honoka'a, then Highway 240 to Waipi'o Valley Lookout. Unless you have a four-wheel-drive vehicle, park at the Lookout and descend into the valley on foot.

From Kailua (Kona) (52 miles), take Highway 190 north to Waimea, then Highway 19 to Honoka'a, and follow directions above.

Kalōpā State Recreation Area

LOCATION: This park is in an upland forest on the northern end of the Hāmākua Coast, about 7 miles from Honoka'a.

DESCRIPTION: Kalōpā is a beautiful, well-maintained park in a deep *'ōhi'a* forest, at an elevation of 2,000 feet. The central area is divided into a campground, picnic ground, and cabin area. The campground is in a grove of tall eucalyptus and *'ōhi'a* trees and is heavily shaded, with thick decaying leaf cover on the ground. The dense shade makes the area slow to dry after a rain. The cabin area is more open, with spacious lawns and landscaped grounds. A 100-acre forest includes hiking and riding trails. Kalōpā means "the tenant farmer" in Hawaiian.

FACILITIES: Tent and cabin camping only; no vehicle camping. A concrete-block building houses all the campground's facilities. It contains rest rooms with cold showers, a covered area with two picnic tables, counter space for camp stoves, and dishwashing sinks. Water is drinkable, and there are electric lights. A large covered pavilion, with several tables, is located in the picnic area, close to the campground. Up the road from the campground are two cabins, each of which contains two bunk rooms accommodating eight persons in four double bunks. Each bunk room has its own toilet, hot shower, and washing sinks. A large dining hall, with a fireplace and an excellent central kitchen with cooking and eating utensils, is shared by all cabin users.

CAMPGROUND ACTIVITIES: The trails in the park are well worth doing, to enjoy the experience of hiking in a native forest. If your time is limited, consider the 45-minute nature loop, which begins near the dining hall. A bulletin board at the parking lot describes the hike, and brochures can sometimes be found in a small kiosk at the trailhead. Points of interest and special trees and plants are numbered along the trail and keyed to the brochure. Some of the largest *'ōhi'a* trees in the state are found along the nature loop and elsewhere in the park.

PERMIT/RESERVATIONS: A permit may be obtained from a state parks office on any island. The following address is for the office on Hawai'i: Division of State Parks, P.O. Box 936, Hilo, HI 96720; phone, (808) 974–6200.

TIME LIMIT: Five nights in any consecutive 30-day period.

COST: Tent camping is free. Cabin bunk rooms rent for $55 per night for one to four persons, $5 for each additional person.

SPECIAL COMMENTS: Kalōpā is the best-maintained park in the state. The lawn area surrounding the cabins and the dining hall is kept in immaculate condition. Hikers making the long backpack into Waimanu Valley like to use Kalōpā, because it is the last place to take hot showers and the first place to get them on the return. Campers should not expect to use the dining hall/kitchen building, because it is kept locked, for the use of cabin renters only.

HOW TO GET THERE: From Hilo (40 miles), take Highway 19 north for about 38 miles to a small sign reading Kalōpā State Park. Turn left and follow signs an additional 2 miles to the park.

From Kailua (Kona) (58 miles), take Highway 190 north to Waimea, then Highway 19 past Honoka'a. Turn right at the sign for Kalōpā State Park and follow signs an additional 2 miles to the park.

Laupāhoehoe Beach Park

LOCATION: This park is on the windward coast, 27 miles north of Hilo.

DESCRIPTION: Laupāhoehoe, meaning "smooth lava flat," is a large, pretty park on a peninsula at the bottom of a steep escarpment. Waves crashing on the rocky shoreline, and the high cliffs behind, make a scenic setting. The park is flat and mostly open, with ironwood trees lining the beach. Tents can be pitched either in the large, grassy area or closer to the shore in the shade of the ironwoods. There is no beach.

FACILITIES: Tent and vehicle camping. There are three separate picnic areas with open tables, and two covered pavilions. The larger pavilion contains five tables, a barbecue, and a dishwashing sink; the second has several tables and a barbecue. Both pavilions have electric lights and drinking water. Rest rooms and outdoor showers are nearby. In addition to the above, three smaller pavilions are located along the south boundary of the park, each with its own table. Another rest room building is in this area. Limited groceries and gas can be obtained in the town of Laupahoehoe; otherwise Honoka'a is slightly closer than Hilo for more extensive needs.

CAMPGROUND ACTIVITIES: *Moi, pāpio,* and *ulua* are caught here.

Tent at Laupāhoehoe Beach Park, Hāmākua Coast. This dramatically situated park sometimes gets heavy day-use from school outings, but normally it has ample room for campers.

PERMIT/RESERVATIONS: Call or write the following: Department of Parks and Recreation, County of Hawai'i, 25 Aupuni Street, Hilo, HI 96720; phone, (808) 961–8311.

TIME LIMIT: Summer months, 1 week; other times, 2 weeks.

COST: Adults, $1 per day; juniors (13 to 17), 50 cents per day; children (12 and under), no charge.

SPECIAL COMMENTS: The monument near the shore is in memory of school children and teachers swept away by the devastating tsunami of 1946.

HOW TO GET THERE: From Hilo (27 miles), take Highway 19 north. After passing through Laupāhoehoe, watch for the sign to Laupāhoehoe Point. Turn right and follow the road down to the beach park.

From Kailua (Kona) (67 miles), take Highway 190 north to Waimea, then Highway 19 through Honoka'a. About 12 miles from Waimea, watch for the sign to Laupāhoehoe Point. Turn left and follow the road down to the beach park.

Keanakolu Cabin

LOCATION: This very isolated cabin is located high on the eastern slope of Mauna Kea, at the end of the Humu'ula Trail, north of Hilo.

DESCRIPTION: Used primarily by hunters, the cabin is for those who really want to get away or hike the several trails in the area. The almost 9,000-foot elevation requires warm clothing and sleeping bags. Keanakolu means "the triple cave" in Hawaiian.

FACILITIES: Cabin only, no tent or vehicle camping. The cabin is spartan, containing nothing but bunks for up to twenty persons. Keanakolu has water and an outhouse toilet. Water should be boiled or treated before use.

CAMPGROUND ACTIVITIES: Hunting, hiking, and exploring the upper slopes of Mauna Kea are all possible, using the cabin as a base.

PERMIT/RESERVATIONS: Call or write the following: Division of Forestry and Wildlife, 1648 Kīlauea Avenue, Hilo, HI 96720; phone, (808) 933–4221.

TIME LIMIT: Two nights.

COST: Free.

SPECIAL COMMENTS: The cabin can be driven to only with a four-wheel-drive vehicle (see directions below). You may also reach the cabin by hiking the 5-mile-long Humu'ula Trail, but finding the trailhead is difficult. It begins 5 miles west of the Niu-Kukui-Milo Village complex, about 15 miles north of Hilo. It is best to ask directions after reaching that area.

HOW TO GET THERE: From Waimea, take Mānā Road east for about 24 miles to the cabin, on the left.

Kolekole Beach Park

LOCATION: This campground is on the windward coast, 12 miles north of Hilo.

DESCRIPTION: This large, attractive campground is scenically located in a deep gulch on a rocky shoreline. A pretty stream borders its north boundary, and a small waterfall enters the stream near the ocean. Most of the park is an open grassy field, but large trees provide some shade along the border. The very narrow beach is mostly pebble and rock, with some patches of black sand. A highway bridge crosses the park 100 feet above the gulch, but there is no traffic noise in the park. Kolekole means "raw" or "scarred" in Hawaiian.

FACILITIES: Tent and vehicle camping. Two large pavilions and four small ones are located in the park. The large pavilion closest to the shore contains three long tables, a barbecue, and rest rooms. The second one contains six large tables, a barbecue, and rest rooms. The four small pavilions, each with a table and grill, are located along the southern border of the park. The only water available is from the outdoor showers or the sinks in the rest rooms. It should be boiled or treated before use. Groceries and gas are best obtained in Hilo, 12 miles south.

CAMPGROUND ACTIVITIES: Rough water and strong currents make ocean swimming dangerous. However, the freshwater stream is usually deep enough for swimming in several places. Threadfin, *pāpio,* and *ulua* can be taken here, but the shoreline is dangerous during periods of high surf.

PERMIT/RESERVATIONS: Call or write the following: Department of Parks and Recreation, County of Hawai'i, 25 Aupuni Street, Hilo, HI 96720; phone, (808) 961–8311.

TIME LIMIT: Summer months, 1 week; other months, 2 weeks.

COST: Adults, $1 per day; juniors (13 to 17), 50 cents per day; children (12 and under), no charge.

SPECIAL COMMENTS: The park is often crowded on weekends, but there is usually plenty of room at other times. Although farther away, Kolekole is probably a better base for exploring Hilo than Onekahakaha, for reasons explained in that section.

HOW TO GET THERE: From Hilo (12 miles), take Highway 19 north and watch for a sign immediately after passing 'Akaka Falls turnoff.

From Kailua (Kona) (75 miles), take Highway 190 north to Waimea, then Highway 19 east through Honoka'a. After the town of Laupāhoehoe, watch for a sign, about 10.5 miles.

NEARBY POINTS OF INTEREST: The stream in the campground comes directly from 442-foot-high 'Akaka Falls. A beautiful walk through lush tropical plantings to view two waterfalls makes this half-mile paved loop trail a must for all visitors. From the campground take the highway toward Hilo. The road to the falls is less than half a mile on the right. Follow this road to its end in the falls parking lot.

For information on Rainbow Falls and Boiling Pots, and Kaūmana Caves, see section on Onekahakaha Beach Park.

Onekahakaha Beach Park

LOCATION: The park is on the ocean, about 2.5 miles east of Hilo on Highway 137.

DESCRIPTION: Onekahakaha, which means "drawing [pictures] sand," is a large, attractive park, with a cove of white sand backing a shallow pond, which is protected by a low wall of stones. A larger pond to the north is deeper, rockier, and more vulnerable to high water and currents. The camping area is located on the western side of the beach park and is flat and mostly grassy, with some bare spots. Pools of standing water are common after heavy rain, so tents should be pitched on higher ground, if available. Shade can be found along the perimeter of the area, which is mostly open.

FACILITIES: Tent and vehicle camping. The camping area itself contains a large rest room area with indoor showers and sinks, plus additional outdoor showers. Another smaller rest room is at the western end, along with several covered pavilions with picnic tables. East of the camping area are two more covered pavilions, another rest room, and outdoor showers. Drinking water is available, and some of the pavilions have electricity. Limited groceries can be obtained at a small store about half a mile toward Hilo on Highway 137, and gasoline is available 2 miles away, at the junction of Highways 137 and 11.

CAMPGROUND ACTIVITIES: The ocean pond behind the rock wall provides safe, but shallow swimming. The northern pond affords good swimming in calm seas, but watch for sea urchins. Snorkeling is fairly good around the rocky areas of the northern pond on calm days. Fishing is good for milkfish, bonefish, mullet, and *'ōpelu*.

PERMIT/RESERVATIONS: Call or write the following: Department of Parks and Recreation, County of Hawai'i, 25 Aupuni Street, Hilo, HI 96720; phone, (808) 961–8311.

TIME LIMIT: Summer months, 1 week; other months, 2 weeks.

COST: Adults, $1 per day; juniors (13 to 17), 50 cents per day; children (12 and under), no charge.

SPECIAL COMMENTS: As of the date of this writing, Onekahakaha was closed for extensive renovation. A decision has not been made as to whether camping will be continued when the park reopens. Check with local authorities. Because it is so close to Hilo, Onekahakaha is popular with local residents and is usually crowded, especially on weekends. There are apt to be lots of small children playing and shouting, so if you are looking for peace and quiet, this may not be the place for you. The campground is often a haven for homeless families, who camp there on a semipermanent basis. They are occasionally required to move, but authorities seem reluctant to force the issue. High winter surf can flood the park, including the camping area.

Because of the above factors, plus its closeness to Hilo, I do not recommend camping at Onekahakaha, in spite of its attractive site. As I have written elsewhere in this book, the closer a campground is to a population center, the greater the possibility of problems. If you want to be close to Hilo, Kolekole Beach Park, about 12 miles north, might be a better selection.

HOW TO GET THERE: From downtown Hilo (2.5 miles), drive east on Kamehameha Avenue, bearing left on Kalaniana'ole Avenue (Highway 137) just past the airport turnoff. Continue about 1.5 miles, watching for the turnoff to the park on the left.

From Kailua (Kona) (94 miles), drive to Hilo, then follow the instructions above.

NEARBY POINTS OF INTEREST: A pretty waterfall and pool right in the suburbs of Hilo, Rainbow Falls gets its name from the rainbows that often appear in its mists. From the campground, return to Hilo, turning left on Waiānuenue Avenue (Highway 200) to Rainbow Drive. After visiting the falls, proceed 2 miles farther to Pe'epe'e Falls Street to see the Boiling Pots, a series of pools connected by underground channels, which make the pools bubble as if they are boiling.

Also close to Hilo are the Kaūmana Caves. These two lava tubes were formed by an eruption of Mauna Loa in 1881. A staircase leads down to the caves. Take a flashlight for the lower cave, which is safe to explore. From the campground, drive to Waiānuenue Avenue, turning left as above. Turn left again on Kaūmana Drive, watching for a sign for the caves on the right, about 3 miles.

James Kealoha Beach Park

LOCATION: The park is on the ocean, about 3 miles east of Hilo on Highway 137.

DESCRIPTION: Kealoha Beach Park borders an open bay with an attractive shoreline area. The western and central parts of the bay are exposed to heavy waves and rip currents during periods of high surf. The eastern section is more protected and contains several small coves of white sand. The area behind the shore is nicely landscaped, with large trees and other plantings. It contains a covered pavilion with picnic tables and modern rest rooms. The campground is located a short distance to the west, in a much less attractive open field, lying between the highway and the sea. The field is flat and mostly grassy with bare patches, and some shade is afforded from trees along its border.

FACILITIES: Tent and vehicle camping. The campground contains rest rooms, outdoor showers, and one open picnic table. Drinking water is available. The much better facilities to the east, mentioned above, are close enough to be used from the campground. Limited groceries can be obtained at a small store about 1 mile west on the road to Hilo. Gas may be purchased at the intersection of Kalaniana'ole Avenue (Highway 137) and Highway 11, about 1.5 miles toward Hilo from the park.

CAMPGROUND ACTIVITIES: On calm days, swimming is excellent from most places off shore. During rough water, swimming may still be possible in the protected eastern end of the bay. Snorkeling is very good, following the above guidelines. A popular local break, known as "Four Miles," sometimes affords good surfing waves, mostly in the winter months. Waters here are good for mullet, threadfin, *pāpio,* goatfish, milkfish, and big-eyed scad.

PERMIT/RESERVATIONS: Call or write the following: Department of Parks and Recreation, County of Hawai'i, 25 Aupuni Street, Hilo, HI 96720; phone, (808) 961–8311.

TIME LIMIT: Summer months, 1 week; other times, 2 weeks.

COST: Adults, $1 per day; juniors (13 to 17), 50 cents per day; children (12 and under), no charge.

SPECIAL COMMENTS: Because of its limited facilities, closeness to a busy road, and proximity to a populated area, I do not recommend that you camp at Kealoha Park. Leleiwi Point, at the east end of Highway 137, appears to be a rendezvous for people involved in suspicious activities. All that traffic will go right by your tent. If you are determined to be close to Hilo without the crowded conditions normally found at Onekahakaha, you might try it, but you have been warned.

HOW TO GET THERE: From downtown Hilo (3 miles), take Kamehameha Avenue east. Bear left on Kalaniana'ole Avenue just after the airport turnoff and watch for a sign.

From Kailua (Kona) (95 miles), drive to Hilo and follow above instructions.

Isaac Hale Beach Park

LOCATION: The park is on the southeast Puna coast, between Cape Kumukahi and the town of 'Opihikao.

DESCRIPTION: Isaac Hale is a 2-acre park centering around a boat ramp, the only one on the Puna coast. It is situated on a small bay and has a modest black-sand beach. The camping area is part grass and partly bare, with some shade from spaced trees.

FACILITIES: The park contains a pavilion with two tables and rest rooms. When I last visited in late 1992, there was no longer any water, and portable toilets had been moved in. The area is run-down and unattractive. There is no electricity.

CAMPGROUND ACTIVITIES: Because the beach contains many pebbles and stones, swimmers and snorkelers usually enter the water at the boat ramp. Kehena Beach is much better for swimming (see below). Mediocre short and long board, and body board surfing can be done on small waves in the center of the bay. Snorkeling is good during calm weather. Goatfish, *pāpio, moi,* and menpachi are most often caught here.

PERMIT/RESERVATIONS: Call or write the following: Department of Parks and Recreation, County of Hawai'i, 25 Aupuni Street, Hilo, HI 96720; phone, (808) 961–8311.

TIME LIMIT: Summer months, 1 week; other times, 2 weeks.

COST: Adults, $1 per day; juniors (13 to 17), 50 cents per day; children (under 12), no charge.

SPECIAL COMMENTS: With the loss of Harry K. Brown Beach Park to the volcano, campers have only Isaac Hale and MacKenzie campgrounds on the northeast side of the lava flows. Neither of them has water. Isaac Hale is one of the few places in the area where swimming is possible, but MacKenzie is the prettier of the two. Because is it only 2 miles away, you might want to check it out before settling down for the night.

Isaac Hale is heavily used by boaters and fishermen and is often crowded with their boats, trailers, and vehicles. This is particularly true on weekends and is another reason to consider camping at MacKenzie.

HOW TO GET THERE: From Hilo (28 miles), take Highway 11 south to the intersection of Highway 130, which bears left at Kea'au. At Pāhoa, bear slightly left on Highway 132. Immediately after passing the entrance to Lava Tree State Monument, watch for Pāhoa-Pohoiki Road to the right. Follow this road to the park.

From Kailua (Kona) (115 miles via Nā'ālehu, 122 miles via Waimea): if coming via Nā'ālehu, turn right onto Highway 130 at Kea'au, about 8 miles past Mountain View, then follow directions above; if coming via Waimea, drive to Hilo and follow directions from there.

NEARBY POINTS OF INTEREST: Pohoiki Warm Springs, behind the beach, is a freshwater pool, heated by Madame Pele. It is well hidden amidst dense vegetation. Ask locally how to find it.

Kehena Beach is a far better place to swim than Isaac Hale and is only 7.3 miles south on Highway 137. A pretty, secluded, black-sand beach, with palm trees and ironwoods for shade, it is difficult to see from the highway. Watch for a small parking pull-off, just past milepost 19. Nudists sometimes frequent this beach.

Lava Tree State Monument is a pretty park in a forest of high trees, formed around an older *'ōhi'a* forest overrun by lava. The lava, swirling around the trees, created grotesque shapes that remained after the trunks of the trees burned out. There are a picnic area and rest rooms. From the campsite (about 6 miles), return on Pāhoa-Pohoiki Road toward Hilo and turn left on Highway 132. The park is on the right.

Wai'ōpae Tide Pools. Wai'ōpae is the only place I know of in the Islands where beautiful coral gardens can be viewed so close to shore, in such shallow water, and with so little effort. A series of connecting pools and the variety of reef fish and coral at Wai'ōpae make you feel as though you are swimming in an aquarium. No lengthy hike or swim is required. Just park the car, walk a few hundred feet to one of the pools, put on your mask, and jump in. From the campground, drive about 3 miles north on Highway 137 to a dirt road on the right named Vacationland Drive. Take this road through Kapoho Beach Lots to the ocean.

MacKenzie State Recreation Area

LOCATION: The campground is on the southeast Puna coast, between the town of ʻOpihikao and Cape Kumukahi.

DESCRIPTION: MacKenzie lies in an ironwood grove on a cliff overlooking the ocean. The ground slopes slightly toward the water and is mostly covered wih ironwood needles. Tent sites are numerous, mostly in heavy shade, although some partially open sites can be found near the water. It is an attractive site.

FACILITIES: Tent camping only. Within the camping area is one open picnic table and enclosed pit toilets. The picnic area contains a small pavilion with one table, several open stone picnic tables, and enclosed pit toilets. There is no water or electricity. Between the two areas is a small water tank with a catchment roof above it. I have always found it empty.

CAMPGROUND ACTIVITIES: Fishing is complicated by the need to haul the catch up over a rocky cliff, which varies from 15 to 25 feet high. Probable catches here include *pāpio, ulua,* and goatfish.

PERMIT/RESERVATIONS: A permit may be obtained from a state parks office on any island. The following address is for the office on Hawaiʻi: Division of State Parks, P.O. Box 936, Hilo, HI 96720; phone, (808) 974–6200.

TIME LIMIT: Five nights in any one consecutive 30-day period.

COST: Free.

SPECIAL COMMENTS: With the loss of Harry K. Brown Beach Park to Madame Pele, campers have only Isaac Hale and MacKenzie campgrounds on the northeast side of the lava flows, which cut the coastal highway in 1990. Without water, neither has much to recommend it. Swimming is possible at Isaac Hale, but a far better place to swim is Kehena Beach, 5.2 miles south (see section on Isaac Hale Beach Park for a description).

HOW TO GET THERE: From Hilo (30 miles), take Highway 11 south to the intersection of Highway 130, which bears left at Kea'au. At Pāhoa, bear slightly left on Highway 132. Immediately after passing the entrance to Lava Tree State Monument, watch for Pāhoa-Pohoiki Road to the right. Follow this road to the coast. On Highway 137 turn right and proceed 2 miles to the park.

From Kailua (Kona) (117 miles via Nā'ālehu, 124 miles via Waimea): if coming via Nā'ālehu, turn right onto Highway 130 at Kea'au, about 8 miles past Mountain View, then follow directions above; if coming via Waimea, drive to Hilo and follow directions from there.

NEARBY POINTS OF INTEREST: For information on Lava Tree State Monument, Wai'ōpae Tide Pools, and Kehena Beach, see section on Isaac Hale Beach Park.

Kalani Honua Conference and Retreat Center

LOCATION: The center is on the southeast Puna coast, about 10 miles south of the town of Pāhoa.

DESCRIPTION: Kalani Honua, which means "sky and land," is a 20-acre secluded cultural and retreat center close to Puna's rugged shoreline, surrounded by lush forests. Although designed to accommodate conferences and groups, the center welcomes individuals and families. Its rates are relatively expensive, but it is the only really clean, comfortable campground north of the recent lava flows.

FACILITIES: Tent camping only, no vehicle camping; cottages, lodge rooms, and multiple occupancy. An attractive, grassy area with some trees is set aside for tents. Rest rooms, hot showers, and picnic tables are provided. Drinking water is obtained from the central kitchen. The center provides three vegetarian meals daily. Gas and groceries can be purchased in Pāhoa, 10 miles north.

CAMPGROUND ACTIVITIES: The grounds contain a swimming pool, tennis court, volleyball court, and a sauna/hot tub, which are available to all guests, including tent campers.

PERMIT/RESERVATIONS: Call or write the following: Kalani Honua, RR 2, Box 4500, Kalapana, HI 96778; phone, (808) 965–7828 or toll free 800–800–6886 (reservations only).

TIME LIMIT: None.

COST: Tent camping costs $15 one person, and $10 for each additional adult per day. Children 3–12 are $5 per day. Camping includes hot showers and use of the pool, hot tub, and sauna. For cottages, one bedroom with double and single bed, bath, and living room is $85 for one, $95 for two persons, $25 each additional. For lodge rooms, a private bath, single is $75, double, $85; shared bath, single is $60, double, $70. For multiple occupancy (may have to share a room), the cost is $45 per person in a room with three twin beds, shared bath. Meals can be purchased individually, or by a $25 per day plan for three vegetarian meals (chicken and fish options usually available). A community kitchen facility is available for cottage and room users, but not for campers. In accommodations, infants under 3 are free. Children 3–12 are $10 per night. Children's meals are half price.

HOW TO GET THERE: From Hilo (32 miles), take Highway 11 to Kea'au, turning left at the traffic light onto Highway 130. Stay on the highway, bypassing Pāhoa, turning left at the next road sign to 'Opihikao. Continue down this road about 5 miles to a **T**, turn right on Highway 137, and proceed another 2 miles to a sign and banner for Kalani Honua on the right.

NEARBY POINTS OF INTEREST: For information on Pohoiki Warm Springs, Kehena Beach, Lava Tree State Monument, and Wai'ōpae Tide Pools, see section on Isaac Hale Beach Park.

Punalu'u Beach Park

LOCATION: The park is on the ocean, along the southeast shore, between the towns of Pāhala and Nā'ālehu.

DESCRIPTION: Punalu'u, which means "coral dived for," is noted for its famed black-sand beach, located on a beautiful, palm-lined bay. The campground is situated adjacent to it, on slightly higher ground to the south. The campsite itself is a grassy, open area on a rocky shoreline. There are a few palm trees, but no real shade. Punalu'u is close to the Aspen Institute for Humanistic Studies and the Seamountain Resort and Golf Course, which together provide the surroundings with attractive landscaping.

FACILITIES: Tent and vehicle camping. Two large, modern pavilions, each with two tables, front a paved parking lot. Two open picnic tables and two barbecues are also provided. A very large pavilion, with kitchen area and dish washup is located just north of the campground. Rest rooms, drinking water, electricity, and public telephone are available. Outdoor showers are provided, but were broken and inoperative when last checked. An excellent restaurant and a souvenir stand are located just behind the beach. Groceries and gas can be obtained in Nā'ālehu, about 8 miles to the south.

CAMPGROUND ACTIVITIES: Not recommended from the camping area, swimming should be done cautiously from the northeast end of the black-sand beach. Strong currents make it advisable to remain inshore of the boat ramp. Snorkeling is good, but only on calm days. The same cautions for swimmers apply to snorkelers. *Pāpio, ulua,* menpachi, and red bigeye are caught here.

PERMIT/RESERVATIONS: Call or write the following: Department of Parks and Recreation, County of Hawai'i, 25 Aupuni Street, Hilo, HI 96720; phone, (808) 961–8311.

TIME LIMIT: Summer months, 1 week; other months, 2 weeks.

COST: Adults, $1 per day; juniors (13 to 17), 50 cents per day; children (12 and under), no charge.

SPECIAL COMMENTS: Because it is a well-known tourist attraction, Punalu'u Beach is often crowded by visitors and local people, particularly on weekends. However, there is usually room in the campground.

HOW TO GET THERE: From Hilo (57 miles), take Highway 11 south past Pāhala, watching for the sign to the park on the left.

From Kailua (Kona) (67 miles), take Highway 11 south past Nā'ālehu, watching for the sign to the park on the right.

Whittington Beach Park

LOCATION: The park is on the southeast shore, between the towns of Pāhala and Nā'ālehu.

DESCRIPTION: Whittington is a very pretty, secluded campground, situated on a dramatic, rocky coastline. The camping area is spacious and grassy, with banyans, palms, *kiawe,* and some ironwood trees affording partial or complete shade. There is no beach, and the shoreline is rocky and usually pounded by heavy waves. An old, abandoned sugar-loading pier is located at the south end of the park. Rough water, difficult entry, and strong currents make swimming dangerous and not recommended.

Whittington Beach Park, quiet and spacious, is the best place to camp in southern Ka'ū and is a good area to fish.

FACILITIES: Tent and vehicle camping. Three covered pavilions each contain two tables, a dishwashing area, a barbecue grill, and electric lights. In addition, there are five open picnic tables. A rest room is located across from the pavilions. Water in the park is not drinkable and should be boiled or treated before use. Groceries and gas can be purchased in Nā'ālehu, 5 miles to the west of the park.

CAMPGROUND ACTIVITIES: This is a good area for *pāpio,* mullet, and red bigeye.

PERMIT/RESERVATIONS: Call or write the following: Department of Parks and Recreation, County of Hawai'i, 25 Aupuni Street, Hilo, HI 96720; phone, (808) 961–8311.

TIME LIMIT: Summer months, 1 week; other months, 2 weeks.

COST: Adults, $1 per day; juniors (13 to 17), 50 cents per day; children (12 and under), no charge.

SPECIAL COMMENTS: Nā'ālehu, 3 miles away, is the southernmost town in the United States, and Whittington is the southernmost campground.

HOW TO GET THERE: From Hilo (61 miles), take Highway 11 south past Pāhala, watching for the sign to the park on the left. The sign is small and comes up suddenly, so it is best to slow down a few miles past the entrance to Punalu'u Beach Park and watch for it carefully.

From Kailua (Kona) (63 miles), take Highway 11 south past Nā'ālehu, watching for the sign to the park on the right. The sign is small and comes up suddenly, so it is best to slow down shortly after passing through Nā'ālehu and watch carefully. The turnoff to the park involves an almost 180-degree angle onto a dirt road going back in the direction of Nā'ālehu.

NEARBY POINTS OF INTEREST: About 20 miles south of the campground is South Point, the southernmost point of the Hawaiian Islands and of the United States. It is well worth a visit for its stark, windswept atmosphere and its archaeological interest, which includes a *heiau,* salt pans, and "canoe holes" in the rock, to which Hawaiians used to tie their canoes while fishing in the strong offshore currents. To reach it from the campground, take Highway 11 southwest to the road to South Point, about 9 miles. Turn left and continue about another 11 miles to the end of the road. You will pass the state's largest wind farm on this road.

Green Sand Beach is one of the most interesting beaches in Hawai'i. Its color comes from olivine crystals eroded from the volcanic cone behind the shoreline. The sea has carved a semicircle out of the cone, providing the beach a dramatic setting. There is no vegetation and consequently no protection from the sun, except in the shadow of a small, rocky ledge. The beach is steep, both on and offshore, creating a strong backwash. Swim with caution. To reach Green Sand Beach, drive to South Point, as above. Unless you have a four-wheel-drive vehicle, park at the eastern end of the point, at the boat ramp. Walk or drive along the rutted coastal road that leads northeast, for 2.5 miles. The beach, which appears below, should be approached from the low sea cliff on its south side, where a rough trail leads to it. Attempting to reach the beach from the steep face of the cone behind the beach is dangerous and causes increased erosion in this fragile area.

LEEWARD SIDE

Manukā State Park

LOCATION: The park is on Highway 11, on the south Kona coast, within the Manukā Natural Area Reserve, 19.3 miles west of Nā'ālehu.

DESCRIPTION: Manukā, which means "blundering," is a state wayside picnic area in the center of a 25,000-acre *'ōhi'a* forest reserve. It consists of just over 13 sloping acres, which are grassy, partially shaded, and landscaped with a collection of native and introduced trees. A nature trail (3.5-mile loop) begins at the parking area and provides an interesting example of the types of plants found in an *'ōhi'a* dry forest. At the top of the loop, just before it turns to make its descent back to the parking area, is a collapsed lava tube filled with native plants. It is possible to climb down into the tube and enter its high, vaulted chamber.

FACILITIES: Tent and vehicle camping is not permitted. Camping is only allowed in a three-sided rock structure with a tin roof, containing a picnic table and rock benches. The park contains a covered pavilion with four picnic tables, two open picnic tables, and rest rooms with flush toilets. There is no drinking water.

CAMPGROUND ACTIVITIES: There is hiking in an upland dry forest.

PERMIT/RESERVATIONS: Permits may be obtained from a state park office on any island. The following address is for the state office on the island of Hawai'i: Division of State Parks, P.O. Box 936, 75 Aupuni Street, Hilo, HI 96720; (808) 974–6200.

TIME LIMIT: Five nights in any one 30-day period.

COST: Free.

SPECIAL COMMENTS: The camping shelter is close to the road, in the lower part of the park, but it is necessary to park in the lot above and walk down to it. I have seen vehicles pulled right up to the shelter on the grass and have also seen small tents pitched beside it. Because the shelter is somewhat removed from the rest of the park, you may be able to get away with this, but keep in mind that, technically, this is not permitted. The shelter does not lend itself to use by more than one camping party, unless they are friends or relatives.

HOW TO GET THERE: From Hilo, drive south on Highway 11 for 84 miles. Watch for the sign about 12 miles after passing the South Point turnoff.

From Kailua (Kona), drive south on Highway 11 about 40 miles and watch for the sign shortly after entering Manukā Natural Area Reserve.

NEARBY POINTS OF INTEREST: The old Hawaiian *kapu* system prescribed severe penalties for violating the rules of the society. The only recourse for a violator was to reach a *pu'uhonua,* a place of refuge, before he was captured and punished. After a ceremonial "cleansing," the violator was allowed to return to his place in society without penalty. Pu'uhonua o Hōnaunau is the only restored place of refuge in the Hawaiian Islands and is now a national historical park. To reach it, drive north from the campground on Highway 11 to the large park sign. Turn left (Highway 160) at the sign and proceed another 3.6 miles to the park.

Kealakekua Bay is the place where Captain James Cook first came ashore on the island of Hawai'i in January, 1779, after sighting the Islands the previous year. It is also the place where he was killed in a dispute over a stolen boat a month later. At the end of the road leading to the bay is a small, gray-sand beach and the remains of a *heiau* where Cook was honored upon his arrival. Visible directly across the bay is a white obelisk that marks the spot where Cook was killed. It is reachable only by boat or a very rough jeep/foot trail from the town of Captain Cook. To reach the bay, drive north on Highway 11 for about 28 miles to a sign marked Kealakekua Bay. Turn left at the sign, following the road down to the shore. A small parking area is situated beside the *heiau,* just before the beach.

For information on 'Āhole Hōlua (slide) at Pu'u Hinahina Bay, see section on Miloli'i Beach Park.

For information on South Point and Green Sand Beach, see section on Whittington Beach Park.

Miloli'i Beach Park

LOCATION: The park is on the south Kona coast, 5 miles off the highway, and 17 miles south of the town of Captain Cook.

DESCRIPTION: Miloli'i is a small beach park located on a lava point adjacent to the Hawaiian fishing village of the same name. Miloli'i means "fine twist" in Hawaiian, referring to the sennit cord made by twisting coconut husk fibers that was formerly produced in the village. The park is mostly hard-packed dirt, with a few patches of grass. A grove of ironwood trees along the water provides partial shade. Two sides of the park are bordered by a seawall. Seaward of the wall, the water is shallow and rocky, with numerous tide pools. A 1926 Mauna Loa lava flow, which destroyed the original settlement, makes an ugly black swath across the landscape and, somehow, still seems menacing. The village, which appears ramshackle and weather-beaten, is one of the last self-supporting communities of its kind in Hawai'i. The people adhere to many of the old traditions, and the Hawaiian language is still spoken by some of the older residents.

FACILITIES: A large pavilion and a smaller one, both roofed with palm fronds, contain picnic tables. One outdoor grill is located near the water's edge. A rest room building with flush toilets is provided, but there is no drinking water in the park. A paved basketball court, a playground, and a dirt parking lot take up more than half the usable space in this small park. A very basic general store with one gas pump is located in the village, but more extensive supplies will have to be purchased in Captain Cook, about 26 miles north.

CAMPGROUND ACTIVITIES: A small fringing reef provides safe conditions for swimming, except during heavy surf, but the water is shallow, and the bottom is rocky. Snorkeling is excellent, except during high surf and storms. *'Ōpelu* (mackerel scad) has long been a mainstay of the village, but *pāpio,* mullet, bonefish, and threadfin can also be hooked. Inquire regarding local restrictions on type of equipment and catch permitted.

PERMIT/RESERVATIONS: Call or write the following: Department of Parks and Recreation, County of Hawai'i, 25 Aupuni Street, Hilo, HI 96720; phone, (808) 961–8311.

TIME LIMIT: Summer months, 1 week; other months, 2 weeks.

COST: Adults, $1 per day; juniors (13 to 17), 50 cents per day; children (12 and under), no charge.

SPECIAL COMMENTS: The local community has virtually taken over this beach park as its own activities center, and it is heavily used, especially by children using the playground and the basketball court. There is not much room for tents, particularly on weekends, when many residents pitch their own. At best, campers are likely to find the park crowded with activity, day or night, and not conducive to camping privacy. Alternatives to camping at Miloli'i are Manukā and Whittington.

HOW TO GET THERE: From Hilo (92 miles), take Highway 11 south past South Point. After passing Manukā State Wayside, watch for the sign to Miloli'i (about 8 miles from Manukā). Turn left on the steep, narrow road and proceed for 5 miles to the town of Miloli'i. The beach park is on the far side of the town.

From Kailua (Kona) (36 miles), take Highway 11 south. After passing the turnoff to Pu'uhonua o Hōnaunau, watch for the sign to Miloli'i (about 14 miles past the Pu'uhonua turnoff). Turn right on the steep, narrow road for 5 miles to the town of Miloli'i. The beach park is on the far side of the town.

NEARBY POINTS OF INTEREST: About 4 miles south of the campground, beside a small, isolated bay, is the best preserved *hōlua* in the Hawaiian Islands, Āhole Hōlua at Pu'u Hinahina Bay. *Hōlua* were giant slides that pre-Contact Hawaiians raced down on wooden sleds. According to legend, Pele, the goddess of fire, often disguised herself and competed with young chiefs in these races. To reach the *hōlua,* walk south on the dirt road from the campground, which soon ends at the water's edge. Continue along the outside of a seawall marking private property. If the tide is in, you will have to wade here. At the end of the seawall, cross the small sandy beach to the wooded area at its south end. The beginning of the trail is difficult to find, but look for a small wooden sign marked Old Trail, with an arrow pointing the way. Starting off poorly defined on black rock, the trail soon becomes easy to follow, and reaches a jeep road at beautiful Honomalino Bay, which you will identify easily by its dark brown sand and the coconut grove that follows the curve of the beach. The jeep road then continues over rugged *'a'ā* lava fields until it reaches the *hōlua*. While you are hiking, watch for segments of the "King's Highway," a trail through the rough *'a'ā* paved with smooth stones, which connected ancient villages to each other all along the west coast of the island. Long sections of this significant archaeological feature parallel the jeep road between Honomalino and Okoe bays. Other signs of former habitation include house foundations and pens that were used to hold cattle while they were waiting to swim out to small ships offshore that would take them to market in Hilo and Honolulu. A worthwhile detour is the beach at Okoe Bay, just a short walk seaward on a branch of the main jeep road, toward a prominent *kiawe* grove on the ocean.

Ho'okena Beach Park

LOCATION: The park is on the south Kona coast, about 10 miles south of Captain Cook.

DESCRIPTION: Ho'okena, which means "to satisfy thirst," is situated on the north side of an open bay. A gray-sand beach, with the remains of an old pier at its north end, is backed by scattered trees. Much of the shoreline is fronted by a rock outcropping, but sandy entrances to the ocean can be found at its north and south ends. The bay is usually calm and safe for water activities except during high surf.

FACILITIES: Tent and vehicle camping is permitted, but see comments below. A pavilion, picnic tables, and rest rooms complete the facilities.

There is no drinking water. Groceries and gas can be obtained at Captain Cook, about 10 miles north.

CAMPGROUND ACTIVITIES: There is good swimming most of the year. The best entry is near the old pier. Snorkeling is good on calm days. *'Ōpelu,* mullet, *pāpio,* bonefish, and threadfin can all be hooked here.

PERMIT/RESERVATIONS: Call or write the following: Department of Parks and Recreation, County of Hawai'i, 25 Aupuni Street, Hilo, HI 96720; phone, (808) 961–8311.

TIME LIMIT: Summer months, 1 week; other times, 2 weeks.

COST: Adults, $1 per day; juniors (13 to 17), 50 cents per day; children (12 and under), no charge.

SPECIAL COMMENTS: As of the date of publication, Ho'okena was closed due to sewage problems. At the time of writing, no decision had yet been made as to whether camping will be continued when the park reopens. Check with local authorities. It is almost impossible to park at Ho'okena. The small lot has room for no more than eight cars and is almost always filled by local residents. Vehicle camping is out of the question, and if you are lucky enough to find a parking spot, and then need to move your car, the spot will be gone when you return. For this reason, plus the lack of showers and drinking water, I do not recommend camping here.

HOW TO GET THERE: From Hilo (109 miles), take Highway 11 south, rounding South Point. Watch for the sign to Ho'okena. Turn left at the sign and follow the road to its end at the beach park.

From Kailua (Kona) (17 miles), take Highway 11 south. After passing the turnoff for the Place of Refuge (Pu'uhonua o Hōnaunau), watch for the sign to Ho'okena. Turn right and follow the road to the beach park.

NEARBY POINTS OF INTEREST: For information on Pu'uhonua o Hōnaunau (Place of Refuge), see the section on Manukā State Wayside.

Mauna Kea State Recreation Area

LOCATION: The park is on the Saddle Road (Highway 200) between Mauna Kea and Mauna Loa, at an elevation of 6,500 feet.

DESCRIPTION: The recreation area on Mauna Kea, which means "white mountain," is used primarily by hunters, by hikers climbing either of the two mountains, and by those who want to get away from it all for a while. Situated in an attractive location in the saddle between Mauna Kea and Mauna Loa, the camp consists of cabins and other associated buildings. Small trees and scrub brush are the main vegetation. The huge bulk of Mauna Kea looms behind the camp, and Mauna Loa occupies almost the entire view to the south.

FACILITIES: Cabins only; no tent or vehicle camping. There are two types of accommodations at Mauna Kea, group cabins and housekeeping cabins. The group cabins can house up to eight persons, dormitory style, in four double bunks. Each cabin has its own rest room, with sinks and hot shower. Bedding and towels are provided. A large recreation/dining hall, with a commercial-size kitchen, is shared by all group cabin users. Cooking and eating utensils are provided. The housekeeping cabins can house up to six persons. They consist of a living/dining room, two bedrooms, kitchen, and bathroom with hot shower. Bedding and eating and cooking utensils are provided. Hot water is available in all kitchens and bathrooms throughout the facility, and all buildings have electricity. Water is drinkable. The dining hall and some of the housekeeping cabins have fireplaces, but firewood is not provided. A public phone is located near the caretaker's residence. The nearest place for groceries and gas is Waimea, 24 miles west and an elevation drop of 4,000 feet.

PERMIT/RESERVATIONS: Permits can be obtained from a state parks office on any island. The following address is for the state office on Hawai'i: Division of State Parks, P.O. Box 936, Hilo, HI 96720; phone, (808) 961–7200.

TIME LIMIT: Five nights in any one consecutive 30-day period.

COST: Housekeeping cabins, $45 per night for one to four persons, $5 for each additional person, up to six. Group cabins, $55 per night for one to four persons, $5 for each additional person.

SPECIAL COMMENTS: Nights are cold at Mauna Kea, with the temperature dropping as soon as the sun goes down. Bring warm clothing and extra blankets or a sleeping bag if you sleep cold. It is best to bring your own firewood, if you plan to use the fireplace. Deadfall is increasingly hard to find, and you will have to range some distance for it. Bring your own ax, saw, machete, or whatever. And, of course, live trees may not be damaged or cut down to obtain firewood.

Many rental companies will not permit their cars to be driven on the Saddle Road. This is an unreasonable restriction, which probably dates from the days when the road was in poor shape, with narrow shoulders and some one-lane stretches. The road is now paved, two-lane, and is in better condition than other roads that have no such prohibitions. If renting a car, you have two choices: talk them out of the restriction or rent a four-wheel-drive vehicle from Harper's Car Rental; phone 969–1478. This is not a bad option, as you may want to drive to the summit of Mauna Kea. (See below.)

A large military training area lies adjacent to the camp. If maneuvers are taking place, artillery and helicopters may disrupt your peace and quiet.

HOW TO GET THERE: From Hilo (28 miles), take Highway 200 (Saddle Road) west, watching for the sign to the park on the right.

From Kailua (Kona) (50 miles), take Highway 190 north about 33 miles to the junction of Highway 200 (Saddle Road). Turn sharp right, follow Highway 200 for another 17 miles, watching for the sign to the park on the left.

NEARBY POINTS OF INTEREST: If you have a four-wheel-drive vehicle, you can go all the way to the summit of Mauna Kea, 13,796 feet, the highest point in the state and the world's premier astronomical observatory. Six nations currently operate nine telescopes on the mountain, and five more are planned or under construction. The largest telescope in the world, the Keck 394-inch mirror, is here. A visitor's center is located at the 9,200-foot level, which is as far as you will be able to go in a conventional vehicle. At the summit area, you can wander around the observatory structures, but as of this writing, only one was partially open to visitors, and you don't see very much. But the view from the top is awesome.

Snow blankets Mauna Kea from about December through March, and active skiing takes place during that period. If you are interested, inquire in Hilo or Waimea. A tour of the observatories is offered one night a week, beginning from the visitor's center. It is free, but participants must provide their own four-wheel-drive vehicle. Tour companies also offer trips to the summit.

It is possible to hike up Mauna Kea from a trail that begins near the visitor's center, or by simply walking up the road. In either case the hike is strenuous, and the altitude will take its toll. Allow at least 8 hours for the round trip. Altitude sickness is possible on Mauna Kea, whether driving or walking to the summit. Headache and nausea can occur. More severe symptoms, such as dizziness or disorientation, require immediate descent to lower altitude.

To reach Mauna Kea from the camp, take the Saddle Road east toward Hilo about 8 miles to a paved road to the left. There is no sign, but the road can be identified by a hunter check-in shack on the right side of the highway. There is no other structure for miles. The road is steep, but paved to the visitor's center.

A trail leads to the summit of Mauna Loa ("long mountain") from a weather observatory at the 11,000-foot level. The trail is steep and rough in places and is entirely over *'a'ā* and *pāhoehoe* lava. The grade and the altitude make this a strenuous hike, but the vistas and the view into the massive 3.5-mile-long summit crater are spectacular. It is 6.4 miles to the 13,679-foot peak, but you should allow 10 to 12 hours for the round-trip. It is dangerous to be on the mountain after nightfall. The lower sections of the trail are marked only by rock cairns, which are impossible to pick out in the dark against the black lava background. As with Mauna Kea, altitude sickness can occur. The same comments as above apply.

To reach Mauna Loa from the camp, take the Saddle Road east toward Hilo about 8 miles to a hunter check-in shack on the right side of the highway. There is no other structure for miles. Less than half a mile from this shack, there is a road on the right, just past a prominent hill. The road is narrow and unpaved except for the final few paved miles, and winds its way up through the lava fields for 19 miles to a parking lot just below the weather observatory. Walk down the rugged jeep road below the weather station a short distance to the trailhead on the left.

Hāpuna Beach State Recreation Area

LOCATION: The park is on the Kohala coast, about 30 miles from Kailua (Kona), and 3 miles south of Kawaihae.

DESCRIPTION: Hāpuna is one of the best white-sand beaches on the island of Hawai'i. It is over half a mile long, more than 200 feet wide, and is beautifully landscaped. Palm and *hala* trees dot the beach and the attractive sloping picnic area behind it. The beach slopes gently, and the offshore bottom is sandy. Hāpuna, which means "spring" in Hawaiian, is located in the driest part of the island, so chances for good beach weather here are excellent. The cabin area is not in the beach area, but on a slope across from the beach parking lot, about a 5-minute walk to the shoreline.

FACILITIES: Cabins only; no tent or vehicle camping. Six A-frame cabins are available for rent about 300 yards uphill from the beach, on an open hillside. The cabins are very basic, each containing two wooden sleeping platforms and a small picnic table. They are screened, but not otherwise protected from the weather. Each cabin accommodates four persons. Two rest room buildings contain toilets, sinks, and cold showers. Drinking water and electricity are available. A central dining hall with a kitchen is shared by all cabin users. Additional facilities at the beach include covered picnic tables overlooking the beach, rest rooms, and outdoor showers. Limited groceries and gas can be obtained in Kawaihae, 3 miles north. More extensive shopping can be done in Waimea, an additional 8 miles to the east.

CAMPGROUND ACTIVITIES: Excellent swimming conditions exist here most of the year. Because the beach slopes gradually, the shorebreak rarely causes a strong backwash, making Hāpuna one of the safest places on the Island to "play in the waves." But caution is necessary during periods of heavy surf, when drownings have occurred. There are no lifeguards. High surf in winter provides very good waves for bodysurfing. Snorkeling is reasonably good along the rocks bordering the south end of the beach. Board surfing and sailboarding are prohibited at Hāpuna. Mullet, *pāpio,* threadfin, and menpachi can all be hooked here. Hiking trails lead north and south from the beach. The more interesting is the short one (20 minutes) north to Kauna'oa Beach, a lovely crescent bay, site of the Mauna Kea Beach Hotel.

PERMIT/RESERVATIONS: Permits can be obtained from a state parks office on any island. Write or call the following: Division of State Parks, P.O. Box 936, Hilo, HI 96720; phone, (808) 974–6200.

TIME LIMIT: Seven days.

COST: $20 per day per cabin.

SPECIAL COMMENTS: Hāpuna has recently received a minor upgrade, including new paint and a new stove in the kitchen. There are no eating or cooking utensils. The small, apartment-size refrigerator is usually overloaded, so it would be wise to bring your own cooler. I also bring a camp stove for reliable cooking. The location is worth putting up with these inconveniences, but if the conditions depress you, consider camping at Spencer Beach Park, about 3 miles down the road.

HOW TO GET THERE: From Hilo (65 miles), take Highway 19 north, through Waimea, to Kawaihae. Continue left on 19 for about 2.5 miles to a sign to Hāpuna on the right.

From Kailua (Kona) (30 miles), take Highway 19 north 30 miles to the sign to Hāpuna on the left.

NEARBY POINTS OF INTEREST: Almost 3,000 petroglyphs (ancient rock carvings) are located in several groupings southwest of Puakō, on old *pāhoehoe* lava flows. *Kiawe* covers the area, the ground is rough, and there are few trails. A large representative petroglyph field can be reached via an easy trail from the Mauna Lani Beach Hotel, 3 miles south of Hāpuna. The former trail from Puakō has been closed.

For information on Pu'ukoholā Heiau, see section on Spencer Beach Park.

Spencer Beach Park

LOCATION: The park is on the Kohala coast just south of Kawaihae.

DESCRIPTION: Spencer is a large park, directly on the ocean, with its own swimming beach. It is the most popular and heavily used campground on the west coast of Hawai'i. Large trees, including some unusually large *kiawe,* provide ample shade, but open, grassy areas are also available for pitching tents. Water conditions are almost always calm, and, because of the presence of an offshore reef, there is very little wave action. The bottom slopes gently off the beach, making it a good place for small children.

FACILITIES: Tent and vehicle camping. A large stone building houses rest rooms, washrooms, changing areas, and cold showers. Picnic tables are located throughout the park, and barbecues can be found near some of them. A large pavilion, with ten long picnic tables, sits directly on the water and has its own rest rooms, dishwashing area, and electric lights. Water is drinkable. The park also provides tennis courts. Gas and limited groceries can be obtained at Kawaihae, about half a mile north. For more extensive shopping, drive to Waimea, 10 miles east.

CAMPGROUND ACTIVITIES: Swimming is almost always safe here, but swimmers need to watch for a few underwater rocks in shallow places close to shore. Snorkeling is usually excellent along the rocks on both sides of the beach, but is sometimes affected by murky water. The area is noted for schools of mullet, especially along the coast north of the park.

PERMIT/RESERVATIONS: For permits write or call the following: Department of Parks and Recreation, County of Hawai'i, 25 Aupuni Street, Hilo, HI 96720; phone, (808) 961-8311.

TIME LIMIT: Summer months, 1 week; other months, 2 weeks.

COST: Adults, $1 per day; juniors (13 to 17), 50 cents per day; children (12 and under), no charge.

Campers at Spencer Beach Park, South Kohala. Spencer, recently improved, is the largest campground on the Kona Coast.

Pavilion at Spencer Beach Park, South Kohala.

SPECIAL COMMENTS: Spencer has the best facilities of any campground on the west coast of the island and recent improvements include a widened beach and a new access road. It is the only campground between Kawaihae and Ho'okena, a distance of over 60 miles. For that reason it is often crowded, especially with foreign campers. Adding to the crowded conditions, homeless people have used the campground in the past as a place to live. However, the county now seems determined to keep them out, and only 68 campers are permitted at a time. The campground now closes two days each month for cleaning, and to insure that would-be squatters move along. This makes for much improved conditions. Reservations for Spencer should be made early, particularly during the summer months.

Spencer is a good base to explore the many attractions of the Kohala coast, including the beaches of Hāpuna, 'Anaeho'omalu, and the tide pools of Kīholo Bay.

HOW TO GET THERE: From Hilo (64 miles), take Highway 19 north through Waimea to Kawaihae. Just after the junction with Highway 270, watch for a large sign to the park on the left.

From Kailua (Kona) (32 miles), take Highway 19 north. Just after the junction with Highway 270, watch for a large sign to the park on the left.

NEARBY POINTS OF INTEREST: Looming directly behind the campground, Pu'ukoholā Heiau was built by Kamehameha, who was told by a famous *kahuna* that he would conquer all the Hawaiian Islands if he built a *heiau* at that location. A small visitor's center provides more information and displays.

For information on Lapakahi State Historical Park, see section on Māhukona Beach Park.

For information on Mo'okini Heiau, see section on Kapa'a Beach Park.

For information on Puakō petroglyphs, see section on Hāpuna Beach State Recreation Area.

Māhukona Beach Park

LOCATION: The campground is on the north Kohala coast about 13 miles north of Kawaihae.

DESCRIPTION: Māhukona, which means "leeward steam" in Hawaiian, is a small, but attractive campground, directly on the water. It lies adjacent to an abandoned pier, once used to load sugar from the former Kohala Sugar Plantation. Māhukona has no beach, and the shoreline is rocky and shallow. A flat, open grassy area, directly back from the shoreline, provides most of the tent sites. Additional sites can be found under large trees on both sides of the pavilion. A good view of Maui can be had from the shoreline.

FACILITIES: Tent and vehicle camping. A large pavilion with electricity contains five long picnic tables and the rest rooms, with cold showers. Water should be boiled or treated before use. Several additional picnic tables are scattered throughout the area, and a barbecue and dishwashing sink are also located outside the pavilion. Groceries and gas can be obtained in Hāwī, about 7 miles to the north.

CAMPGROUND ACTIVITIES: Although Māhukona has no beach, swimmers usually enter the water from the abandoned pier, a short walk down the road from the campground. Swimming is usually safe in the pier basin and the waters nearby, except during heavy surf. Very good snorkeling is found along the rocky shore and in the vicinity of the old pier, where railroad and industrial artifacts can be seen. Most often caught here are mullet, threadfin, menpachi, and *pāpio*.

PERMIT/RESERVATIONS: Permits may be obtained by writing or calling the following: Department of Parks and Recreation, County of Hawai'i, 25 Aupuni Street, Hilo, HI 96720; phone, (808) 961–8311.

TIME LIMIT: Summer months, 1 week; other months, 2 weeks.

COST: Adults, $1 per day; juniors (13 to 17), 50 cents per day; children (12 and under), no charge.

SPECIAL COMMENTS: Māhukona can be crowded on weekends, sometimes by young folks with boom boxes. If this bothers you, try Kapa'a or Kēōkea, both farther north.

HOW TO GET THERE: From Hilo (77 miles), take Highway 19 north through Waimea to Kawaihae. Turn right on Highway 270 and watch for a sign, about 13 miles from Kawaihae.

From Kailua (Kona) (46 miles), take Highway 19 north. At Kawaihae, bear left along the coast on Highway 270. Proceed another 13 miles, watching for the sign.

NEARBY POINTS OF INTEREST: Lapakahi State Historical Park, the remains of an ancient fishing village, lies along the ocean about a mile south of the campground. A brochure at the entrance allows you to make a self-guided tour.

For information on Mo'okini Heiau, see section on Kapa'a Beach Park.

Kapa'a Beach Park

LOCATION: The park is on the north Kohala coast between the towns of Kawaihae and Hāwī.

DESCRIPTION: Kapa'a, which means "the closing" or "the solid," is an isolated, dry campsite on a rocky shoreline, backed by *kiawe* trees. The park is often windswept. Much of the area is covered by high grass, which is brown most of the year. The ground is hard and rocky and slopes toward the ocean. An attractive miniature cove, surrounded by *kiawe,* lies below the parking lot. There is a fine view of Maui across the channel.

FACILITIES: A large, weather-beaten pavilion houses four big picnic tables and rest rooms. An additional open picnic table stands beside the parking lot. There is no water or electricity. Only a few tent sites are available, in high grass under *kiawe* trees. Groceries and gas are available at Hāwī, 5.5 miles north.

CAMPGROUND ACTIVITIES: Although there is no beach, swimmers can enter the water at the small, sheltered cove. Swimming is dangerous in the winter months and during periods of high surf, when strong currents build offshore. Snorkeling is very good on calm days, with the same warning as above. This is a good place for mullet, *pāpio,* threadfin, and menpachi.

PERMIT/RESERVATIONS: Permits may be obtained by writing or calling the following: Department of Parks and Recreation, County of Hawai'i, 25 Aupuni Street, Hilo, HI 96720; phone, (808) 961–8311.

TIME LIMIT: Summer months, 1 week; other months, 2 weeks.

COST: Adults, $1 per day; juniors (13 to 17), 50 cents per day; children (12 and under), no charge.

SPECIAL COMMENTS: Kapa'a is a dry, almost arid location. Camping here is suitable for a small group seeking privacy, but considering the lack of water, most campers will be happier at Māhukona, about 1.5 miles to the south.

HOW TO GET THERE: From Hilo (79 miles), take Highway 19 north through Waimea to Kawaihae. Turn right on Highway 270 and watch for a sign, about 15 miles from Kawaihae.

From Kailua (Kona) (48 miles), take Highway 19 north. At Kawaihae, bear left along the coast on Highway 270. Proceed another 15 miles, watching for a sign.

NEARBY POINTS OF INTEREST: Most *heiau* remaining in Hawai'i are simply large piles of rock, representing the foundation, or base, upon which other religious buildings stood. Mo'okini Heiau is different. It is a walled enclosure, 30 feet high in places, encompassing an area almost the size of a football field. Oral chants date the *heiau* from a.d. 480. The stones for its construction are said to have come from Pololū Valley, 14 miles away, passed hand to hand in a single night. Mo'okini is undergoing restoration and is easily the most interesting *heiau* in the state. To reach it from the campground, drive north on Highway 270 to the turnoff for the small airport at 'Upolu Point, about 4 miles. Turn left and proceed another 1.5 miles to a dirt road bearing right, just before the airport. Continue on this poorly maintained road, watching for the *heiau* on the left. The reputed birth site of King Kamehameha I is located a little over half a mile past the *heiau,* on the same poor road.

Maui

Maui has a reputation for being overbuilt. A drive along its western shores tends to confirm that reputation. From Lahaina north to Kapalua, and from Kīhei south to Wailea, a seemingly uninterrupted line of hotels and condominiums marches relentlessly along the seashore. Yet, much of Maui's lovely shoreline as well as a good deal of its beautiful backcountry remains wild and unspoiled. There are lots of parks, both on the ocean and upland. And even in the thickest part of the condo/hotel forest, shoreline access easements guarantee that everyone, not just hotel guests, is able to enjoy the beautiful beaches of Kā'anapali and Wailea.

The second largest of the main islands, Maui is 48 miles long and 26 miles wide, covering a land area of 729 square miles. The island as it exists today was formed by two volcanoes, giving it its "figure 8" shape. But Maui was once part of a much larger island, containing six volcanoes, that geologists call Maui-nui (Big Maui), which included the islands of Moloka'i, Lāna'i, and Kaho'olawe. Politically, Maui nui still exists, because these islands now form Maui County. Maui is the second youngest of the Hawaiian chain, between 800,000 and 1.3 million years old. Its two distinct parts, joined by an isthmus created by lava flows, are alike in some ways, different in others.

West Maui's peak, Pu'u Kukui, is one of the wettest spots in the Hawaiian Islands, with over 400 inches of rainfall per year. East Maui's summit, Haleakalā, rarely receives more than 30 inches. On the other hand, West Maui's Kā'anapali/Kapalua beaches, and East Maui's Kīhei and Wailea beaches, are close copies of each other. Both East and West Maui have roads that go all the way around their circumference, albeit they are very narrow and winding. West Maui has its Kā'anapali condos; East Maui its Kīhei ones. The west has its upscale resort at Kapalua, the east at Wailea. East Maui has lava flows; West Maui has none. But East Maui does have the oldest of the only two wineries in the state, in the middle of Kula's cool upcountry ranch land. West Maui has Lahaina, once the whale-hunting and now the whale-watching capital of the state. East Maui has Hāna, a sleepy town at the end of a tortuous drive that tourists flock to, finding nothing but a sleepy town and a beach after they get there. And so it goes.

Maui is called "The Valley Isle" in tourist brochures—why, I don't know. Its valleys are no more beautiful than those of Kaua'i or Hawai'i.

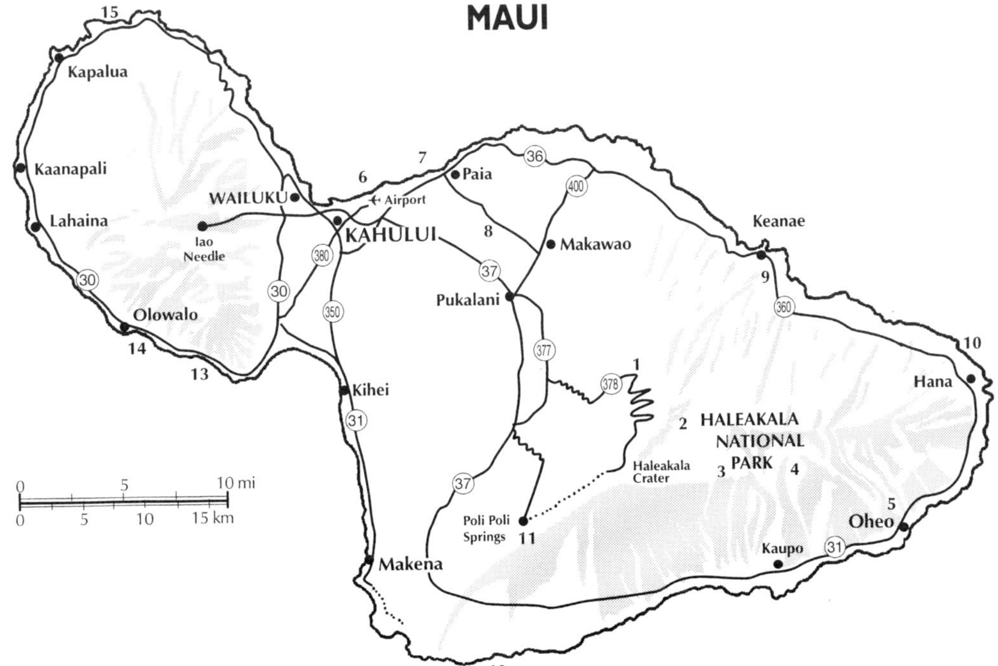

Maui Campgrounds

1. Hosmer Grove
2. Hōlua Cabin and Campground
3. Kapala'oa Cabin
4. Palikū Cabin and Campground
5. Kīpahulu ('Ohe'o Pools) Campground
6. Kanahā Beach Park
7. H. A. Baldwin Beach Park
8. Rainbow Park
9. Camp Ke'anae
10. Wai'ānapanapa State Park
11. Polipoli Springs State Recreation Area
12. Kanaio Beach
13. Pāpalaua Beach Park
14. Camp Pecusa
15. Windmill Beach

Maybe it has more of them, but I haven't counted to find out. As is the case on the other Islands, Maui's main industry is now tourism. Sugar and pineapple are the main agricultural crops, and most of Maui's population of 91,000 people work in one of those three activities. There is no public transportation on the island, and hitchhiking is illegal. People do hitch rides by standing on the side of the road, facing traffic and looking sad. But don't put your thumb out.

Despite all its public parks, Maui County is definitely inhospitable to campers. The county allows camping in only three of its seventeen parks. Compare this with Kaua'i County with seven campgrounds, Hawai'i County with thirteen, and O'ahu with twelve, and it is evident that Maui County wants its visitors to be hotel guests, not campers. But thanks to state and federal authorities, camping on Maui is almost as varied and rewarding as elsewhere in the state.

THINGS TO SEE AND DO: You will find more information about the points of interest listed below in the sections on individual campgrounds. Distances on Maui tend to be farther than on other Islands, not because Maui is so much larger, but because of its extended "figure 8" shape. Also, some roads, such as between Kula and Mākena, have no convenient connection with each other. You may want to take this into account when deciding where to camp.

Point of Interest	**Nearest Campground**
Haleakalā Summit and Crater	Haleakalā campgrounds
'Īao Valley and Needle	Kanahā Beach Park
Ke'anae Arboretum	Camp Ke'anae
Lahaina	Camp Pecusa
'Ohe'o Gulch (Seven Pools)	Kīpahulu ('Ohe'o Pools) Campground
Olowalu petroglyphs	Camp Pecusa
Wai'ānapanapa Caves	Wai'ānapanapa State Park

HALEAKALĀ NATIONAL PARK

Haleakalā National Park, the "House of the Sun," reaches from Maui's highest peak, 10,023 feet, to the ocean at Kīpahulu, almost 20 miles away. It includes one of the largest volcanic craters in the world, 7.5 miles long and 2.5 miles wide. Its 21-mile circumference encompasses 19 square miles. For outdoor enthusiasts there are 36 miles of trails, four campgrounds, and three cabins. It is the only place in the world to easily view the silversword. Its flora zones are so varied that one botanist called a hike from the park summit to the sea the equivalent of walking from Alaska to Mexico.

Sliding Sands Trail is the gateway to Haleakalā Crater and its cabins and campgrounds.

The drive to the summit of Haleakalā is an experience in itself. The lush pasture land of up-country Maui provides a perfect foreground frame for stunning views of West Maui and the islands of Lāna'i, Molokini, Moloka'i, and Kaho'olawe. From the summit, the peaks of Mauna Loa and Mauna Kea on the island of Hawai'i are added to the panorama. Four overlooks on the way up afford spectacular views into the crater, including ones at the Visitor Center and the summit just above it. Cinder cones that appear small from the crater rim rise as high as 600 feet from the crater floor.

Temperatures on the mountain and in the crater range from 26 to 77 degrees Fahrenheit, and high winds are frequent on the upper slopes of the mountain. Annual rainfall varies from 20 inches at the west end of the crater to over 200 on its eastern side. It can be cold, wet, or windy at any time, and conditions can change quickly.

No visitor should leave Maui without a trip to the crater rim, and no outdoor lover should miss hiking in the crater, preferably camping within it at least one night. Use the next sections to plan your hiking and camping trip.

Hosmer Grove

LOCATION: This campground is on the slopes of Haleakalā, at an elevation of 6,800 feet, just off Haleakalā Crater Road.

DESCRIPTION: Hosmer Grove is a small, but very attractive campground in an open, grassy area, surrounded by the tall trees of an upland forest. The trees are mostly nonnative and were introduced in the 1920s as an experiment to see if a lumber industry could flourish in Hawai'i. The area is protected from the high winds that assault other parts of the mountain at this altitude, but nights can be cold.

FACILITIES: Tent and vehicle camping. Vehicle campers are limited to the small parking lot. A covered pavilion containing two picnic tables and two small grills is located at the entrance to the campground, and several other picnic tables are found throughout the area. Two chemical toilets are provided and are well maintained. The faucet at the pavilion provides water that is safe to drink, but it has an unpleasant taste. No groceries or gas are available except back down the mountain at Pukalani.

CAMPGROUND ACTIVITIES: A half-mile-long nature trail makes a loop from the end of the parking lot and returns near the pavilion. Brochures are usually available at the trailhead or can be picked up at Park Headquarters.

PERMIT/RESERVATIONS: None. Occupancy is limited to twenty-five persons, with no more than twelve persons in one group.

TIME LIMIT: Three nights per month.

COST: Free.

HOW TO GET THERE: From Kahului (about 28 miles) take Highway 37 southeast through Pukalani (about 7.2 miles), turning left at the sign to the crater (Highway 377). Continue to watch for crater signs, and another left turn will put you on Haleakalā Crater Road (Highway 378). Watch for a sign to Hosmer Grove, just under 10 miles from the Crater Road turnoff.

NEARBY POINTS OF INTEREST: Hosmer Grove is a jumping-off place for hikers and campers descending into Haleakalā Crater. It is also a good place to spend the night before rising early to see the sunrise over the crater.

Hōlua Cabin and Campground

LOCATION: This campground is inside Haleakalā Crater, on the Halemau'u Trail, just behind the Hōlua Cabin.

DESCRIPTION: Hōlua, which means "sled" in Hawaiian, is situated at an elevation of almost 7,000 feet with spectacular views of the crater walls and lava flows. Vegetation is sparse and limited to dry grass and scrub. There are no trees. The area in the vicinity of the cabin is grassy, but the campground is rocky and uneven, but it is large enough so that you will be able to find a site. A covered shed for horses provides flat, smooth ground for a tent, as well as shelter from the elements. I have camped here occasionally when horses were not in residence.

FACILITIES: Tent and cabin camping. Pit toilets and water are the only facilities available to the tent camper. Water is obtained by catchment from the roof of the cabin and is collected in a tank at the rear. Water for the campground is provided by a spigot on the trail between the cabin and the campground. It should be treated before use. The cabin has bunks with mattresses for twelve people, but bedding is not provided. A table, chairs, some cooking utensils, and a wood-burning cook stove with firewood are provided.

PERMIT/RESERVATIONS: Tent camping permits are issued at Park Headquarters on a first-come, first-served basis on the day of use. Occupancy is limited to twenty-five persons, with groups restricted to twelve persons. A lottery system is in effect for cabin reservations. Requests for cabins must be made 3 months in advance, and alternate dates should be included. You may request more than one cabin within the prescribed time limit. For example, you may request Hōlua for two nights and another cabin for one night or all three cabins for one night each. Another way to secure a cabin is to pick up a cancelled reservation. This can be done by calling the number below between 1:00 and 3:00 p.m. Monday through Friday. For reservation requests and information, call or write the following: Haleakalā National Park, P.O. Box 369, Makawao, HI 96768; phone, (808) 572–9306.

TIME LIMIT: Two consecutive nights, with an overall camping limit within the crater of three nights per month.

COST: Free for tent campers. Cabins cost $40 per night for one to six persons, and $80 for seven to twelve.

SPECIAL COMMENTS: Hōlua is a great place to see the *nēnē,* the Hawaiian state bird. Driven to the point of extinction by hunting and predators, *nēnē* are being reared in captivity and released in the wild. Because they remember the hand that fed them while they were young, they will dog your footsteps at Hōlua, looking for a handout.

The water supply at Hōlua is limited, particularly during the dry summer months. Check its status at Park Headquarters and use only what you need for drinking and cooking. No open fires are allowed in the crater, so you must bring a stove if you want hot food. Be sure to pack out everything you pack in.

Except for the use of the water tank and the pit toilets, the cabin and its vicinity is for the exclusive use of those who have paid for it. Although it is inviting, you may not camp on the grassy lawn in front of the cabin. Your tent is restricted to the rocky campsite or the horse stable.

HOW TO GET THERE: Follow driving directions to Haleakalā Crater (see the section on Hosmer Grove). There are two ways to reach Hōlua from the Crater Road. The first is via the Halemau'u Trail, a switchback trail that reaches the cabin in just under 4 miles from the trailhead at 8,000 feet. To reach the trailhead, continue past Hosmer Grove and Park Headquarters to the sign for the Halemau'u Trail parking area.

The second trail, Sliding Sands, starts at the summit and intersects with a trail to Hōlua, for a total distance of 7.4 miles. The best way to make the hike, if you can arrange the transportation, is to hike in via Sliding Sands and out by way of Halemau'u.

NEARBY POINTS OF INTEREST: Just under a mile along the trail to Palikū, the Silversword Loop Trail leads through a silversword garden that is well worth the small detour. Unique to Hawai'i, this high-altitude plant grows only here, and on Mauna Loa and Mauna Kea on the island of Hawai'i. It takes between 7 and 20 years to bloom, and it can produce hundreds of flowers on its crowning stalk. The plant dies after blooming, scattering its seeds to the wind, starting the growing cycle again. The blooming season is generally from May to October. Some years ago Silversword Loop was within a fenced enclosure, to protect it from browsing goats that had almost eliminated the silversword from the crater. Fortunately, a combined fencing and hunting program has eliminated the goats instead, and the silversword has made a dramatic comeback. You will now see it growing in many other locations along the trail.

An additional 1.4 miles on the same trail brings you to the Bottomless Pit, a wire-enclosed hole. Its 65-foot depth is hardly even close to what its name implies.

Closer to Hōlua than either of the above, but unmarked on any brochure, is a quarter-mile-long lava tube that you can hike through from one end to the other if you have a flashlight and don't mind squeezing around a few tight spots. The trail to the tube leads off the main trail to Hōlua, but is faint and unmarked. Get directions at Park Headquarters if you plan to look for it.

Kapala'oa Cabin

LOCATION: This cabin is inside Haleakalā Crater, just off Sliding Sands Trail at an elevation of 7,250 feet.

DESCRIPTION: Kapala'oa, which means "whale tooth," is situated in a flat, desertlike part of the crater. There is little vegetation in the vicinity, and what is there is usually dry and brown. The area surrounding Kapala'oa is not as attractive as that of the other two cabins, but it is more centrally located for exploring the crater than either of the other two.

FACILITIES: Cabin only, no tent camping. Water is obtained by catchment from the roof of the cabin and is collected in a tank. It should be treated before use. The cabin has bunks with mattresses for twelve people, but bedding is not provided. A table, chairs, some cooking utensils, and a wood-burning cook stove with firewood are supplied. A pit toilet is located outside the cabin.

PERMIT/RESERVATIONS: A lottery system is in effect for cabin reservations. Requests for cabins must be made 3 months in advance, and alternate dates should be included. You may request more than one cabin within the prescribed time limit. For example, you may request Kapala'oa for two nights and another cabin for one night or all three cabins for one night each. Another way to secure a cabin is to pick up a cancelled reservation. This can be done by calling the number below between 1:00 and 3:00 p.m. Monday through Friday. For reservation requests and information, call or write the following: Haleakalā National Park, P.O. Box 369, Makawao, HI 96768; phone, (808) 572–9306.

TIME LIMIT: Two consecutive nights, with an overall camping limit within the crater of three nights per month.

COST: Cabins cost $40 per night for one to six persons, and $80 for seven to twelve.

SPECIAL COMMENTS: The water supply at Kapala'oa is limited, particularly during the dry summer months. Check its status at Park Headquarters and use only what you need for drinking and cooking. Be sure to pack out everything you pack in.

HOW TO GET THERE: Follow driving directions to Haleakalā Crater (see the section on Hosmer Grove). There are two ways to reach Kapala'oa from the Crater Road. The first is via the Halemau'u Trail (7.7 miles), down the switchback, past Hōlua Cabin, and intersecting with Sliding Sands Trail just before reaching the cabin. To reach the Halemau'u trailhead, continue past Hosmer Grove and Park Headquarters to the sign for the Halemau'u Trail parking area.

The second route is via Sliding Sands Trail, starting at the summit and reaching Kapala'oa after 5.8 miles. The best way to make the hike, if you can arrange the transportation, is to hike in via Sliding Sands and out by way of Halemau'u. Better yet, if you have the time, from Kapala'oa hike to Palikū, camp overnight, and hike out the next day via the Halemau'u Trail.

NEARBY POINTS OF INTEREST: A side trail just west of the cabin leads north to the Bottomless Pit, a wire-enclosed hole that, despite its name, is only 65 feet deep.

Palikū Cabin and Campground

LOCATION: This campground is inside Haleakalā Crater, at its western end, just before the Kaupō Gap, at an elevation of 6,380 feet.

DESCRIPTION: After hiking over the harsh, dry, cinder and lava landscape on either Halemau'u or Sliding Sands trails, the lush green meadows of Palikū are a welcome oasis. It is like entering another world. Unlike the barren western end, which receives only about 20 inches of rainfall per year, Palikū gets over 200. Palikū means "vertical cliff," and here the cliffs are green, not gray or brown, as the crater walls are elsewhere. Trees grow tall, and the grass is thick as a carpet. It's beautiful, but make sure you bring your rain gear.

FACILITIES: Tent and cabin camping. Pit toilets and water are the only facilities available to tent campers. Water is obtaned by catchment from the roof of the cabin and is collected in a tank. It should be treated before use. The cabin has bunks with mattresses for twelve people, but bedding is not provided. A table, chairs, some cooking utensils, and a wood-burning cook stove (firewood supplied) just about complete the furnishings.

PERMIT/RESERVATIONS: Tent camping permits are issued at Park Headquarters on a first-come, first-served basis on the day of use. Occupancy is limited to twenty-five persons, with groups restricted to twelve persons. A lottery system is in effect for cabin reservations. Requests for cabin occupancy must be made 3 months in advance, and alternate dates should be included. You may request more than one cabin within the prescribed time

Palikū campground and cabin is a lush change from the stark volcanic landscape of the rest of the crater.

limit. For example, you may request Palikū for two nights and another cabin for one night, or all three cabins for one night each. Another way to secure a cabin is to pick up a cancelled reservation. This can be done by calling the number below between 1:00 and 3:00 p.m. Monday through Friday. For reservation requests and information, call or write the following: Haleakalā National Park, P.O. Box 369, Makawao, HI 96768; phone, (808) 572–9306.

TIME LIMIT: Two consecutive nights, with an overall camping limit within the crater of three nights per month.

COST: Cabins cost $40 per night for one to six persons, and $80 for seven to twelve. Free for tent campers.

SPECIAL COMMENTS: No open fires are allowed in the crater, so you must bring a stove if you want hot food. Be sure to pack out everything you pack in. Except for the use of the water tank and the pit toilets, the cabin and its vicinity is for the exclusive use of those who have paid for it.

HOW TO GET THERE: Follow driving directions to Haleakalā Crater (see the section on Hosmer Grove). As is the case with Hōlua, there are two ways to reach Palikū from the Crater Road. The first is via the Halemau'u Trail, a distance of 10.2 miles. The trail proceeds down the switchback, past Hōlua Cabin, Silversword Loop, and Bottomless Pit. Follow the signs to Palikū. To reach the trailhead, continue past Hosmer Grove and Park Headquarters to the sign for the Halemau'u Trail parking area.

The second trail, Sliding Sands, starts at the summit and goes straight for 9.8 miles to Palikū, passing Kapala'oa Cabin on the way. As is the case with Hōlua, if you can arrange the transportation, the best way to see as much of the crater as possible is to hike in via Sliding Sands and out by way of Halemau'u.

NEARBY POINTS OF INTEREST: The premier hike in the crater is from the summit to the sea, via Sliding Sands Trail and the Kaupō Gap, overnighting at Palikū. Botanists have called it the equivalent of hiking from Alaska to Mexico. Although difficult to arrange because it requires a pickup or a prepositioned vehicle at Kaupō, the hike is memorable if you can manage it. If not, you may want to hike a few miles down the Kaupō Trail for great views all the way to the ocean. But don't go too far. Remember, all those downhill steps must be repeated uphill.

Kīpahulu ('Ohe'o Pools) Campground

LOCATION: This campground is on Highway 31, about 10 slow, winding miles past Hāna, 62 miles southeast of Kahului.

DESCRIPTION: One of the meanings of 'Ohe'o is "gathering of pools," an apt description of this enchanting but heavily visited area of Haleakalā National Park. A series of waterfalls cascade down the gulch, forming more than twenty separate pools as the 'Ohe'o Stream makes its way to the ocean. One of the best overviews of the pools is from the bridge across the 'Ohe'o Stream. The campground is in an attractive grassy meadow on the ocean side of the road, about two-tenths of a mile past the bridge.

FACILITIES: Tent and vehicle camping. Rest rooms and a few picnic tables and grills are available, but there is no drinking water. Water from the stream must be treated before drinking and should be obtained as far upstream as possible because of the large number of people swimming in the pools near the road. Gas and groceries are available back at Hāna.

CAMPGROUND ACTIVITIES: The major activity is pool-hopping and swimming. For a real adventure, hike up the trail to Makahiku Falls, about half a mile. Follow the ditch behind the overlook to the head of the falls and swim up the stream through a steep-sided gorge to a delightful waterfall and small pool. Ocean swimming is not recommended here, because powerful currents run near the shore. Local fishermen have reported that sharks frequent the area.

A "must" for camper/hikers at ʻOheʻo is the 4-mile round-trip hike to Makahiku and Waimoku falls. The trail begins across the road from the parking area and makes its way gradually uphill through a wide meadow. After the Makahiku Falls overlook, the trail crosses the stream and winds through a wet forest and a bamboo grove so thick that day is almost turned to night. A boardwalk traverses a small bog; after another small stream crossing, you will find yourself at Waimoku, a beautiful bridal-veil falls, with a pool at its base for a refreshing dip.

PERMIT/RESERVATIONS: None.

TIME LIMIT: Three nights.

COST: Free.

SPECIAL COMMENTS: For many years ʻOheʻo Pools were known as "Seven Sacred Pools," a name apparently invented to attract tourists to the Hāna area and then perpetuated on maps and in tour brochures. The pools were never sacred, and, as your visit will show, there are many more than seven. Efforts by the National Park Service and the Hawaiʻi Council for Truth in Advertising are slowly changing things back to the way they should be. Many maps and brochures now show the name as I have done in the title to this section, retaining the Seven Pools designation only because most tourists do not recognize the name Kīpahulu or ʻOheʻo. Eventually, "Seven Sacred Pools" should pass into the oblivion it deserves.

HOW TO GET THERE: From Kahului, take Highway 36, which becomes Highway 360, to Hāna, and then Highway 31 to ʻOheʻo. After Hāna, the highway soon turns into a winding, narrow, rutted road, one way in places. It is slow going, especially when meeting oncoming vehicles. You will know you have reached ʻOheʻo when you cross the bridge and see the pools on both sides. Continue on to the parking lot on the left.

NEARBY POINTS OF INTEREST: Palapala Hoʻomau Church is the site of the grave of Charles Lindbergh. The famous aviator spent many of the last years of his life in Hāna and selected the churchyard as his final resting place. The church is located 1.2 miles past ʻOheʻo, off the ocean side of the road. Watch for it through the trees and turn on the dirt road by a wooden water tank.

OTHER EAST MAUI

Kanahā Beach Park

LOCATION: The park is situated on Kahului Bay, just east of town and adjacent to the airport.

DESCRIPTION: Kanahā, which means "the shattered thing," is a mile-long white sand beach very close to both Kahului and the airport, yet with a feeling of isolation. Most of the park itself is undeveloped, and only the eastern portion has any facilities. *Kiawe* trees provide most of the shade. Immediately offshore, the water is shallow, with a sand and rock bottom. The park has a fine view of the West Maui mountains.

FACILITIES: Tent camping only. Picnic tables, drinking water, rest rooms, showers, and outdoor grills are available in the eastern end of the park. A large pavilion stands on a sandy hill, at its highest point. All shopping facilities are available in Kahului, 2 miles west.

CAMPGROUND ACTIVITIES: Swimming is only fair, due to the shallow, rocky bottom. *Ulua,* goatfish, and threadfin can be caught here. Recently, Kanahā has become a favorite windsurfing site, especially when conditions are not favorable elsewhere.

PERMIT/RESERVATIONS: A county parks permit is required and can be obtained at the following address: Department of Parks and Recreation, War Memorial Center, Wailuku, HI 96793; phone, (808) 243–7389.

TIME LIMIT: Weekends only, until further notice. Check for update when applying for a permit.

COST: $3 per person per night; 50 cents per person under 18.

HOW TO GET THERE: From Kahului, drive east on Ka'ahumanu Avenue (Highway 32) to the T intersection with Hobron Avenue (Hwy 361). Turn left a short distance to Amala Place, which becomes Alahao Street before entering the park.

NEARBY POINTS OF INTEREST: Kanahā Pond Wildlife Sanctuary was formerly an ancient Hawaiian fishpond. An observation point has been established at the intersection of Highways 36 and 37. For other points of interest, see H. A. Baldwin Beach Park and Rainbow Park.

H. A. Baldwin Beach Park

LOCATION: The park is on the ocean, about 7 miles east of Kahului on Highway 36 (Hāna Highway).

DESCRIPTION: A long white-sand beach, backed by a flat, grassy field, make Baldwin a very spacious park. Palms and ironwood trees line the beach, which has a good view of West Maui. A baseball field and a soccer field lie between the beach and the road. Unfortunately, the campground is also located here, completely removed from the beach park proper and set off by itself on a flat, rectangular site enclosed by a chain-link fence. One writer referred to this campsite as "a cage full of tents." There is no view of the ocean or the beach or anything else except the highway, with Haleakalā off in the distance.

FACILITIES: Tent camping only. A large pavilion at the beach park contains eighteen picnic tables, with four additional tables nearby. Two broken barbecue grills are usable, and rest rooms, outdoor showers (without shower heads), and public phones are provided. At the campsite itself are a separate parking lot, a water faucet with drinking water, and two portable chemical toilets. The busy highway is only about 100 feet away. Groceries and gas can be purchased in Pā'ia, about half a mile east.

CAMPGROUND ACTIVITIES: Swimming is good, but be alert for currents and heavy shorebreak. Safest swimming is in two natural pool-like areas, one in front of the pavilion behind a narrow ledge of beach rock, and the other at the west end of the beach. Baldwin is probably the best bodysurfing beach on the island. Conditions are almost always good, but they can become dangerous for the inexperienced. Board surfing is also possible, but conditions are not as reliable as they are for bodysurfing. One of the best sailboarding areas in Hawai'i is at Ho'okipa Beach Park, 2.5 miles east. Board and bodysurfing are also enjoyed here, with caution. Surf can range from 2 to 18 feet. Goatfish, *ulua,* and threadfin are the most common catches.

PERMIT/RESERVATIONS: A county permit is required and can be obtained from the following address: Department of Parks and Recreation, War Memorial Center, Wailuku, Maui, HI 96793; phone, (808) 243–7389.

TIME LIMIT: Three nights. Camping is limited to 15 days per year.

COST: $3 per person per night; 50 cents per person under 18.

SPECIAL COMMENTS: Baldwin is a very popular park and is usually crowded; good surfing conditions make it a gathering place for young people. Also, the two ball fields are near the campground and could make things fairly noisy. Considering all this and the relatively unattractive location of the campground area, there is little reason to stay here unless you are an avid bodysurfer or fall in love with the beach. If you are on the way to Hāna, I recommend driving farther on and camping at Wai'ānapanapa State Park.

HOW TO GET THERE: From Kahului, drive east on Highway 36, the Hāna Highway, until you come to signs for the park, about 7 miles.

NEARBY POINTS OF INTEREST: 'Īao Needle, Maui's unofficial landmark, is an obelisklike peak rising 2,250 feet in a valley surrounded by high, fluted green walls. The valley also contains an outdoor cultural park and a rock formation that resembles the profile of John F. Kennedy. To get there from the campsite, drive back to Kahului on Highway 36, which becomes Highway 32 at Ka'ahumanu Avenue. Continue on Highway 32 through Wailuku, and follow the signs to 'Īao Needle.

Rainbow Park

LOCATION: The park is about 8 miles east of Kahului, between the towns of Pā'ia and Makawao.

DESCRIPTION: Rainbow Park is a very pretty glen, partly shaded by mature trees, including poinciana, mango, and monkeypod. Its grassy ground slopes gently, but there are several flat areas for tents. It is close to the road, which is above the park, but traffic is not heavy.

FACILITIES: A small roofed pavilion contains one picnic table with a bench on only one side. Drinking water may be obtained from a faucet in the sprinkler line on the left side of the pavilion. Several benches, not tables, are scattered throughout the park. A single chemical toilet is located in the center of the dirt parking lot.

PERMIT/RESERVATIONS: A county permit is required and can be obtained from the following address: Department of Parks and Recreation, War Memorial Center, Wailuku, Maui, HI 96793; phone, (808) 243–7389.

TIME LIMIT: Three nights. Camping is limited to 15 days per year.

COST: $3 per person per night; 50 cents per person under 18.

HOW TO GET THERE: From Kahului (8 miles), drive east on Highway 36 to Pā'ia, just under 5 miles. At the stoplight, turn right on Baldwin Avenue, proceeding 2.9 miles to the park. Watch carefully for a small, round sign on a tree on the right, reading Rainbow Park. A dirt road drops sharply from here to the parking area.

NEARBY POINTS OF INTEREST: The towns of Makawao and Pā'ia are worth a short stroll, even though they have become rather touristy.

Camp Ke'anae (YMCA)

LOCATION: The camp is on Highway 360 (Hāna Highway) about 34 miles east of Kahului.

DESCRIPTION: A YMCA camp just off the highway at the turnoff to the Ke'anae Peninsula, the camp consists of a group of buildings primarily for the use of members. The location is close to the road, but there are good views of the Ke'anae Peninsula below. Ke'anae means "the mullet" in Hawaiian.

FACILITIES: Tent camping, dormitories, and group cabins. Rest rooms and hot showers are available, and the water is drinkable. Dormitories are cabins with double bunks, holding about twenty persons each. Bunks have mattresses, but users must provide own bedding. The entire camp, including several lodging buildings and a kitchen/dining building, can be rented by large organizations.

PERMIT/RESERVATIONS: For information and reservations, contact the following: Maui YMCA, 250 Kanaloa Avenue, Kahului, Maui, HI 96732; phone, (808) 242–9007.

TIME LIMIT: Three nights.

COST: Dormitories, cabins, and tent camping, $10 per person per night.

SPECIAL COMMENTS: Unless you are tired of driving or slowly exploring the windward coast, there is not much reason to stop at Ke'anae. The dorms are not particularly attractive, and if you are looking for indoor accommodations, the cabins at Wai'anapanapa State Park are a much better choice.

HOW TO GET THERE: From Kahului (34 miles), take Highway 36 (Hāna Highway), which becomes Highway 360. Continue to the Ke'anae cutoff on the left. Watch for the sign for the YMCA camp, also on the left.

NEARBY POINTS OF INTEREST: Ke'anae Arboretum is an attractive botanical garden exhibiting both native and introduced plants. It offers a large area devoted to several varieties of taro, growing in typical flooded paddies. At the end of the arboretum plantings, a mile-long trail continues into a native forest.

Wai'ānapanapa State Park

LOCATION: The park is on the ocean, off the Hāna Highway (Highway 360), about 53 miles east of Kahului Airport.

DESCRIPTION: A beautiful, remote park in a wild, coastal setting, Wai'ānapanapa is an ideal camping place for visiting Hāna or for stopping overnight en route to Kīpahulu ('Ohe'o Pools). Meaning "glistening water," Wai'ānapanapa is named for a cave in the park that contains a freshwater pool. A crescent-shaped black-sand beach lies at the head of a small bay, accessible by trail from the parking lot. The campground is in an open grassy field, surrounded by tropical almond, *hala*, and palm trees. The field can become soggy in wet weather, and it will hold pools of standing water if it really rains. Tenting under the trees is somewhat restricted by rocky ground and hundreds of fallen tropical almond nuts.

FACILITIES: Tent and cabin camping only. Picnic tables and some outdoor grills are located throughout the tent campground and in a separate picnic area. Rest rooms, outdoor showers, and drinking water are provided. Twelve housekeeping cabins are located at the east end of the park, accommodating up to six persons each. They include a kitchen, living room, one bedroom, and bathroom with hot shower and come furnished with bedding, linen, towels, dishes, and cooking and eating utensils. Gas and groceries are available in Hāna, about 4 miles southeast.

CAMPGROUND ACTIVITIES: Heavy surf and frequent rip currents require caution at all times, and only good swimmers should enter the water. Threadfin, *pāpio,* and *ulua* are sometimes caught here.

A paved loop path beginning at a sign near the parking lot leads to the two Wai'ānapanapa Caves. The main entrance to the first is filled with fresh water, which is usually at a level high enough to permit swimming to its back reaches. With a mask and an underwater flashlight, it is possible to enter a second chamber on the left side of the cave, but you will need to swim a short distance under water. A less scary and drier way to enter this chamber is by a second entrance to the cave, a small "window" above and to the left of the main entrance. Exploring this second chamber is for experienced spelunkers only or those in the company of a local guide and should never be attempted alone.

A segment of the "King's Highway," an old Hawaiian trail built to allow foot travel over areas of rough lava, passes by the park. It can be followed north for 1 mile to the airport or south 3 miles to Hāna. In either direction, the trail passes dramatically close to waves smashing against low sea cliffs, spraying geysers of water high into the air. Sections of smooth stones, marching in single file, still form part of the trail. The trail to Hāna passes the remains of a *heiau* and ends at a rocky beach. From here it is possible to take a dirt road for a short distance to Hāna.

PERMIT/RESERVATIONS: Permits may be obtained from a state parks office on any island. The following address is for the office on Maui: Division of State Parks, P.O. Box 1049, Wailuku, Maui, HI 96793; phone, (808) 984–8109.

TIME LIMIT: Five nights in any one 30-day period.

COST: Free for tent camping. Housekeeping cabins, $45 per night for one to four persons, $5 per night each additional person, up to six. Group cabins, $55 per night for one to four persons, $5 per night each additional person.

SPECIAL COMMENTS: The cabins at Wai'ānapanapa are usually reserved far in advance, particularly in the summer months and on weekends. A needed facility that is lacking in the camping area is a covered pavilion, where people can cook and eat out of the rain, which it does a lot at Wai'ānapanapa. When this happens you can take your food and stove and head for the covered pavilions at Hāna Beach Park.

HOW TO GET THERE: From Kahului (53 miles), drive east on Highway 36, which becomes Highway 360 after its junction with Highway 40. Continue on Highway 360 until you pass the road to the Hāna Airport on the left, then watch for a large sign to the park.

NEARBY POINTS OF INTEREST: Hāna is a small, very quiet town that many tourists insist on seeing, only to wonder why after they arrive. Maybe it's to buy an "I Survived the Hāna Highway" T-shirt, a memento of 617 curves and 56 bridges on a narrow, precarious road. Hāna Bay, with its brown-sand beach, is lovely, and swimming is usually safe. The original Hasegawa General Store, famed in song and story, burned down in 1990. It is occupying rental space until a new building is completed.

For information on ʻOheʻo Pools, see the section on Kīpahulu Campground.

Polipoli Springs State Recreation Area

LOCATION: The park is at 6,200 feet elevation, on the northwest slope of Halekalā, in the Kula Forest Reserve.

DESCRIPTION: A beautiful, heavily forested park, Polipoli is reminiscent of northern California and the Pacific Northwest. When the area was reforested in the 1920s, instead of the typical tropical *ʻōhiʻa* and *koa,* Polipoli was seeded with redwoods, Monterey cypress, sugi cedars, ash, eucalyptus, and cedar. The park and its trails afford sweeping views of West Maui, Kahoʻolawe, Lānaʻi, Molokaʻi, and both Mauna Kea and Mauna Loa on the island of Hawaiʻi.

FACILITIES: Tent and cabin camping only. A small open, grassy field next to the parking lot is available for picnic use, but tents must be pitched under the tall trees. Several picnic tables are located throughout the area, as are a few outdoor grills. Pit toilets and drinking water are provided, but there are no showers.

The lone cabin contains three bedrooms, a bathroom, and a kitchen/dining/living area. It is without refrigeration or electricity, but contains a gas stove and lanterns and a gas water heater, which, unfortunately, does not heat the shower. Cooking and eating utensils and bed linens are provided. The cabin accommodates up to ten people.

In addition to the cabin there are several trail shelters located throughout the park, which can accommodate overnight hikers. They require no permits and are on a first-come, first-served basis. They are located as follows: an old CCC barracks at the end of the Redwood Trail; at the junction of the Redwood and Tie trails (four bunks); near the junction of the Plum and the Haleakalā Ridge trails (sleeps four); at the junction of the Waiohuli and Boundary trails; at the end of Kahua Road (sleeps four and has water). In addition, at the end of the Haleakalā Ridge Trail, a dry cave containing a flat ledge is often used as a trail shelter.

CAMPGROUND ACTIVITIES: Hiking and hunting are the main activities here. The park has an extensive trail system, including the Skyline Trail, which goes to the summit of Haleakalā. A good guide to the trails can be found in my *Adventuring in Hawaii* (Sierra Club Books).

PERMIT/RESERVATIONS: Permits may be obtained from a state parks office on any island. The following address is for the office on Maui: Division of State Parks, P.O. Box 1049, Wailuku, Maui, HI 96793; phone, (808) 984–8109.

TIME LIMIT: Five nights in any one 30-day period.

COST: Free for tent camping. Cabin, $45 per night for one to four persons, $5 per night each additional person, up to six.

SPECIAL COMMENTS: Polipoli cabin is the most difficult cabin to reserve in the state system. Local Maui residents, especially hunters, keep it virtually fully occupied. If you want this cabin, be sure to reserve as far in advance as possible and provide alternate dates. Between May and July, Polipoli is a good place to pick plums. The best spots are the old CCC camp, the ranger's cabin area, and along Plum Trail.

HOW TO GET THERE: From Kahului (31 miles), drive southeast on Highway 37 through Pukalani and south to the second junction with Highway 377. Turn sharp left on Highway 377 and proceed four-tenths of a mile to Waipoli Road on the right. A narrow, switchback road climbs steeply through pasture and scrub until it reaches a more level section, which is unpaved and rough. This road ends at the park. Although conventional cars can negotiate this road carefully, a four-wheel-drive vehicle is recommended, and is required in wet weather or if you intend to hike the Skyline Trail or drive to Kahua.

Kanaio Beach

LOCATION: The campsite is at the extreme western end of Maui's south coast, about 3.5 miles east of the beginning of La Pérouse Bay.

DESCRIPTION: This is a primitive campsite area, unmarked in any way. Camp in the general area as described below. Rough *'a'ā* lava fields dominate this area, the site of the last volcanic eruption on Maui, about 1790. *Kiawe* trees and other dryland plants make up the sparse vegetation. The landscape is stark and arid, and there is little refuge from the sun beating on the black lava. The coast contains many small coves with coral or pebble beaches.

FACILITIES: None. Tent camping only. No water is available anywhere in this area.

CAMPGROUND ACTIVITIES: Swimming is good on calm days, but is complicated by finding safe entries. The same comments apply to snorkeling. Shoreline fishing can be very good here, because of the isolation of the area and few fishermen. Catches include *pāpio,* mullet, bonefish, milkfish, big-eyed scad, and sometimes *ulua.*

PERMIT/RESERVATIONS: None.

TIME LIMIT: None, but your stay will be limited by the amount of water you can pack in.

COST: Free.

SPECIAL COMMENTS: Do not drive a vehicle beyond the western approach to La Pérouse Bay. Even the hardiest four-wheel drives have gotten stuck in the jagged, deeply rutted lava. About the only reason to use this campground is if you are hiking the "King's Highway" and want to make it an overnight trip. The terrain is hot and inhospitable and there is little protection from the sun and absolutely no water except from the sea.

HOW TO GET THERE: From Kahului, take Highway 380 south to its junction with Highway 30. Watch for the sign to Kīhei (Highway 31), which comes up quickly. Take Highway 31 south through Wailea and Mākena as far as you can go before encountering conditions too rough for your vehicle. Continue on foot along the "King's Highway" (see below) for about 5 miles.

NEARBY POINTS OF INTEREST: The "King's Highway" is a section of an ancient Hawaiian trail that begins at La Pérouse Bay and can be followed on state land for about 5.5 miles. It includes portions where the original smooth stepping-stones were placed in the rough *'a'ā* lava to protect barefoot travelers.

WEST MAUI

Pāpalaua Beach Park

LOCATION: The park lies between Highway 30 and the ocean about midway between Kahului and Lahaina.

DESCRIPTION: Pāpalaua is a former state wayside park that has been turned over to Maui County. At the time of publication, it was being developed as a county beach park and campground. The name means "rain fog," which is hard to understand in a location that gets as much sun as this one. The park consists of a long, narrow stretch of gray sand directly off the highway. The beach is shaded by *kiawe* trees and the water offshore is shallow. A long reef lies offshore, reaching north to Olowalu. The water is almost always calm, and there is no shorebreak. The island of Kahoʻolawe is visible to the south.

FACILITIES: Picnic tables, outdoor grills, and portable toilets were the only facilities at the time of writing. The county plans to make improvements, including rest rooms, showers, and drinking water. Limited groceries at Olowalu Store. Groceries and gas in Wailuku or Lahaina.

CAMPGROUND ACTIVITIES: Swimming, except for children, is only fair, due to the shallow bottom, but snorkeling is excellent along the offshore reef. Whales can often be seen between November and April, but are usually far enough offshore to require binoculars for good viewing.

PERMIT/RESERVATIONS: At the time of this writing, Pāpalaua was not yet open for camping. Once open, a county parks permit will be required and can be obtained at the following address: Department of Parks and Recreation, War Memorial Center, Wailuku, HI 96793; phone, (808) 243–7389.

TIME LIMIT: Three nights. Camping is limited to 15 days per year.

COST: $3 per person per night, 50 cents per person under 18.

HOW TO GET THERE: From Kahului/Wailuku, take Highway 30 south about 12 miles to the park on the left.

NEARBY POINTS OF INTEREST: See Camp Pecusa.

Camp Pecusa

LOCATION: The camp is on the ocean along Highway 30, on Maui's west coast, 6.5 miles south of Lahaina.

DESCRIPTION: Pecusa is a private camp owned and operated by the Episcopal Church. It is a grassy area, located in a pretty grove of mostly mature trees, including palms, sea grape, *milo,* monkeypod, and *kiawe.* The camp is fronted by a narrow, gray-sand beach strewn with small, gravel-sized stones. The water offshore is flat and calm with no shorebreak and a shallow, rocky bottom. From the beach there are fine views of Haleakalā and the islands of Molokini and Kahoʻolawe.

FACILITIES: Cabin, tent, and vehicle camping. The camp is divided into two distinct sections, one for cabin users, and one for tenters. The tent area sits in a grove of *kiawe* and young *milo* trees. It contains picnic tables, faucets for drinking water, a fire pit, a dishwashing sink, an outdoor solar-heated shower, and two portable chemical toilets. A pay phone and a clothesline complete the facilities.

Six A-frame cabins, each containing six cots and mattresses, are available for rent to groups. The package includes a completely equipped kitchen with cooking/eating utensils and dishes, a dining hall, and bathrooms with hot showers. Cabin users must provide their own bedding or sleeping bags.

CAMPGROUND ACTIVITIES: Swimming is almost always safe, although care must be taken in the shallow, rocky water near the shoreline. Very good snorkeling can be found about 100 yards offshore, where a submerged reef is located. Commercial snorkeling boats carrying tourists frequently anchor here.

From November through April, humpback whales from Alaska visit Hawaiian waters. They are so popular that they have been designated the official state mammal. Sightings off Camp Pecusa beach are frequent during the season. Binoculars or telescopes provide the best viewing.

PERMIT/RESERVATIONS: Tent camping is on a first-come, first-served basis; cabins by reservation. Prospective tent campers may call to see if the campground is full. Write or call the following: Camp Pecusa, 800 Olowalu Village, Lahaina, Maui, HI 96761; phone, (808) 661–4303.

TIME LIMIT: Seven days for tent and vehicle camping; none for cabin users.

COST: Tent camping, $5 per person per night. Cabins, $9 per person per night; $240 minimum per night. Cabin rental provides exclusive use of all six cabins (accommodating 42 persons), the grounds, the kitchen and dining hall, and the rest rooms and showers.

SPECIAL COMMENTS: Until Pāpalaua Beach Park opens, Camp Pecusa is the only campground on Maui's entire beautiful west coast. From Līpoa Point in the north to La Pérouse Bay in the south, there's not another place to pitch a tent. A fatal shark attack occurred near the campground in November, 1991, when a snorkeler was killed by a large tiger shark.

HOW TO GET THERE: From Kahului (16 miles), follow the signs to Lahaina, taking Highway 380 until it intersects with Highway 30. Turn left at Highway 30, continuing toward Lahaina. From the exit of the highway tunnel, it is 4 miles to the Camp Pecusa sign on the left. Follow the dirt road a short distance to the parking lot.

From Lahaina, drive south on Highway 30, 6.5 miles. The sign for the camp is on the right, about half a mile past the Olowalu Store.

NEARBY POINTS OF INTEREST: An interesting group of petroglyphs can be seen at Olowalu on a cliff face, where a ramp has been constructed for close viewing. From the campground, turn left on Highway 30 toward Lahaina. In half a mile, you will reach the Olowalu Store on the right. A dirt road behind the store leads to the petroglyphs, about another three-quarters of a mile. Watch for the ramp on the right.

Lahaina, an old whaling town and former capital of the Hawaiian Kingdom, is well worth a visit. It has many historic buildings, good shopping, and excellent restaurants. Have a drink in the Whaler's Bar of the Pioneer Inn and go aboard the *Carthaginian,* a replica of a nineteenth-century brig similar to the *Thaddeus,* which brought the first missionaries to Hawai'i. Across from the Pioneer Inn is one of the most sprawling banyan trees in the state, covering over half an acre.

During the winter and early spring, humpback whales are numerous in the waters between Maui and Lāna'i. Boats for whale watching leave from Lahaina and from Mā'alaea Harbor to the south. Some boat captains are so confident that you will sight whales that they offer a second cruise free if you don't see them. Boats of all types are required to maintain a certain distance from the whales, so bring a pair of binoculars and a telephoto lens for your camera if you have them.

Windmill Beach

LOCATION: This beach is on the northern tip of West Maui, on the ocean, just off Highway 30.

DESCRIPTION: Windmill is an isolated white-sand beach, strewn with coral rubble and backed by an attractive ironwood grove. A long flat reef extends the entire length of the beach, making a shallow, rocky bottom offshore. This shelf is pounded by heavy waves on all but the calmest days. There is a good view of the rugged coastline to the west. The true name of this area is Punalau Beach, which means "many springs" in

Hawaiian, referring to freshwater springs that once existed near the shoreline. The popular name for the beach comes from a water-drawing windmill that formerly occupied the east end of the beach.

FACILITIES: None.

CAMPGROUND ACTIVITIES: Swimming is only possible on calm days, which are few, and then only on the east end of the beach, where there are several channels through the reef. Care should be taken even here, because strong currents may build up in these channels at any time. The same comments apply to snorkeling. Shoreline fishing is probably the safest activity on this beach, except for beachcombing and sunbathing. Goatfish, *pāpio,* leatherback, and milkfish can all be taken here.

PERMIT/RESERVATIONS: Windmill Beach is private property, but a camping permit may be obtained from the following: Maui Land and Pineapple Company, Honolua Division, Lahaina, Maui, HI 96761; phone, (808) 669–6201.

TIME LIMIT: Three days.

COST: $5 per person per night.

SPECIAL COMMENTS: Although the lack of facilities is an inconvenience, Windmill Beach is the only camping spot anywhere in this vicinity. Drinking water, rest rooms, and showers are available at D. T. Fleming Beach Park, a short distance away. Be sure to bury any human wastes and pack out all trash.

HOW TO GET THERE: Proceed north from Lahaina on Route 30 to a point 3.5 miles past D. T. Fleming Beach Park where a dirt road on the left side of the highway angles back and drops sharply. You will be able to see the ironwood grove and parts of the beach. The dirt road is steep and is usually too slippery for conventional-drive cars in wet weather.

NEARBY POINTS OF INTEREST: Just 1.4 miles back toward Lahaina from Windmill Beach is Honolua Bay, an excellent snorkeling site that is calm most of the year. Although the water near the shore is muddy, it clears quickly, especially on the right side of the bay, where beautiful coral formations can be seen. Watch for parked cars on the ocean side of the highway, and walk down the dirt road through a dense forest. A deteriorated concrete boat ramp on a boulder beach will tell you that you are in the right place. Honolua Bay is also a favorite surfing spot.

Moloka'i

For those who feel that much of Hawai'i is too commercial and overdeveloped, Moloka'i offers a great alternative. Even residents of other parts of the state like to come here when they want to get away from it all. The sparse population, dense upland forests, and miles of deserted beaches provide an outdoor experience far removed from other tourists, hikers, and campers.

Although this might sound like paradise regained, there are some problems. Much of the island is either ruggedly inaccessible or in private ownership. The north shore of Moloka'i, boasting the highest waterfalls and some of the most spectacular scenery in the state, is reachable only by boat or rough, difficult trails. Much of the western third of the island, including the seashore, is owned by Moloka'i Ranch Company. Most of the upland forest reserve, containing many of the hiking trails, can be reached only by four-wheel-drive vehicle. Yet with the right equipment and the necessary permits, the camper can enjoy all of these one-of-a-kind wilderness experiences.

The fifth largest of the main Islands, Moloka'i is 38 miles long and about 10 miles wide, encompassing 261 square miles. Its age is between 1.3 and 1.8 million years, and it was formed by two volcanoes. A third, posterosional eruption, occurring much later, added the Makanalua Peninsula (Kalaupapa) to the island. The two distinct geographic regions of Moloka'i are so different from each other that they could easily be two separate islands. In fact, when seen from O'ahu, Moloka'i does appear exactly that way. West Moloka'i, the part closest to O'ahu, is dry and relatively flat, reaching a maximum altitude of 1,381 feet. The "Desert Strip," on the northwest coast, has large sand dunes extending as far as 4 miles inland. East Moloka'i, on the other hand, is lush and mountainous. Verdant valleys send streams and waterfalls rushing toward the sea, and Kamakou, its highest peak, reaches well into the clouds at almost 5,000 feet.

The population of Moloka'i, roughly 6,700, contains a higher percentage of Hawaiians than any other place in the state, with the exception of privately owned Ni'ihau. Unfortunately, the island also has the state's second highest unemployment rate, 7.3 percent, compared with a statewide average of just over 4 percent, caused mainly by the phaseout of pineapple farming. It was hoped that tourism would take up the slack, particularly at the resort complex on beautiful Pāpōhaku Beach. This has been only par-

MOLOKA‘I

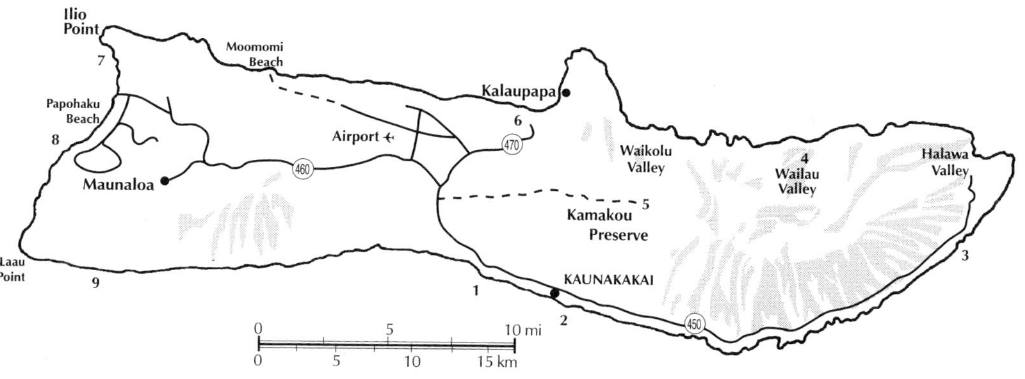

Moloka‘i Campgrounds

1, Kiowea Beach Park
2. Oneali‘i Beach Park
3. Waialua Congregational Church
4. Wailau Valley
5. Waikolu Lookout
6. Pālā‘au State Park
7. Kawākiu Bay
8. Pāpōhaku Beach Park
9. Hālena Camp

tially successful, and Moloka'i continues to have the second lowest hotel occupancy rate of all the Islands. When the hotel company, Kaluako'i, was first formed, six hotels were planned, and rosy projections proclaimed that the population of Moloka'i would reach 30,000 within 20 years. The 20 years have passed, only one hotel was built, and the population of Moloka'i has remained essentially the same.

The tourist nickname of Moloka'i is "The Friendly Isle." Why this particular name was picked, I have no idea. I have found residents of Moloka'i neither more nor less friendly than those of the other Islands. If they in fact are, it might be because they have less tourism to contend with. There is no public transportation on the island, and hitchhiking is not legal.

Moloka'i is known for its former leper colony. Made famous by Father Damien, who worked and died there, it is located at Kalaupapa, on the almost inaccessible north shore of the island. Before Father Damien's arrival, lepers were dumped on the isolated peninsula and left to fend for themselves. The priest brought order, care, and hope to the colony. Modern drugs have now arrested the disease, and, unlike in the past, residents are free to leave if they wish. The settlement may only be visited by making prior arrangements (call Damien Tours, 808 567–6171). There is a $30 charge per person for the tour, and persons under 16 are not permitted. Access is by plane or by hiking down a steep trail (see the section on Pālā'au State Park). It is also possible to ride a mule down the trail to the settlement. The cost is $120 per person, which includes the settlement tour and lunch.

There are not many public campgrounds on Moloka'i. Camping is allowed in only two locations on state forest lands and in two county parks and one state park. Adding to the problem, four private campgrounds have closed since the previous edition of this book. Camping is no longer permitted at Mo'omomi Beach, Ranch Mo'omomi, Pu'uhakina Beach, or Hale o Lono Harbor.

THINGS TO SEE AND DO: Points of interest are few, but some of them are unique. Those listed below are described in more detail in the sections on campgrounds located nearest to them. Distances on Moloka'i are not great. If you plan to hike down to the former leper colony at Kalaupapa, for example, but would prefer to camp on the beach instead of in the forest at Pālā'au, it is only about a 30-minute drive from Oneali'i Beach Park to the Kalaupapa trailhead.

Point of Interest	**Nearest Campground**
African Wildlife Park	Kawākiu Bay
Hālawa Valley and Moa'ula Falls	Waialua Congregational Church
'Ili'ili'ōpae Heiau	Waialua Congregational Church

Kalaupapa Settlement	Pālā'au State Park
Mo'omomi Sand Dunes	Pālā'au State Park
Phallic Rock	Pālā'au State Park
Sandalwood Pit	Waikolu Lookout
South shore fish ponds	Oneali'i Beach Park
Waikolu and Pelekunu lookouts	Waikolu Lookout

EAST MOLOKA'I

Kiowea Beach Park

LOCATION: The park is on Highway 460, 1 mile west of Kaunakakai, on the south shore.

DESCRIPTION: Kiowea, which is the Hawaiian name for a migratory shoreline bird, occupies a flat grass and sand site, directly off the highway and on the ocean. It is surrounded by the Kapuāiwa Coconut Grove, named for a Hawaiian chief who later became King Kamehameha V. The park also contains several small banyans and *kamani* trees. The palm trees, extending almost to the water line, provide a lovely setting. However, they leave space for only a narrow sand beach, which fronts the park. The water is shallow, and the offshore bottom is rocky and muddy. The island of Lāna'i is clearly visible across the Kalohi Channel.

FACILITIES: Tent and vehicle camping. A covered pavilion, with electric lighting, houses seven picnic tables, sinks, drinking water, and barbecue grills. Rest rooms and showers are in a separate building. Groceries and gas can be purchased in Kaunakakai, 1 mile east.

CAMPGROUND ACTIVITIES: Shallow water and a muddy, rocky bottom make swimming unattractive except wading for small children. The water is normally calm and safe. Goatfish, *manini,* mullet, and an occasional parrotfish or *pāpio* compose the usual catch, but the fishing is mediocre.

PERMIT/RESERVATIONS: Kiowea is a private park, primarily for the use of homesteaders on Hawaiian Home Lands. It is available to others on a space-available basis. Permits provide exclusive use of the park and its facilities and may be obtained by writing or calling the following: Department of Hawaiian Home Lands, P.O. Box 198, Ho'olehua, Moloka'i, HI 96729; phone, (808) 567–6104.

Kiowea Beach Park campground, a little over a mile east of Kaunakakai, provides exclusive use to permit holders.

TIME LIMIT: Day-to-day. Hawaiian homesteaders have priority, but reservations are accepted from others.

COST: $5 per night for a group of any size.

SPECIAL COMMENTS: The best chance to get a camping permit here is during the winter months. Homesteaders keep it very busy at other times, especially during the summer and on holidays. Warning! Do not pitch your tent under a bearing coconut tree. Coconuts can fall with a deadly effect.

HOW TO GET THERE: Proceed 1 mile west of Kaunakakai on Highway 460.

NEARBY POINTS OF INTEREST: See section on Oneali'i Beach Park.

Oneali'i Beach Park

LOCATION: The park is on Highway 460, 3 miles east of Kaunakakai, on the south shore.

DESCRIPTION: Oneali'i, which means "royal sands" in Hawaiian, occupies a flat, open, 12-acre grassy field directly off the highway and on the ocean. A narrow, sandy beach lined with palms fronts the park and the camping area, but the offshore bottom is shallow and muddy. Partial shade is provided by *hau* and palm trees and several small banyans. There is a fine view of Lāna'i directly across the Kalohi Channel.

FACILITIES: Tent and vehicle camping. A large covered pavilion with picnic tables, a dishwashing area, and electricity services the entire park, with several outdoor tables throughout the area. A broken concrete barbecue platform, along with a small pavilion, is located near the shore in a shady grove at the west end of the park. Drinking water is available, and rest rooms and enclosed showers are provided. Groceries and gas may be obtained in Kaunakakai.

Oneali'i Beach Park, east of Kaunakakai, has rarely more than one or two tents.

CAMPGROUND ACTIVITIES: Because of shallow water and a rocky, muddy bottom, wading, rather than swimming, is the water activity here. Enjoyed mainly by children, the water is calm and safe. It is a mediocre to average fishing spot, where goatfish and mullet are the usual catches.

PERMIT/RESERVATIONS: Permits may be picked up at the County Parks and Recreation Office at the Pau'ole Center Multipurpose Building in Kaunakakai, but it is better to get one in advance by writing or calling the following: Maui County Parks Department, P.O. Box 526, Kaunakakai, Moloka'i, HI 96748; phone, (808) 553–3204, or call the Maui office, (808) 243–7389.

TIME LIMIT: Camping is limited to 3 days, but longer stays can usually be arranged.

COST: $3 per person per night.

SPECIAL COMMENTS: Even though it is the closest public beach park to Kaunakakai, Oneali'i is rarely crowded, even on weekends. However, part of the park consists of a large ball field, which can be noisy when in use.

HOW TO GET THERE: Proceed east from Kaunakakai 3 miles on Highway 450.

NEARBY POINTS OF INTEREST: At one time the Moloka'i shoreline was dotted with 58 fish ponds, the largest number of any of the Islands. These ponds, belonging exclusively to the *ali'i,* or chiefs, were used to trap and keep fish until ready for use. Many of them can still be seen by driving east on Highway 450, between Kaunakakai and Waialua.

Hālawa Valley is the only one of the four amphitheater valleys of Moloka'i that is accessible by vehicle. Hālawa means "curve" in Hawaiian. It is at the end of Highway 450, about 28 miles east of Kaunakakai. The valley was once used extensively for taro growing, but declining population and two devastating tsunamis ended all taro production by 1957. A county beach park located at the end of the road has a small pavilion, picnic tables, rest rooms, and running water, which should be treated before drinking. Two sandy beaches line the bay. They are both safe for swimming, although the water is shallow and sometimes muddy.

From the parking area near the beach park, it is possible to hike to twin waterfalls at the head of the valley, although the trail to Hīpuapua, the farthest, is difficult and often overgrown. Moa'ula Falls, however, is easily reached by a 2-mile-long trail and is a lovely spot. The pool at its base is deep enough for a brisk dip, if you can stand the temperature. At the beach park roadside parking area, there is a sign pointing down the road to "Secure Parking." If you are hiking to the falls, it might be a good idea to take advantage of this, if the price is not too high. This beach park parking area is the only place in Hawai'i where I have had my car broken into.

Waialua Congregational Church

LOCATION: The campground is on Highway 450, 18 miles east of Kaunakakai, on the south shore.

DESCRIPTION: Waialua, which means "two waters," is a small, grassy picnic area on the ocean, directly across from the church. Palm trees, *hala,* and *naupaka* on the shoreline make a very attractive setting. A narrow sandy beach fronts the site. The water is shallow for about 100 yards out to a submerged reef. The islands of Lāna'i and Maui can be seen from the shore.

FACILITIES: Tent and vehicle camping. A large pavilion contains a kitchen and picnic tables. A separate building houses showers and rest rooms. The campground has drinking water and electric lighting. The nearest gas and groceries are in Kaunakakai.

CAMPGROUND ACTIVITIES: Inside the reef, the shallow water makes swimming suitable mostly for children and then only on calm days. Outside the reef, on calm days, swim with caution. Snorkeling is good along the reef on calm days. Shoreline fishing is good for threadfin, mullet, and goatfish, but *pāpio* and *ulua* sometimes come by.

PERMIT/RESERVATIONS: The entire campground is rented to a single group only, which then has exclusive use of the grounds. Reservations must be accompanied by one night's deposit and can be made by contacting the caretaker at the following address: Jo-Ann K. Simms, Star Route 335, Kaunakakai, Moloka'i, HI 96748; phone, (808) 558–8150.

TIME LIMIT: None; subject only to prior commitments.

COST: $85 per night for the first three nights; $70 for each night thereafter.

SPECIAL COMMENTS: Because of the narrowness of the site, camping here puts you close to the road. However, this is not the problem that it would be in other areas, because traffic on the east end of Moloka'i is light. Also, this spot is pretty enough to overlook its proximity to the road.

HOW TO GET THERE: From Kaunakakai (18 miles), drive east on Highway 450, watching for the Waialua Congregational Church on the left. The picnic area is on the right, clearly visible from the road.

NEARBY POINTS OF INTEREST: For information on Hālawa Valley and the south shore fish ponds, see the section on Oneali'i Beach Park.

About 3.5 miles back toward Kaunakakai are the remains of 'Ili'ili'ōpae Heiau, one of the major *heiau* in Hawai'i. Nothing is left but the foundation, but it is worth a visit if you have not seen one before, and it is close to the campground. For directions, see the section on Wailau Valley or inquire locally.

Wailau Valley

LOCATION: On the spectacular north shore of the island, this wild and uninhabited valley lies east of Hālawa.

DESCRIPTION: Wailau is a huge amphitheater valley, the largest on Moloka'i. The valley walls are steep, rising to over 4,900 feet, and numerous waterfalls cascade down its sides. Wailau means "many waters" in Hawaiian, and the valley floor contains several watercourses fed by the waterfalls, springs, and a very heavy rainfall. Some open space remains in the valley, as a result of long-ceased taro farming, but second-growth forest continues to claim the land. Older, denser forest is encountered in the valley's upper reaches. Wailau Beach consists mainly of boulders, although in summer a small sand beach accretes on its western corner, near the mouth of Wailau Stream. Heavy surf pounds the beach in winter, making access from the sea hazardous and sometimes impossible.

FACILITIES: There are no facilities of any kind in Wailau. Water from the stream can be used for drinking, but should be treated before use. Despite the valley's size, camping in the area immediately behind the beach is restricted by boulders and soggy ground. The best sites are on a slight rise behind the beach on the western side of the stream. Numerous campsites can be found farther up the valley. Care should be taken to dispose of human wastes by burying them well away from running water.

CAMPGROUND ACTIVITIES: Wailau is for the camper who wants to get away from it all. It is beautiful and isolated. Hiking and exploring the valley are the main activities. Little evidence is left of former habitation, except for some taro terraces. The tsunami of 1946 wiped out what remained of the village of Wailau. Swimming can sometimes be dangerous because of strong currents, and fishing is poor as a result of centuries of scouring of the ocean bottom by heavy freshwater flow from the stream.

PERMIT/RESERVATIONS: Camping permits must be obtained in advance from the state forestry office on Maui. Write or call the following: Division of Forestry and Wildlife, P.O. Box 1015, Wailuku, Maui, HI 96793; phone, (808) 984–8100.

You can obtain a permit on Moloka'i; however, the Forestry office there is only open part-time.

TIME LIMIT: Two nights. Longer stays may be allowed at the discretion of the Forestry Division.

COST: Free.

SPECIAL COMMENTS: When I last visited Wailau in the early 1980s, our group camped in a large marijuana patch on the rise behind the beach mentioned above. When the "planter" appeared to complain, we explained that we had been camping in this spot for years and there was no place else for a group of our size. An agreement was finally reached in which he let us stay there if we did not disturb any more of his plants. Marijuana may not be growing there now, because of the state's eradication efforts. Incidentally, in all my hiking and camping in the Islands, this is the only place I have ever come across a marijuana field.

HOW TO GET THERE: There are two ways to enter Wailau Valley—by boat or by way of the Wailau Trail. Usually, boats can enter only during the summer months, and even then they cannot land people directly on the rocky beach. You will have to wade or swim ashore through the surf, carrying whatever luggage you have. There are several private boat owners who can be hired to take groups in and out of Wailau. Most of them live in Hālawa Valley. Ask around in Kaunakakai, at the police station, and at the county and state offices.

The Wailau Trail begins on the south shore, crosses the mountains, and then follows the valley floor to Wailau Beach. It is 8 miles long, and part of it is on private property. The trail is not maintained and is a strenuous hike over rugged terrain. It begins at the 'Ili'ili'ōpae Heiau, 15.7 miles east of Kaunakakai on Highway 450. When you have driven about 14 miles, watch for The Lady of Seven Sorrows Church, on the left side of the road. Proceeding nine-tenths of a mile from the church, you will come to a small bridge with white pipe railings. Turn left immediately after crossing the bridge, onto the overgrown, one-way dirt road. The road ends in about half a mile, with a house on the right and a small wooden sign marking the trail on the left. The sign, which reads "Wailau Trail, dangerous, 12 hours minimum, landowner assumes no liability," implies permission to use the trail. If you prefer to secure more formal permission, call Pearl Petro, (808) 558–8113. There is no parking area here, so it is best to park your car somewhere along the highway and hike the half mile to the trailhead.

The trail leads immediately to the *heiau,* then climbs 3 miles over fairly steep terrain, traverses a bog, and then descends steeply from the ridge-top at 2,800 feet. On reaching the valley floor, it crosses the stream and follows its east bank to the beach, a distance of about 4.5 miles.

When I last hiked this trail, in 1984, we found the part from the summit to the floor of Wailau Valley almost completely washed out, and we had to make our own way down. The going was rough and, in some places, dangerous. We also had a problem finding the trail again once we reached the valley floor and had to bushwhack along the stream before we connected with it. Talking to people who hiked it in 1991 revealed that it is in about the same shape now. I would not recommend this hike to any but the most experienced hikers, in good physical condition. Even then, make sure to obtain the latest information about trail conditions. Hiring a local guide, if you can find one, is probably the surest and safest way to go. A hiker disappeared in Wailau Valley in March 1993 after giving his pack to a Forestry employee and stating that he intended to hike out.

Waikolu Lookout

LOCATION: The campground is on Moloka'i Forest Reserve Road, about 13.5 miles northeast of Kaunakakai.

DESCRIPTION: This combined campsite and picnic area is located deep within an upland forest, at an altitude of 3,600 feet. The campground is situated in a grassy clearing, which can be soggy if it has been raining, and is surrounded by a dense forest. Cold, misty winds often blow in from the north, which can make Waikolu a very chilly place. The campsite is across the road from the Lookout, which provides a magnificent panorama of Waikolu Canyon. Waikolu, which means "three waters," drops dramatically between steep green walls from its upper reaches all the way to the sea. It is best to visit the overlook in the morning, because the view is frequently obscured in the afternoon by mists and clouds that cover the upper canyon.

FACILITIES: The picnic area contains a picnic table in the grassy area and another at the Lookout. Rest rooms with pit toilets are provided, but there is no water, potable or otherwise.

CAMPGROUND ACTIVITIES: Hiking and exploring are possible in the upland forest, including a native bog.

PERMIT/RESERVATIONS: Camping permits should be obtained in advance from the state forestry office on Maui. Write or call the following: Division of Forestry and Wildlife, P.O. Box 1015, Wailuku, Maui, HI 96793; phone, (808) 984–8100.

If you arrive on Moloka'i without a permit, one can be obtained at the state offices in Kaunakakai. However, they do not keep regular office hours, so it would be better to obtain the permit in advance.

TIME LIMIT: Two nights. Longer stays may be allowed at the discretion of the Forestry Division.

COST: Free.

SPECIAL COMMENTS: The Moloka'i Forest Reserve Road is unpaved and is marked for use by four-wheel-drive vehicles only. Some guide books will tell you that the road can be negotiated by a conventional-drive car if it is dry. I do not recommend that you do this. You could find the road dry at the beginning, only to get mired down in some serious mud farther up the ridge. In any event, do not attempt to drive past the campsite with an ordinary car. Beyond this point, the road is deeply rutted and difficult even for a four-wheel-drive.

The pavilion mentioned in the state Recreation Map for Moloka'i no longer exists.

HOW TO GET THERE: From Kaunakakai, drive west on Highway 460 for about 3.5 miles to a dirt road on the right, just before a white bridge. Turn right and proceed another 10 miles to the campground. Stay on the main road, bearing left, and avoid the many side roads.

NEARBY POINTS OF INTEREST: The Sandalwood Pit is a depression in the ground, dug to the measurements of the hull of a nineteenth-century sailing ship, that was used to determine how much sandalwood was necessary to make a boatload. When the pit was full, the wood was taken down the mountain to a waiting cargo vessel. This practice ended in about 1840, when the supply of sandalwood became exhausted. The pit is located 9.2 miles from the highway, on the left side of the Moloka'i Forest Reserve Road. It is another eight-tenths of a mile to the Waikolu Lookout campground.

There are several hiking trails in this area, all within the Kamakou Preserve managed by The Nature Conservancy. The Hanalilolilo Trail begins two-tenths of a mile from the campsite, on the left side of the road. It passes through a native *'ōhi'a*/fern forest, leads to a lookout over Pelekunu Valley, and joins the Pēpē'ōpae Trail, a boardwalk through a native bog. For access and information about these and other trails, contact the following: Manager, Kamakou Preserve, P.O. Box 40, Kualapu'u, Moloka'i, HI 96757; phone, (808) 567–6680.

Pālā'au State Park

LOCATION: The park is at the end of Highway 470, about 10 miles northwest of Kaunakakai.

DESCRIPTION: Pālā'au, which means "wooden fence" in Hawaiian, is a 233-acre heavily wooded park at an elevation of 1,600 feet. It sits about 300 yards back from the edge of steep cliffs that drop to the sea on the north shore of the island. The campground is located in a eucalyptus and ironwood grove just off the highway on the left, near the end of the road. The trees provide full shade, and because not much sun penetrates the site, the campground can be chilly and damp. A dramatic lookout over Kalaupapa Peninsula is just a short walk, as is a well-known phallic rock, both described below.

FACILITIES: Tent camping only. Picnic tables and outdoor grills in the open are located throughout the campsite. A small rest room building has running water, which must be treated before drinking. A large, covered pavilion is situated about 200 yards back down the road toward the park entrance. It has picnic tables, rest rooms, and nonpotable water. In February 1992 it suffered from a heavy dose of graffiti, but it is a good place to cook and eat if it rains. Gas and groceries can be obtained at Kaunakakai, 10 miles back down the road. Limited items are available at the general store in Kualapu'u, 3 miles south.

CAMPGROUND ACTIVITIES: Hiking and exploring are possible in the dense upland forest. Pālā'au is an ideal starting place for the hike down to Kalaupapa, described below.

PERMIT/RESERVATIONS: Permits may be obtained from a state parks office on any island. The following address is for the parks office on Maui, which issues advance permits for Moloka'i: Division of State Parks, P.O. Box 1049, Wailuku, Maui, HI 96793; phone, (808) 984–8109. If you arrive on Moloka'i without a permit, one can be obtained at the state office in Kaunakakai.

However, they do not keep regular office hours, so it is better to get the permit in advance.

TIME LIMIT: Five nights in any 30-day period.

COST: Free.

SPECIAL COMMENTS: The state Recreation Map for Molokaʻi incorrectly describes the campground as having drinking water and cabins available, which is not the case.

HOW TO GET THERE: From Kaunakakai, proceed west on Highway 450 to the junction of Highway 470 on the right, about 4.5 miles. Follow Highway 470 to the end, an additional 5.5 miles.

NEARBY POINTS OF INTEREST: The Phallic Rock is startlingly realistic. This large fertility symbol is just a short walk from the campsite, along a trail that begins at the end of the road. It is said that in ancient times Hawaiian women came here to make offerings to ensure successful childbirth.

The Kalaupapa Lookout is also reached from a trail at the end of the road. It is a striking overlook of the entire Kalaupapa Peninsula, including the settlement and Kauhakō Crater.

Kalaupapa Settlement, the former leper colony made famous by Father Damien, is located on the western shore of the Kalaupapa peninsula. Only about 100 or so patients remain in the settlement. Modern drugs have now arrested the disease, and, unlike in the past, patients are free to leave if they wish. Those who stay do so mainly because of long association with the town and lack of family and friends elsewhere.

The best hike on Molokaʻi descends the cliff from Pālāʻau to the settlement. The trail is steep and moderately strenuous, but it is wide and well maintained, and the view is marvelous. It is 2 miles long and should take no more than an hour and a half each way. The beginning of the trail down to Kalaupapa is not marked. From the campsite, turn right on the road, as if leaving the park. Take the first road to the left, which will be marked by a stop sign and a notice telling unauthorized persons to keep out. There is usually a chain across the road, so you will have to park and walk from this point. Proceed to the edge of the cliff, where the trail begins on the east side of a communication station.

The gray-sand beach at the bottom of the trail can be dangerous for swimming, so care should be exercised. At the eastern end of the beach, a road leads into Kalaupapa. You may proceed this far without any special permission. However, entry into the settlement is strictly prohibited to all persons unless previous arrangements for a guided tour have been made. This can be done by calling Damien Tours, (808) 567–6171. It would be a shame to descend the trail without visiting the settlement, which includes a bus tour of the settlement, a visitor's center, Father Damien's church, and Kalawao Park, where you will enjoy an unequaled view of the spectacular north shore of the island. There is a $30 charge per person for the tour, and those under 16 are not permitted.

WEST MOLOKA'I

Kawākiu Bay

LOCATION: The campground is on the extreme northwest shoreline, just south of 'Ilio Point, about 22 miles northwest of Kaunakakai.

DESCRIPTION: Kawākiu, which means "spy time" or "spy place" in Hawaiian, is a lovely, crescent-shaped beach of white sand, backed by a grove of *kiawe* trees. The bay has a sandy bottom, that deepens quickly. On the north end of the beach, a rocky shelf is uncovered at low tide. The area is subject to strong winds and heavy surf, particularly in the winter months. The *kiawe* grove is a great place to camp, but watch out for thorns. A muddy stream behind the *kiawe* grove is usually blocked from entering the bay by sand dunes. On a clear night, the lights of O'ahu are visible across the channel. Kawākiu Bay is properly Kawākiunui Bay, to distinguish it from the smaller Kawākiuiki, the next bay to the north.

FACILITIES: None. Tent and vehicle camping. Restaurant and coffee shop at the Kalua Ko'i Hotel, about 1.5 miles south. Limited groceries and gas available in Maunaloa, about 6 miles southeast.

CAMPGROUND ACTIVITIES: Swimming is good when the ocean is calm, mostly during the summer. A pounding shorebreak and dangerous currents make swimming unsafe on many occasions during the winter and spring months. Goatfish, threadfin, and *pāpio* can be caught here.

PERMIT/RESERVATIONS: No written permit is required; however, call Moloka'i Ranch, (808) 552–2681, and let them know the dates and length of your stay. If they are running cattle in the area, you will not be able to camp, and the gate will be locked.

Kawākiu Bay, an isolated and lovely spot on Moloka'i's west coast, is reached by four-wheel drive or a 30 minute hike.

TIME LIMIT: Four days.

COST: Free.

HOW TO GET THERE: From Kaunakakai, drive west on Highway 460 to the turnoff for the Kalua Ko'i Hotel, about 14 miles. At 4.5 miles from the turnoff, a road to the right is marked for Paniolo Hale. Turn here, and four-tenths of a mile farther will be another sign for Paniolo Hale, to the left. Do not turn, but proceed straight for another one-tenth of a mile, where you will see a pavilion on the right. Unless you have a four-wheel drive, park here and hike 30 minutes to the bay. Driving past the pavilion, you will see a dirt road straight ahead. When it forks, go left. After driving five-tenths of a mile, you will come to a gate. Close the gate behind you and continue another seven-tenths of a mile to the bay.

NEARBY POINTS OF INTEREST: The African Wildlife Park is a 1,500-acre animal preserve, just southeast of Kawākiu, situated on terrain similar to the Serengeti Plain in Africa. More than 1,000 animals roam wild, including giraffes, impala, oryx, kudu, antelope, and ibex. Visitors are given a narrated vehicle tour, which makes stops for picture taking. Tours begin at the tour desk, in the Kalua Ko'i Hotel complex, leave four times daily (8 and 10 a.m. and 1 and 3 p.m.) Reservations are required. Cost: $30 for adults; $20 for children.

Pāpōhaku Beach Park

LOCATION: The park is just off Kaluako'i Road, about 20 miles northwest of Kaunakakai, on the western shore.

DESCRIPTION: Pāpōhaku, which means "stone fence," is the largest beach on Moloka'i. Almost 3 miles long and 100 yards wide, it is one of the state's largest white-sand beaches. Low sand dunes and patches of grass back the beach, along with several small groves of *kiawe* trees. Other than these, the area is mostly treeless, and shade is sparse. The beach park is a welcome oasis of shade trees and grassy lawn. There is usually a powerful shorebreak and a correspondingly strong backwash. Although the Kalua Ko'i Hotel is located at its north end, the beach is usually deserted, except for occasional strollers and fishermen. It is an ideal place for those seeking an isolated location that is accessible by car.

FACILITIES: Tent and vehicle camping. The beach park was renovated in 1990, and the improvements include rest rooms, drinking water, outdoor showers, picnic tables, and barbecue grills. Grass was planted, and trees were brought in for shade. A restaurant and a coffee shop are located at the hotel, 1 mile north. Limited groceries and gas can be purchased in Maunaloa, 6 miles east.

CAMPGROUND ACTIVITIES: Do not be deceived by its peaceful appearance, or by what you may have read in other publications. Pāpōhaku is not safe for swimming. In addition to the heavy shorebreak mentioned above, strong offshore currents are prevalent year-round. The shoreline is especially dangerous for young children, because of waves rushing inland and the strong seaward backwash that follows. Goatfish, *pāpio,* and threadfin can be taken here. Be on the lookout for strong waves sweeping suddenly up the flat beach. Beachcombing is often very good because of the lack of an offshore reef, especially after storms or periods of heavy surf.

PERMIT/RESERVATIONS: Permits may be picked up at the County Parks and Recreation Office at the Pau'ole Center Multipurpose Building in Kaunakakai, but it is better to get one in advance by writing or calling the following: Maui County Parks Department, P.O. Box 526, Kaunakakai, Moloka'i, HI 96748; phone, (808) 553–3204.

TIME LIMIT: Camping is limited to 3 days, but longer stays can usually be arranged.

Grassy campsite at Pāpōhaku Beach Park is shaded by mature *kiawe* trees.

COST: $3 per person per night.

HOW TO GET THERE: Take Highway 460 west from Kaunakakai to the turnoff to the Kalua Ko'i Hotel, about 14 miles. At the hotel, continue left along Kaluako'i Road, about 1 mile to the park.

NEARBY POINTS OF INTEREST: For information on the African Wildlife Park, see section on Kawākiu Bay.

Hālena Camp

LOCATION: The camp is on the south shore, about 14 miles west of Kaunakakai.

DESCRIPTION: Hālena, which means "yellowish" in Hawaiian, is named for the yellow-tinted beach rock in the area. The beach is white sand, fronted at the water's edge by a layer of flat rock. Hālena is part of a 12-mile section of undeveloped shoreline, and there is something magical about camping in this lonely, uninhabited area. Low sand dunes back the beach, and *kiawe* trees cover the land as it rises gradually from the shoreline. The island of Lāna'i is visible across the channel.

FACILITIES: Tent and vehicle camping. A cluster of small, weather-beaten buildings, a former Boy Scout Camp, is located in a grassy field directly behind the beach. The largest building (called the pavilion) can be used for sleeping, although it has no furnishings and campers must provide their own bedding. Water, showers, and toilets are available. Limited groceries and gas can be purchased in Maunaloa, 4 miles north.

CAMPGROUND ACTIVITIES: Shallow water and a rocky bottom make for mediocre swimming. This is a good area for mullet, *pāpio,* threadfin, and goatfish. There are no specific hiking trails here, but a dirt road goes east and west along the shoreline, and some jeep trails head upland.

PERMIT/RESERVATIONS: Obtain a permit in advance from Moloka'i Ranch Company, P.O. Box 259, Maunaloa, HI 96770; phone, (808) 552–2681.

TIME LIMIT: Camping is permitted only on weekends, from 3 p.m. Friday to 5 p.m. Sunday.

COST: The cost of camping on Moloka'i Ranch property is relatively high, but the experience is worth it. At Hālena, the fee is $10 per person per day. There is also a $50 deposit, a $5 key deposit (both refundable), and a mandatory $30 charge for use of the pavilion.

SPECIAL COMMENTS: As of the date of writing, Hālena was temporarily closed for renovation. Check with the Ranch for completion information. If you don't mind the walk, a small cove of white sand lies just east of Hale o Lono, 1 mile west. Although the water is shallow here also, the bottom has sandy pockets and the swimming is better than at Hālena. Hālena is a popular weekend spot for local residents and Moloka'i Ranch employees, particularly during the summer months. Make reservations as far in advance as possible.

HOW TO GET THERE: Specific directions are given when you pick up your permit at the Moloka'i Ranch Office, because it involves use of private roads and ranch gates. The usual route is south from the town of Maunaloa, about 16 miles west of Kaunakakai. A four-wheel-drive vehicle is best, because the road from Maunaloa down to the coast is very rutted and bumpy. Also, there are spots along the beach where the road might be impassable for a conventional-drive car in wet weather.

NEARBY POINTS OF INTEREST: Hale o Lono Harbor, the start of the annual Moloka'i to O'ahu canoe race, is 1 mile west, along the shore road. There are no facilities here, and the harbor is used mainly by sailboats cruising interisland.

Lāna'i

Except for Ni'ihau, which is privately owned and off-limits to visitors, Lāna'i is the least populated and least visited of the main Hawaiian Islands. Even among residents of the state, those who travel to Lāna'i are mainly hunters, fishermen, and a few scuba divers. The island's reputation for being mainly a pineapple plantation has much to do with this, as does the fact that until recently, the only hotel on the island had a mere ten rooms. With the opening of two new luxury hotels and their associated golf courses, tourism is increasing, but only for the affluent. By normal standards, these are very expensive hotels.

The sixth largest of the main Islands, Lāna'i is 18 miles long, 13 miles wide, and encompasses 140 square miles. It is a shield volcano, between 1.3 and 1.8 million years old. It is drier than most of the other main Islands, because it lies in the wind shadow of Maui, which restricts its rainfall. The population of 2,200 is about half Filipino in origin, most of whom worked in the pineapple fields for the Dole Food Company, which owns virtually the entire island. Its unemployment rate of 12 percent is the highest in the state and due to go higher. Dole ceased all pineapple growing on the island on 31 October 1992. Lāna'i, which is still known as "The Pineapple Island," will have to find a new nickname for itself.

Paradoxically, Lāna'i has always had a great outdoor environment, but it has been difficult to take advantage of it. It has some great beaches, but four-wheel drive is required to reach most of them. Hunting and fishing are good, but accommodations have been few. Lāna'i is heaven for hikers, but hell for campers. There are miles of hiking and jeep trails and long stretches of deserted beach, but camping is restricted to one small campground. It is located on one of the prettiest beaches on the island, but shares it with one of the luxury hotels—a possibly precarious status. This is really disappointing, because there is so much on Lāna'i for outdoor enthusiasts to see and do. Residents of the island are allowed to camp almost anywhere, so if you are fortunate enough to know someone who lives there, you can camp with him. If you are renting a jeep, you might check with the rental company. As residents, they might be able to make some arrangement. But don't count on it.

THINGS TO SEE AND DO: Garden of the Gods is a somewhat overblown name for an area of eroded rock and soil formations, but it is worth a visit

LĀNA'I

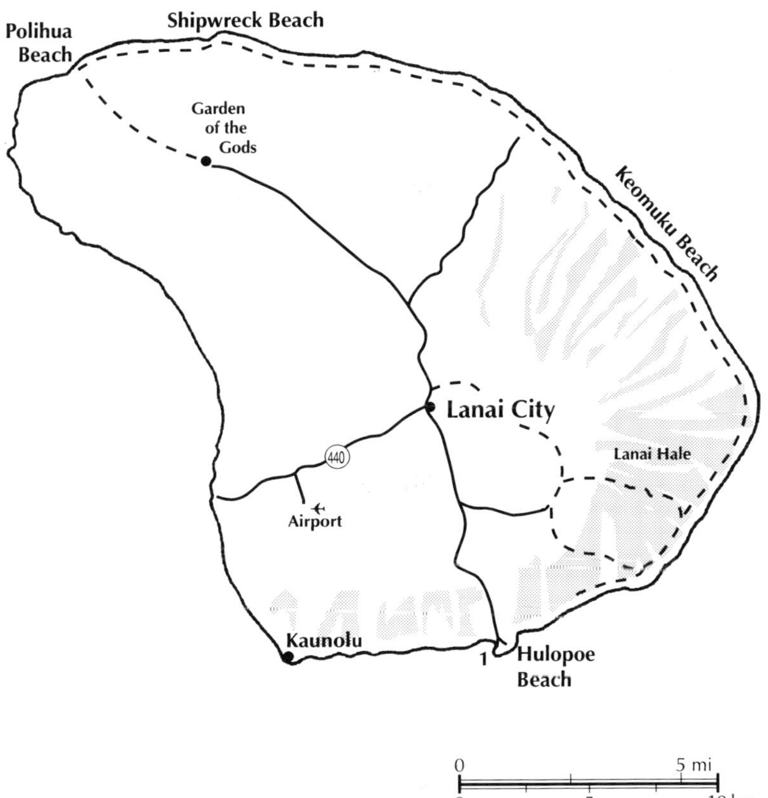

Lāna'i Campground

1. Hulopo'e Beach Park

if you don't expect too much and have a four-wheel drive. Interesting patterns and colors appear at sunrise and sunset. Don't be fooled by the many rock cairns. Despite what local residents may tell you or what you have read, they are of very recent origin and were put there by people just like you. It is located about 6.6 miles northwest of Lāna'i City by a dirt road through the pineapple fields. There may be small signs. Ask directions.

Hulopo'e Bay is the location of the campground, and it is described in that section.

Kaunolū Village is one of the most important sites of ancient Hawai'i. The ruins of this fishing community are situated on a desolate bluff overlooking the sea on the south shore of the island. There is a trail through the village and signs explain the various archaeological sites. Take Highway 440 west from Lāna'i City to Kaupili Road, just past the airport (about 3.4 miles). Turn left and proceed another 2.5 miles to a jeep road (Kaunolū Road) on the right, which goes down to the site. A four-wheel-drive vehicle is required.

The Luahiwa petroglyphs are located about 2 miles south of Lāna'i City via Highway 440. This site has some excellent examples of ancient Hawaiian rock carvings on clusters of boulders. It is not easy to find, so ask directions locally. A trail to the site is being constructed, which will solve the problem.

Shipwreck Beach is a great place for beachcombing, especially if you are interested in driftwood and junk, but glass balls and paper nautilus shells have been found. Two major wrecks lie visible just offshore, and the remains of others litter this 8-mile stretch of beach on the north shore of the island. From Lāna'i City, take Highway 430 and proceed north to the coast, about 8 miles. A dirt road turns west (left) at the beginning of Shipwreck Beach. The road soon disintegrates to four-wheel status, but you can walk as far as you want. There is not much chance for snorkeling or swimming, because of shallow water.

Hulopo'e Beach Park

LOCATION: The park is at the end of Highway 440 (Mānele Road), about 6 miles south of Lāna'i City.

DESCRIPTION: Hulopo'e Bay boasts a beautiful, crescent-shaped white-sand beach, considered by most people to be the best on the island. Hulopo'e has no specific meaning in Hawaiian, and the area is believed to have been named after a fisherman who lived here. It is sometimes called "White Mānele" by local residents. Mānele Bay, which lies immediately east of Hulopoʻe, used to have a black-sand beach before the construction of its small boat harbor, and it was referred to as "Black Mānele." An ancient fishing village existed at Mānele, which means "sedan chair" in Hawaiian, and its ruins can still be seen in the camping area.

The beach is backed by a grove of *kiawe* trees and by a new luxury hotel, which restricts much of the area behind the central part of the beach to hotel guests. Offshore, the bottom is sandy, except for a portion on the east side of the bay, where a lava shelf is host to colorful coral formations. The bay is part of the Mānele-Hulopoʻe Marine Life Conservation District, which restricts fishing and boating activities.

FACILITIES: Tent camping only. There are only three individual campsites at Hulopoʻe, each one limited to six persons. Rest rooms and showers are provided, and drinking water is available, as are picnic tables and outdoor grills. *Kiawe* trees provide partial shade. Groceries and gas are available only in Lānaʻi City.

CAMPGROUND ACTIVITIES: The protected bay and moderate surf make for excellent, safe swimming most of the year, except during *Kona* storms and periods of heavy southern swells. Caution should be taken with small children and by nonswimmers, because the bottom drops off quickly in the shorebreak area. A shallow wading pool has been excavated in the rocky terrace near the bay's eastern point. On calm days, snorkeling is excellent, especially in the coral gardens along the shelf on the east side of the bay, although these seem to have been damaged by Hurricane ʻIniki in September 1992. Both board and bodysurfing can be enjoyed when the surf is suitable, usually during winter and spring. Because of the conservation district, fishing is restricted to shoreline casting for fin fish. Spear fishing is not allowed. Signs posted in the area provide more specific information. *Ulua,* bonefish, and threadfin can be caught here.

PERMIT/RESERVATIONS: Because of the small number of campsites, permits should be obtained as far in advance as possible, from the following: Lānaʻi Company, P.O. Box 310, Lānaʻi City, HI 96763, Attn: Camping Permits; phone, (808) 565–8206.

TIME LIMIT: Seven days.

COST: There is a $5 registration fee and a charge of $5 per person per night.

SPECIAL COMMENTS: With only three permits issued per day, the campground is usually filled up months in advance. Do not come to Lānaʻi hoping to get a permit after arrival. Remember, this is the only campsite on the island. It is privately owned, and a warden checks campers to see that they have permits.

HOW TO GET THERE: From Lāna'i City, drive south on Highway 440 to the end of the road, about 6 miles.

NEARBY POINTS OF INTEREST: A short hike around the eastern point of the bay will bring you to a smaller version of Hulopo'e. Pu'u Pehe Cove is the remains of a volcanic cinder cone; it has a small white-sand beach. Swimming and snorkeling are good here, the fishing is the same as at Hulopo'e, and there are usually fewer people.

For other points of interest, see the preceding section on Lāna'i.

O'ahu

For most visitors to the Islands, Hawai'i is Waikīkī. Nearly 75 percent of tourism centers on its wall-to-wall hotels and relatively narrow beach. Many of these tourists never go anywhere else, except for a visit to the Arizona Memorial and a brief drive around the island. Most of them never visit another island. But O'ahu is far more than just Waikīkī, and you don't have to fly to another island to enjoy magnificent scenery, deserted beaches, or a true tropical atmosphere.

O'ahu need not take a back seat to the other Islands when it comes to the sheer, breathtaking beauty of its natural endowment. Its majestic mountains, silent rain forests, and miles of uninterrupted sandy beaches rival those of any of its neighbors. The fluted cliffs of the Pali, plunging like a giant green theater curtain to the plain below, are as awesome in their own way as those of the Nā Pali coast of Kaua'i. The beaches at Mokulē'ia and Kahuku are as free of people as those on the south shore of Moloka'i. O'ahu has more forest trails than Hawai'i, which is over six times larger. And quiet, mirror-still Kāne'ohe Bay, the only true lagoon in Hawai'i, is unequaled anywhere in the Islands.

If the natural grandeur of O'ahu is often overlooked or unseen, it is because of one thing—its population. People, and the things they need, have detracted much from the scenic splendor of O'ahu. Monolithic buildings block views of the shoreline and the mountains. Freeways gouge giant paths through formerly pristine valleys. Insatiable demands for water dry up flowing mountain streams. Waves of sugarcane disappear under the developer's ax. Los Angeles–style gridlock freezes long lines of cars entering and leaving Honolulu every day. O'ahu, with only 10 percent of the land area of the Islands, must support almost 82 percent of the population.

The third largest of the main Islands, O'ahu was formed by two volcanoes. It is between 2.2 and 3.4 million years old. The island is 44 miles long, 30 miles wide, and 594 square miles in all. Over 840,000 people live here, most of them in Honolulu. Tourism is the major industry, with federal government spending running a close second in the amount of money brought into the state. Agriculture is still important, with pineapple leading the way. Sugar, for more than one hundred years O'ahu's leading crop, saw its last harvest in 1996. What to do with these lands is now the subject of intense study. Corn, coffee, and oriental vegetables are already growing on some of this acreage, and macadamia nuts and a forest industry are under

O‘AHU

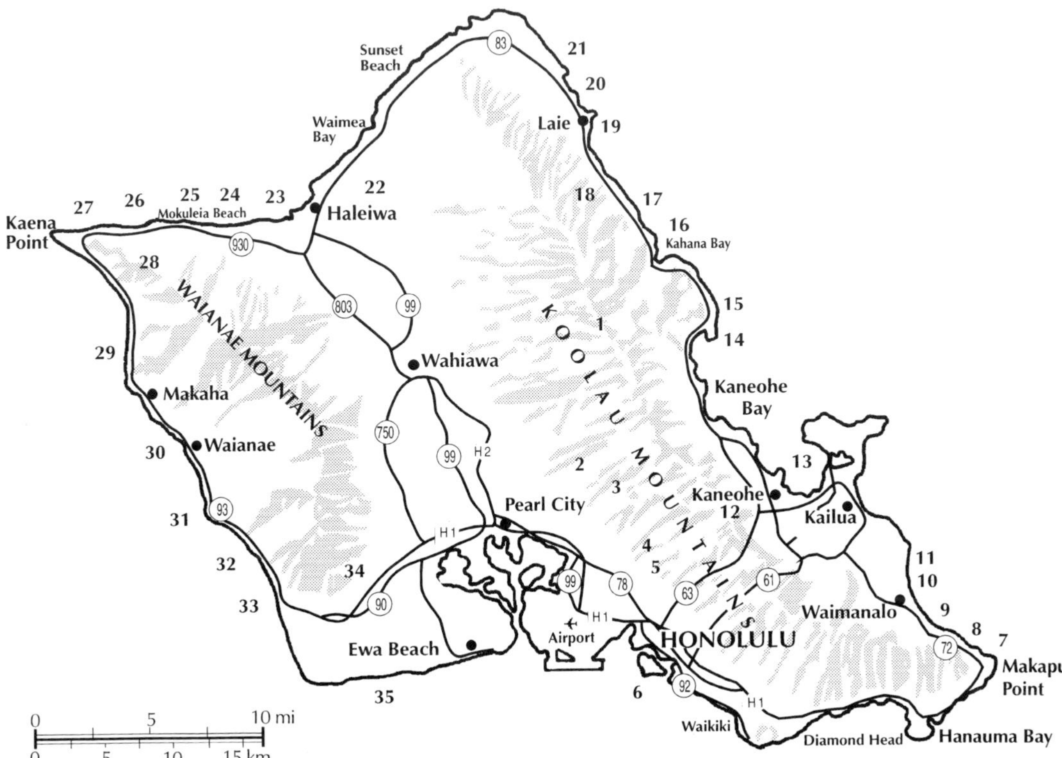

O‘ahu Campgrounds

1. Poamoho Trail Shelter
2. Mānana Trail
3. Waimano Trail
4. Keaīwa Heiau State Recreation Area
5. Camp H. M. Smith
6. Sand Island State Recreation Area
7. Makapu‘u Beach Park
8. Waimānalo Beach Park
9. Waimānalo Bay Beach Park
10. Bellows Beach Park
11. Bellows Air Force Station
12. Ho‘omaluhia Botanical Garden
13. Marine Corps Base Hawaii
14. Kualoa Beach Park
15. Swanzy Beach Park
16. Kahana Valley State Park
17. Hau‘ula Beach Park
18. Hau‘ula Trail System
19. Kokololio Beach Park
20. Mālaekahana State Recreation Area
21. Kahuku Section: Mālaekahana State Recreation Area
22. Pālama Uka Camp
23. Kaiaka Bay Beach Park
24. Mokulē‘ia Beach Park
25. Camp Mokulē‘ia
26. Mokulē‘ia Army Beach
27. Camp Erdman
28. Peacock Flat Campground
29. Kea‘au Beach Park
30. Wai‘anae Army Recreation Center
31. Lualualei Beach Park
32. Nānākuli Beach Park
33. Kahe Point Beach Park
34. Camp Timberline
35. Barbers Point Naval Air Station

consideration. Federal spending is mostly for defense, and over 60,000 military personnel are stationed here. All services are represented: the navy at Pearl Harbor, the army at Schofield Barracks, the air force at Hickam, and the marines at Kāne'ohe. These are just the major installations; there are others.

Politically, O'ahu differs from the other Islands in one significant aspect. The island of Kaua'i is Kaua'i County. The island of Hawai'i is Hawai'i County. The islands of Maui, Moloka'i, Lāna'i, and Kaho'olawe comprise Maui County. The island of O'ahu, however, is not O'ahu County but rather the City and County of Honolulu. Thus politically, the city of Honolulu encompasses the entire island, although geographically it is limited to its southeast corner. Towns such as Kailua, Waipahu, and Pearl City are only neighborhoods, without any self-government, although they have district representatives in the city council.

The tourist nickname of O'ahu is "The Gathering Place," but you will never hear anyone but a tour guide or an airline flight attendant refer to it that way. The Hawaiians did not use the term, because the island did not have a significant population until fairly recent times and was historically subordinate to Hawai'i and Kaua'i. The word "O'ahu" does not *mean* "the gathering place," as some tour guides will tell you it does. O'ahu, like the names of all the other main Islands except Lāna'i, does not have a specific meaning in Hawaiian or, if it did, that meaning has been lost.

Unlike the other Islands, O'ahu has a good public transportation system. "The Bus" serves virtually the entire island on regularly scheduled runs. Timetables are available free, and bus maps and guides can be purchased at a reasonable cost. By calling (808) 848–5555 you can get bus schedules, times, and route information. One problem campers will have with The Bus is that luggage larger than you can hold on your lap or place under your seat is not permitted. Metal-frame packs are specifically prohibited, and large backpacks will probably not get aboard. Drivers are allowed discretion in the matter, so a lot depends on the driver and the location of the particular run. You are much more likely to get your backpack aboard an uncrowded rural bus than one on a busy, downtown route. Hitchhiking is legal if done from a bus stop.

SPECIAL RULES FOR CAMPING ON O'AHU. Camping on O'ahu suffers from what O'ahu in general suffers from—lots of people, lots of buildings, lots of cars. And because of the congestion, O'ahu has camping rules that do not apply on the other Islands. There is good news and bad news.

The good news is that, although permits are required, camping in both state and city and county campsites is free.

The bad news is that camping is no longer permitted at the following beach parks: Hale'iwa, Hukilau, Ka'a'awa, Kākela, and Punalu'u.

The maximum consecutive stay at a public campground is 5 days. There is no camping at state or city and county campgrounds on Wednesdays and Thursdays. That means that on Wednesday morning you must pack your gear, vacate the campground by 8 a.m., and find other accommodations. You cannot go to another campground. The proffered reason for this requirement is maintenance and cleanup of the campsite. Another reason is to discourage extended or "permanent" camping by individuals who would otherwise opt to live on the beach, including homeless families.

You may not apply for a city and county camping permit earlier than two Fridays before the day you want to camp, and you must apply in person; neither reservations nor applications are accepted over the phone. Permits may be obtained at the Department of Parks and Recreation, 650 South King Street, Honolulu, HI 96813; phone, (808) 523–4525 or at any of the satellite city halls listed below.

Ala Moana—Ala Moana Shopping Center; phone, 973–2600
Fort Street Mall—1000 Fort Street Mall; phone, 532–2500
Kailua—302 Ku'ulei Road; phone, 261–8575
Kalihi—Pālama—2295 North King Street; phone, 832–2900
Kāne'ohe—46–018 Kamehameha Highway; phone, 235–4571
Wahiawā—830 California Avenue; phone, 621–0791
Wai'anae—85–555 Farrington Highway; phone, 696–6371
Waipahu—94–144 Farrington Highway; phone, 671–5638

You may not apply for a state permit earlier than 30 days before your camping date; however, you may do so by mail or phone.

From the above, you can see that you will not be able to make plans centered on staying at a city and county park until after your arrival and after checking on availability. This is not as discouraging as it sounds. Except for weekends, you will usually be able to get a permit for the park of your choice, even though you cannot apply more than two Fridays in advance. Even if your first choice is full, you will probably get another, either nearby or with similar amenities. The real problem is not being able to camp on Wednesdays and Thursdays, which requires that you check into a hotel for those days or stay at one of the private campgrounds mentioned in this book. The Kahuku Section of the Mālaekahana Bay State Recreation Area does permit camping on these days. It is concession operated, and a fee is charged.

Camping is permitted in most of O'ahu's forest reserve with a permit from the Division of Forestry and Wildlife, 1151 Punchbowl Street, Room 325, Honolulu, HI 96813; phone, (808) 587–0166. This is backcountry camping, with no facilities of any kind. Mānana, Waimano, and Hau'ula Trails are examples of this type of camping. For more information, check with the Forestry Division.

Several authorities recommend that visiting campers avoid the beach parks on the leeward coast of O'ahu. These parks are Kahe, Nānākuli, Lualualei, and Kea'au. This area is one of the more economically deprived on the island, and there have been incidents directed against touring campers. Also, homeless people may use these beaches from time to time. It is too bad, because the weather is perfect, the beaches lovely, and the sea cobalt blue. If you want to camp here, it would be best to check with the city and county park office above for the latest status. And it would be best not to camp alone. Ask other campers how they are faring and then camp nearby.

THINGS TO SEE AND DO. Obviously, there are far more things to see and do on O'ahu than are shown below. Those listed are only some of the major ones, and those that might be of special interest to campers and hikers. Keep in mind that distances on O'ahu are short and that a particular point of interest may be convenient to several campgrounds, not just the closest.

Point of Interest	**Nearest Campground**
Arizona Memorial	Keaīwa Heiau State Recreation Area
Bishop Museum	Sand Island State Recreation Area
Blowhole	Makapu'u Beach Park
Diamond Head	Sand Island State Recreation Area
Hanauma Bay	Makapu'u Beach Park
'Iolani Palace	Sand Island State Recreation Area
Ka'ena Point Natural Area Reserve	Kea'au or Mokulē'ia Beach Park
Polynesian Cultural Center	Mālaekahana State Recreation Area
Punchbowl	Keaīwa Heiau or Sand Island State Recreation Area
Sacred Falls	Hau'ula Beach Park
Sea Life Park	Makapu'u Beach Park
Waimea Falls Park	Kaiaka Bay Beach Park

CENTRAL O'AHU AND THE SOUTH SHORE

Poamoho Trail Shelter

LOCATION: The cabin is in the Ko'olau Mountains, 7 miles east of Wahiawā.

DESCRIPTION: This very basic cabin sits high on the Ko'olau summit ridge, just off the Summit Trail. Views in the vicinity can be spectacular, but the summit is often cloudy, windy, and rainy. The cabin contains no furniture of any kind, just four walls, a roof, and a floor.

FACILITIES: None. Water can be obtained from a stream about a quarter of a mile down the trail, and should be treated before drinking.

PERMIT/RESERVATIONS: Access to the cabin is via the Poamoho Trail, which crosses private land and requires a permit from the Forestry Division. Write or call the following: Division of Forestry and Wildlife, 1151 Punchbowl Street, Room 325, Honolulu, HI 96813; phone, (808) 587–0166.

TIME LIMIT: Poamoho may be used on weekends only, because it lies within a military maneuver area.

COST: Free.

HOW TO GET THERE: From Honolulu (24 miles), take H-1 Freeway to H-2 to Wahiawā, about 18 miles. Drive through Wahiawā, and watch for the Dole Pineapple stand and parking lot on the right. Take the first right turn past the stand, at the Na Ala Hele trail sign, and drive up the dirt road until you can go no farther. The road becomes a jeep road and, finally, a trail.

Mānana Trail

LOCATION: The trail is on the western slope of the Ko'olau Mountains northeast of Pearl City, at the end of Komo Mai Drive.

DESCRIPTION: This rough, heavily forested trail is ideal for those who really want to get away. After walking less than half a mile, all sense of civilization disappears, and it is hard to believe that people, cars, and freeways are so near. Along the lower elevations the trail is lined with strawberry guava and then passes through several vegetation zones, including guava, eucalyptus, and *koa*. From the end of the trail at the Ko'olau summit, there is a fine panoramic view of the windward coast. Mānana is not often used and can be fairly overgrown.

FACILITIES: None. Tent sites can be found at the bottom of the trail near the water tank at the beginning of the hike. Once the trail begins to ascend the ridge, suitable camping sites are few and far between. Water can only be obtained by hiking down one of the side trails to Mānana Stream on the north or Waimano Stream to the south, and should be treated before drinking. These trails are mostly steep and not maintained.

CAMPGROUND ACTIVITIES: Swimming is possible only by descending one of the trails to the streams mentioned above. You can usually find a spot deep enough to soak in. Hiking is mostly restricted to the trails, because of steep ridges and heavy vegetation. Botany enthusiasts will enjoy the variety of plants and trees in the area, including quite a few native species.

PERMIT/RESERVATIONS: No permit is required to hike the trail. Camping permits are required. An ID, such as a social security number, is required for each person camping. Permits are not issued by mail, but must be picked up in person at the following address: Division of Forestry and Wildlife, 1151 Punchbowl Street, Room 325, Honolulu, HI 96813; phone, (808) 587–0166.

TIME LIMIT: Two weeks.

COST: Free.

SPECIAL COMMENTS: The Mānana Trail traverses a public hunting area, so caution should be exercised. It can be very windy at the summit of the Ko'olau Range, so be prepared with a jacket if hiking to the top. A connection exists between the Mānana Trail and the Waimano Trail to the south. This connecting trail, which follows the Ko'olau Summit for about a mile, is narrow, precipitous, and dangerous. Only experienced hikers, with no fear of heights, should consider this route. It should not be attempted by anyone in rain or fog.

HOW TO GET THERE: From Honolulu (13 miles), take the H-1 Freeway to Pearl City (Exit 10). Bear right on Moanalua Road to its end at Waimano Home Road. Turn right and proceed seven-tenths of a mile to Komo Mai Drive on the left. Turn left and go to the end of the road. Park outside the locked gate and continue on foot along the paved walkway to a water tank, where the trail begins.

Waimano Trail

LOCATION: This trail is located along the slope of the mountains northeast of Pearl City, near the end of Waimano Home Road.

DESCRIPTION: This beautiful, well-maintained trail passes through several vegetation zones and affords fine views of the Wai'anae Mountains, Pearl Harbor, and the windward coast. For much of its 7-mile length it follows an old irrigation ditch, with tunnels and dams along the way. Although there are shorter routes to the Ko'olau summit from leeward O'ahu, Waimano is one of the easiest grades to ascend, rising gradually over long ridges and moderate switchbacks. At the beginning, the trail divides into a lower and an upper trail, with the lower portion rejoining the upper after about a mile. Along the lower elevations the trail is lined with strawberry guava. Mango trees dot Waimano ("many waters") Valley to the left, with some of the larger ones eventually reaching the trail. Midway along the trail, a *koa* forest begins, interspersed with several clumps of royal palms, and a large eucalyptus grove is located just after the stream crossing. About two-thirds of the way up the trail, *'ōhi'a* trees take over, with tree ferns *(hāpu'u)* sheltering in their shade. The final mile to the summit ridge is relatively open, with ferns, such as *uluhe,* predominating. From here, a sweeping view of Kāne'ohe Bay unfolds, all the way from Chinaman's Hat to the Mōkapu Peninsula.

FACILITIES: None. Water is available from Waimano Stream at the bottom of the lower trail and again farther up the trail where it crosses the stream. It should be treated before drinking. Water should not be taken from the irrigation ditch along the trail. The ditch is no longer in use and the water is mostly stagnant and filled with rotting vegetation. Several tent sites can be found at the bottom of the lower trail near the beginning of the hike. Suitable camping sites farther along the trail are few and far between. Room for two or three tents can be found in a small clearing just past the eucalyptus grove mentioned above.

CAMPGROUND ACTIVITIES: Swimming is usually possible in several small pools along the lower trail, and a pool where the upper trail crosses the stream is sometimes deep enough to soak in. Hiking is mostly restricted to the trail, because of steep ridges and heavy vegetation. Botany enthusiasts will enjoy the variety of plants and trees in the area, including quite a few native species.

PERMIT/RESERVATIONS: No permit is required to hike the trail. Camping permits are required. An ID, such as a social security number, is required for each person camping. Permits are not issued by mail, but must be picked up in person at the following address: Division of Forestry and Wildlife, 1151 Punchbowl Street, Room 325, Honolulu, HI 96813; phone, (808) 587–0166.

TIME LIMIT: Two weeks.

COST: Free.

SPECIAL COMMENTS: The Waimano Trail traverses a public hunting area, so caution should be exercised. It can be very windy at the summit of the Ko'olau Range. It is a good idea to be prepared with a jacket if hiking to the top. A connection exists between the Waimano Trail and the Mānana Trail to the north. This connecting trail, which follows the Ko'olau Summit for about a mile, is narrow, precipitous, and dangerous. Only experienced hikers, with no fear of heights, should try this route. It should not be attempted by anyone in rain or fog.

HOW TO GET THERE: From Honolulu (14 miles), take the H-1 Freeway to Pearl City (Exit 10). Bear right on Moanalua Road to its end at Waimano Home Road. Turn right and proceed 1.7 miles to a security post at the entrance to Waimano Home. Park outside the fence. The trail begins on the left side of the fence at an old trail registry and a new trail marker.

Keaīwa Heiau State Recreation Area

LOCATION: The park is in south-central O'ahu, above Hālawa Heights.

DESCRIPTION: This attractive wooded park consists of almost 385 acres of forest in the foothills of the Ko'olau Mountains. Mature eucalyptus, ironwood, and Norfolk Island pine dominate the campground area. Keaīwa, which means "the mystery," offers a cool, mountain alternative to the warm, sunny beach campgrounds along the coast. Campers have a choice of a flat, open, grassy area or sloping, shaded sites on bare ground with fallen leaf cover.

FACILITIES: Tent camping only. The campground is divided into two sections, one above the other along the road. The lower section, called Campground 3, is further divided into two areas, one below a parking lot and a smaller site above it. The lower site is flat, open, and grassy. It contains six scattered picnic tables, enclosed rest rooms with cold showers, outdoor grills, and a dishwashing area. The site above the parking lot is heavily shaded by large trees, slopes toward the parking lot, and contains three picnic tables and a barbecue (without grill).

The upper campground section is unnumbered and is reached by walking up the road another 10 minutes. Tent sites here are shaded by large trees and are generally on bare ground. Several picnic tables are located here, as is a covered pavilion with an additional four large tables. There is another rest room at the top of the hill, but its showers have been turned off. Drinking water is available at both sections. A public telephone is located near the caretaker's cabin at the park entrance. Groceries and gas must be purchased in 'Aiea, about 2 miles back down the hill.

CAMPGROUND ACTIVITIES: The 'Aiea Loop Trail (4.8 miles) begins in the upper campground. It is a moderate hike with good views of Pearl Harbor and the mountains. The ruins of the Keaīwa Heiau can be visited near the park entrance.

PERMIT/RESERVATIONS: Permit applications are accepted no earlier than 30 days before the period requested. Permits may be obtained from a state parks office on any Island. The following address is the state office on O'ahu: Division of State Parks, P.O. Box 621, Honolulu, HI 96809; phone, (808) 587–0300.

TIME LIMIT: Five nights; Fridays, 8 a.m. to Wednesdays, 8 a.m. (no camping Wednesdays and Thursdays because of maintenance). Another camping permit for the same park will be issued only after 30 days have elapsed.

COST: Free.

SPECIAL COMMENTS: Park gates close at 6:45 p.m. and do not open again until 7 a.m. Cars cannot enter or leave the park during this period.

HOW TO GET THERE: From Honolulu (11 miles), take the H-1 Freeway west to Highway 78 (Moanalua Freeway), exiting at 'Aiea (Exit 13A). Follow Moanalua Road to 'Aiea Heights Drive on the right. Proceed up the hill to the end of the road, where the park begins. The campground is reached by driving past the picnic area at the park entrance and continuing up a one-way loop road.

NEARBY POINTS OF INTEREST: See Camp H. M. Smith.

Sand Island State Recreation Area

LOCATION: The park is on the south shore, just south and west of Honolulu Harbor. It is the only campground within the Honolulu metropolitan area.

DESCRIPTION: A large waterfront park directly on the ocean, Sand Island has 102 acres of spacious grass lawns, partially shaded by medium-sized ironwoods and sea grape. Palm trees line the long, uncrowded sandy beach. The sand here is coarser than at other O'ahu beaches, and the offshore bottom is rocky and uneven. Sand Island boasts a fine view of the Honolulu coastline from the harbor to Diamond Head and is noted for beautiful sunsets.

FACILITIES: Tent camping only. Covered and open picnic tables dot the area, but there is no central pavilion. Rest rooms include enclosed cold showers, and the water is drinkable. Groceries and gas are available in Kalihi, 3 miles away.

CAMPGROUND ACTIVITIES: The beach has been improved in recent years, but swimmers must still take care because of the rocky bottom. *Pāpio,* goatfish, and bonefish can be taken here. Fishing is best along the park's undeveloped western shoreline.

PERMIT/RESERVATIONS: Permits may not be requested more than 30 days in advance and may be obtained from a state parks office on any island. The following address is the state office on O'ahu: Division of State Parks, P.O. Box 621, Honolulu, HI 96809; phone, (808) 587–0300.

TIME LIMIT: Weekends only, Fridays 8 a.m. to Mondays 8 a.m. Another camping or lodging permit for the same park will be issued only after 30 days have elapsed.

COST: Free.

SPECIAL COMMENTS: Prospective campers are sometimes put off by the industrial area that they are required to drive through to reach Sand Island. Keep going, and the park will provide a welcome oasis from all the docks, warehouses, and junkyards. Homeless people sometimes camp here, and authorities can be slow to move them out. Unlike some other O'ahu campsites, Sand Island is big enough to accommodate them without interfering with the enjoyment of the recreational camper, but you still may want to check this when you apply for your permit. The park gates close at night at 6:45 p.m. and reopen at 7 a.m. Cars cannot enter or leave the park during this period. Sand Island is very popular and often all permits are taken on the first day of the 30-day advance application period.

HOW TO GET THERE: Take Ala Moana Boulevard (Highway 92) west until it becomes Nimitz Highway. Turn left on Sand Island Access Road (Highway 64) to its end at the park.

NEARBY POINTS OF INTEREST: Sand Island is a good base to explore the various visitor attractions of downtown Honolulu, Waikīkī, and Pearl Harbor. It is the closest campsite to the Bishop Museum and the Tantalus/Mānoa Trail complex in the Ko'olau Mountains behind Honolulu.

Camp H. M. Smith

LOCATION: This military installation sits on a ridge overlooking Honolulu, near the Aloha Stadium.

DESCRIPTION: There are two campgrounds on the base for the use of members of the armed forces, active and retired, their dependents and guests, and certain Department of Defense civilian personnel. Camp Hawkins is located in a quiet, wooded part of the base, with a panoramic view over Pearl Harbor and Honolulu all the way to Diamond Head. The helipad site is higher up the ridge, with an even more awesome view.

FACILITIES: Tent and vehicle camping. There are only two camping sites at Camp Hawkins, but both sites are large, each capable of accommodating up to twenty or more persons. The helipad site is also a large one, but it is restricted to occupancy by only one party. Thus, no more than three groups can occupy the sites, making for maximum privacy and surrounding space. Portable toilets are provided at both locations, and only Camp Hawkins has running water. Gas and limited grocery shopping are available on the base, more extensive shopping in Pearl City/Pearl Ridge.

CAMPGROUND ACTIVITIES: Hiking and horseback riding trails lead from the campground area, and an on-base stable, close to the campground, rents horses. Base sports activities include tennis courts, swimming pool, gym, and fitness center.

PERMIT/RESERVATIONS: Reservations may be made by mail or phone to: MWR Office, P.O. Box 64123, Camp H. M. Smith, HI 96861; phone, (808) 484–9417.

TIME LIMIT: None.

COST: Free.

HOW TO GET THERE: From Honolulu, take the H1 Freeway west. When H1 and Highway 78 divide, follow 78 to the Stadium/Camp Smith exit. Head uphill on Hālawa Heights Road, to Camp Smith, on the right. At the main gate, ask for directions to Camp Hawkins, or the helipad site, as appropriate.

NEARBY POINTS OF INTEREST: Arizona Memorial, Honolulu and its tourist attractions.

WINDWARD SIDE

Makapu'u Beach Park

LOCATION: The park is on the windward shore at the southeastern tip of O'ahu, just off Highway 72.

DESCRIPTION: Lying on an exposed, rocky shoreline, Makapu'u gives an impression of isolation despite its proximity to the highway. Sweeping views of the ocean and offshore islands and a mountain backdrop make a dramatic setting. The sandy beach, about 1,000 feet long, is bordered on the west by a rocky point and on the east by a steep sea cliff. The offshore bottom is sandy and slopes gradually, but the shorebreak is among the heaviest on O'ahu. It can be dangerous from September through April, with strong currents adding to the hazards. The camping area is adjacent to the beach park on the northwest and has its own vehicle entrance. The area is devoid of trees, so there is no shade available. Makapu'u is exposed to the northeast trades, making it often windy. The name means "bulging eye" in Hawaiian, derived from the name of a supernatural woman.

FACILITIES: Tent and vehicle camping. The campground is divided into specific numbered sites, each with its own picnic table and parking spot. A rest room is located near the campground entrance, as are outdoor showers. Additional rest rooms, showers, and picnic tables can be found at the beach park, where a public phone is also available. Groceries and gas may be obtained in Waimānalo, about 4.5 miles northwest.

CAMPGROUND ACTIVITIES: Water entry at the campground section is dangerous, because of the rocky shore and pounding surf. Swim from the beach park, using caution in the winter months. Snorkeling is good, on calm days only, in the vicinity of the rocky point on the west end of the beach. Makapu'u is probably the most famous bodysurfing beach in the Islands, with waves that can reach up to 12 feet. Body boards are permitted, but other surfboards or sailboards are not allowed. *Pāpio* and *ulua* are the best probable catches in this usually rough water.

PERMIT/RESERVATIONS: Permit applications are accepted no earlier than two Fridays before the period requested. Requests for permits are not taken over the phone, nor are reservations accepted. Applicants must appear in person at the following address or at any satellite city hall listed at the beginning of the section on O'ahu: Department of Parks and Recreation, 650 South King Street, Honolulu, HI 96813; phone, (808) 523–4525.

TIME LIMIT: Five nights; Fridays, 8 a.m. to Wednesdays, 8 a.m. (closed Wednesdays and Thursdays for maintenance).

COST: Free.

SPECIAL COMMENTS: The campground itself is somewhat barren and exposed, but Makapu'u Beach Park is a lovely sandy beach. Spend your time at the park, and sleep at the campground.

HOW TO GET THERE: From Honolulu (14 miles), take the H-1 Freeway east to its end, continuing on Highway 72 to the sign for Makapu'u Beach Park. Turn right at the next road and proceed about one-tenth of a mile farther.

NEARBY POINTS OF INTEREST: Sea Life Park, a popular outdoor aquarium with performing dolphins and whales is just across the road from the western end of the park. Sandy Beach Park, another well-known bodysurfing beach, is only about 2 miles south of the park, around Makapu'u Point. Koko Crater Botanical Garden, a pretty spot inside an old volcanic crater, is 3 miles south of Makapu'u. At the Hālona Blowhole, a parking area and overlook allow you to watch water spouting high from a crack in the reef to your front. The height of the spout depends on wave conditions. It is 3 miles from the campground. Hanauma Bay is the premier snorkeling and diving spot on O'ahu. This beautiful beach, in a crater open to the sea, is a must, even if you don't snorkel. It is less than 5 miles south of Makapu'u.

Waimānalo Beach Park

LOCATION: The park is on the windward shore, on Highway 72 about 2 miles south of the town of Waimānalo.

DESCRIPTION: Waimānalo, which means "potable water," is situated on one of the finest sandy beaches on O'ahu. The beach fronting the park is part of a 3.5-mile-long sandy crescent stretching from Wailea Point south past Kaiona Beach Park. It is a wide beach, backed most of its length by ironwood trees. The sandy ocean bottom slopes gently into deeper water, and the shorebreak is almost always small. The campground is a pleasant, open, grassy area, with partial shade available from a few scattered trees.

FACILITIES: Tent and vehicle camping. Rest rooms, outdoor showers, and picnic tables are provided. Drinking fountains were out of order as of this writing, but water in the rest rooms and showers is drinkable. A large covered pavilion is located at the north end of the beach park, but as of this writing it contained no tables. Perhaps you could move one in the event of rain. A public telephone is available. Groceries and gas can be obtained in Waimānalo, about 2 miles north.

CAMPGROUND ACTIVITIES: Swimming is excellent and safe all year. Milkfish, bonefish, goatfish, and sometimes *pāpio* can be caught here. For beachcombers, the long, uninterrupted beach ensures that you will find something, especially after a storm.

PERMIT/RESERVATIONS: Permit applications are accepted no earlier than two Fridays before the period being requested. Requests for permits are not taken over the phone, nor are reservations accepted. Applicants must appear in person at the following address or at any satellite city hall listed at the beginning of the section on Oʻahu: Department of Parks and Recreation, 650 South King Street, Honolulu, HI 96813; phone, (808) 523–4525.

TIME LIMIT: Five nights; Fridays, 8 a.m. to Wednesdays, 8 a.m. (no camping Wednesdays and Thursdays because of maintenance).

COST: Free.

SPECIAL COMMENTS: Homeless people sometimes camp at this location, which can interfere with its use by recreational campers. But it is a pretty site and worth checking out. However, if this bothers you, go to Waimānalo Bay Beach Park or Bellows Beach Park.

HOW TO GET THERE: Take the H-1 Freeway east to its end, continuing on Highway 72 to a wooden sign on the right indicating the park (16 miles).

NEARBY POINTS OF INTEREST: Waimānalo Beach Park is close to Sea Life Park, Makapuʻu and Sandy bodysurfing beaches, Koko Crater Botanical Garden, and Hanauma Bay for excellent snorkeling. All of these may be reached from the campground by driving southeast on Highway 72.

Waimānalo Bay Beach Park

LOCATION: The park is on the windward coast, off Highway 72, about 1 mile south of the town of Waimānalo.

DESCRIPTION: Beautifully situated in an ironwood grove on one of the finest beaches on O'ahu, this campground is one of the best on the island. A backdrop of steep cliffs contrasts with offshore views of Rabbit Island and the Mokoluas. From the shore you can see the entire three-and-a-half-mile sweep of the sandy beach as it curves north and south of the campground. Offshore, the sandy bottom slopes gradually; although the shorebreak is rougher than at other locations on this long beach, it is still relatively modest. An open, grassy area extends behind the trees along the shoreline, and the facilities are located here.

FACILITIES: Tent camping only. Campsites are individually numbered and assigned that way. They are all under the trees. Each has its own picnic table, grill, and trash receptacle and is swept clear of pine needles—a good idea, because insect pests like to burrow in them. A central rest room building also contains five showers and a changing room. Picnic tables and water fountains are spaced throughout the area, and there is a dishwashing sink. Groceries and gas can be obtained in Waimānalo, 1 mile north. A public telephone is located near the caretaker's house.

CAMPGROUND ACTIVITIES: Swimming is excellent and mostly safe all year. Strong currents can occur during the winter months. The consistent but small shorebreak makes surfing of interest primarily to beginning board and bodysurfers. Milkfish, bonefish, goatfish, and sometimes *pāpio* can be caught here. The long, uninterrupted beach ensures that beachcombers will find something, especially after a storm.

PERMIT/RESERVATIONS: Permit applications will be accepted no earlier than two Fridays prior to the period requested. Requests for permits are not taken over the phone, nor are reservations accepted. Applicants must appear in person at the address below, or at any satellite city hall listed at the beginning of this section on O'ahu: Department of Parks and Recreation, 650 South King Street, Honolulu, HI 96813; phone, (808) 523–4525.

TIME LIMIT: Five nights; Fridays, 8 a.m. to Wednesdays, 8 a.m. (no camping Wednesdays and Thursdays because of maintenance).

COST: Free.

SPECIAL COMMENTS: Because there are only about twelve campsites, the park is never crowded. However, applications should be made as far in advance as allowable, especially for weekends. Gates to the park close at 6:45 p.m. and do not open again until 7 a.m. Vehicles cannot enter or leave the park during this period.

HOW TO GET THERE: From Honolulu (17 miles), take the H-1 Freeway east to its end, continuing on Highway 72 to the sign to the park. Turn right and proceed two-tenths of a mile to the park.

NEARBY POINTS OF INTEREST: Waimānalo Bay Beach Park is close to Sea Life Park, Makapu'u and Sandy bodysurfing beaches, Koko Crater Botanical Garden, and Hanauma Bay for excellent snorkeling. All of these may be reached from the campground by driving southeast on Highway 72.

Bellows Beach Park

LOCATION: The park is on the windward shore, within Bellows Air Force Station, about 2.5 miles northwest of Waimānalo.

DESCRIPTION: This large park is beautifully situated in an ironwood forest along one of the finest sandy beaches on O'ahu. Views of offshore islands and backdrops of steep cliffs add to its spectacular setting. The beach fronting the park is part of a 3.5-mile-long sandy crescent stretching from Wailea Point south past Kaiona Beach Park. It is a wide beach, backed for most of its length by ironwood trees. The sandy ocean bottom slopes gently into deeper water, and the shorebreak is almost always small.

FACILITIES: Tent camping only. Fifty numbered campsites are scattered in an ironwood grove, affording shade and partial shade. Each of the fifty campsites has its own picnic table. Rest rooms are somewhat run-down, but adequate. Outdoor showers and dishwashing areas are provided. Water is drinkable. Groceries and gas can be obtained in Waimānalo, about 2.5 miles south.

CAMPGROUND ACTIVITIES: Swimming is excellent and safe all year. The consistent but small shorebreak makes Bellows of interest primarily to beginning board and bodysurfers. Milkfish, bonefish, goatfish, and sometimes *pāpio* can be caught here. The long, uninterrupted beach ensures that beachcombers will find something, especially after a storm.

PERMIT/RESERVATIONS: Permit applications are accepted no earlier than two Fridays before the period requested. Requests for permits are not taken over the phone, nor are reservations accepted. Applicants must appear in person at the following address or at any satellite city hall listed at the beginning of the section on O'ahu: Department of Parks and Recreation, 650 South King Street, Honolulu, HI 96813; phone, (808) 523–4525.

TIME LIMIT: Camping at Bellows is permitted only on weekends and holidays that adjoin weekends. Hours are from noon on Friday to 8 a.m. Monday.

COST: Free.

SPECIAL COMMENTS: Bellows is a popular campground, especially in the summer months. Applications for these months should be made as far in advance as allowable. Because of its location on a military reservation, the campground and beach park are sometimes subject to additional restrictions. Check with the city and county park office at the above address or phone number.

HOW TO GET THERE: From Honolulu (19 miles), take the H-1 Freeway east to its end and continue on Highway 72 to the sign for Bellows Air Force Station on the right. Follow the road to the beach park and campground, about another 2 miles.

NEARBY POINTS OF INTEREST: See the section on Waimānalo Beach Park.

Bellows Air Force Station

LOCATION: The base is on the ocean about 2.5 miles northwest of Waimānalo, off Highway 72.

DESCRIPTION: Bellows provides cottages on the beach for active-duty and retired military personnel, Department of Defense (DOD) civilian employees, and their guests. The base is beautifully situated in an ironwood forest along one of the finest beaches on O'ahu. Views of offshore islands and backdrops of steep cliffs add to its spectacular setting.

FACILITIES: Cottages only; no tent or vehicle camping. All cottages are two-bedroom with kitchen and bath and sleep four comfortably. They are completely furnished, including dishes, utensils, and bedding. A small BX, club, and a snack bar are located nearby. More extensive shopping and gas are available in Waimānalo.

CAMPGROUND ACTIVITIES: Swimming is excellent and safe all year. The consistent but small shorebreak makes Bellows of interest primarily to beginning board and bodysurfers. Milkfish, bonefish, goatfish, and sometimes *pāpio* can be caught here. The long, uninterrupted beach ensures that beachcombers will find something, especially after a storm.

PERMITS/RESERVATIONS: DOD ID card or other authorized documentation is required. Reservations are accepted on a first-come, first-served basis, according to the following priorities: active-duty Air Force personnel, 90 days in advance; other active-duty personnel, 75 days; retired personnel, 60 days; DOD civilians, 45 days. Bellows prefers to take reservations by telephone, (808) 259–8841. If for some reason a phone call is not possible, write Bellows Reservation Office, 220 Tinker Road, Waimānalo, HI 96795.

TIME LIMIT: Fourteen days.

COST: Oceanfront cottages are $50 per day; back cottages, $45.

SPECIAL COMMENTS: If you are looking for reasonable cottage-type accommodations on the windward side and Bellows Air Force Station is full or you are not eligible, Mālaekahana State Recreation Area, another long, lovely beach, also offers cabins.

HOW TO GET THERE: From Honolulu (19 miles), take the H-1 Freeway east to its end and continue on Highway 72 to the sign for Bellows Air Force Station on the right. Follow the road past the beach park and through the security gate, another 2.5 miles.

NEARBY POINTS OF INTEREST: See the section on Waimānalo Beach Park.

Ho'omaluhia Botanical Garden

LOCATION: The botanical garden is on the windward side, on the outskirts of the town of Kāne'ohe.

DESCRIPTION: Ho'omaluhia, "to cause or give peace and tranquility," does exactly that. Situated right at the base of the spectacular Ko'olau Pali, this beautiful, 400-acre botanical garden seems so removed from the noise, traffic, and crowds of O'ahu that you might think you are on one of the neighbor islands. Surrounded by rare and exotic plants, your tent pitched on a spacious green lawn, dramatic green cliffs soaring into a bright blue sky, it is hard to believe that Honolulu is less than half an hour away. Five camping areas, well removed from other activities and from each other, ensure

The Ko'olau mountains provide a dramatic backdrop for Ho'omaluhia, the only botanical garden in the state that allows camping.

privacy and quiet enjoyment. This is further enhanced by separating group campers from individual and family sites. There is even an area, complete with corral, for campers who come on horseback!

FACILITIES: Tent camping only. Facilities here are better and are better maintained than anywhere else on O'ahu. Each of the five camping areas has its own rest rooms, with sinks and cold showers. Two separate dishwashing stations are provided at each rest room. Picnic tables, outdoor grills, and water spigots are located throughout each area. A visitor center at the entrance to the garden provides information, displays, and activities. A public phone is available here. Two shopping malls, restaurants, supermarkets, and gas stations are available in Kāne'ohe, 1 mile away.

CAMPGROUND ACTIVITIES: Hiking and browsing among the plantings are the main activities here. The garden is laid out geographically, with areas devoted to tropical American, native Hawaiian, Polynesian, Indian/ Sri Lankan, and African plants and trees. Many of the plants are endangered and rare. A map showing hiking trails through all these areas is available at the visitor center. A 32-acre lake adds to the setting, but there is no swimming or boating allowed. The garden sponsors various activities, such as guided walks, art exhibits, ancient Hawaiian plant usage, and moon walks. Schedules are available at the visitor center.

PERMIT/RESERVATIONS: Permits are required to camp. Write or call the following: Hoʻomaluhia Botanical Garden, 45–680 Luluku Road, Kāneʻohe, HI 96744; phone, (808) 233–7323.

TIME LIMIT: Five nights. There is no camping on Tuesdays and Wednesdays.

COST: Free.

SPECIAL COMMENTS: All campers are required to check in at the visitor center for campsite assignment and to pick up a vehicle parking pass. The garden's gate is locked at 4 p.m. and opens at 9 a.m. Although you may *exit* the grounds at certain other specified times, you may not *re-enter* the park between these hours. As of this writing, Hoʻomaluhia is underutilized. The day I was there, four of the five camping areas were empty, and only two tents were in the fifth.

HOW TO GET THERE: From Honolulu (10 miles), take the H-1 Freeway to Likelike Highway (Highway 63), proceeding through the Wilson Tunnel to the windward side. At the first major intersection, Kamehameha Highway (Highway 83), turn right and then right again on Luluku Road, which leads to the visitor center.

NEARBY POINTS OF INTEREST: Unless you insist on being on the beach, Hoʻomaluhia is an ideal place from which to explore all of the windward coast.

Marine Corps Base Hawaii

LOCATION: The facility is located on the northwestern side of Mōkapu Peninsula within the Marine base in Kāneʻohe.

DESCRIPTION: The campground occupies a portion of Hale Koa Beach, a beautiful, small beach directly on Kāneʻohe Bay. It sits just behind the beach in a grove of ironwood trees, with a magnificent view over the bay and mountain vistas beyond. The beach is white sand, has no shore break, and the bottom slopes gently, making it ideal for small children. The cottages are located about a mile north, on a rise above the bay. They also have lovely views from decks overlooking the bay but do not have a beach. Pyramid Rock Beach is a short walk from the cabins.

FACILITIES: Tent camping and cottages. The campground has eight individually assigned sites, some with picnic tables. Two covered pavilions contain other tables. Portable toilets are located in two locations and outdoor showers are situated around the site. Drinking water is available from the showers. Cottages are two-bedroom, sleep four, and are completely furnished to include dishes, utensils, and bedding. Complete shopping and recreational facilities are available on the base, including gas station, clubs, and restaurants.

CAMPGROUND ACTIVITIES: Swimming is excellent at the campground, and snorkeling is good. Swimming and surfing are excellent at Pyramid Rock Beach. Fishing is not good at Hale Koa Beach, but *pāpio,* milkfish, and goatfish can sometimes be caught at Pyramid Rock Beach. Golf, tennis, boat and kayak rental, bowling, and other recreational activities can be found on base.

PERMIT/RESERVATIONS: Department of Defense ID card or other authorized identification is required. Priority is given to active-duty, retired, and Department of Defense civilian personnel, in that order. Reservations may be made by mail or phone. For the campground, contact Marine Corps Base Hawaii, Outdoor Recreation Center, Bldg 1698, Kāne'ohe, HI 96863; phone, (808) 254-7666. For cottages, contact Marine Corps Base Hawaii, MWR Department, Kāne'ohe, HI 96863; phone, (808) 254-2716.

TIME LIMIT: None for campground, seven days for cottages.

COST: Campground, $8 per night, two tents and up to ten people permitted. Cottages, $55 per night.

HOW TO GET THERE: Take the H-3 Freeway directly to the main gate of the base. From here it is best to ask directions, since the route crosses an active airstrip.

NEARBY POINTS OF INTEREST: Ho'omaluhia Botanical Garden, Sea Life Park, Sacred Falls.

Kualoa Beach Park

LOCATION: On the windward shore, Kualoa is a peninsula on Kāne'ohe Bay, 2.5 miles south of the town of Ka'a'awa.

DESCRIPTION: A beautifully situated park directly on the quiet waters of Kāne'ohe Bay, Kualoa has a spectacular mountain backdrop and affords sweeping views over the bay, distant mountains, and Mōkapu Peninsula.

Kualoa Beach Park, Campground B, with Chinaman's Hat offshore.

Mokoli'i Island (Chinaman's Hat) lies 500 yards directly offshore. Broad, grassy fields with young palms border a long, narrow beach. The waters of the bay lap gently on the shore. There are no waves or shorebreak.

Kualoa was one of the most sacred places in ancient Hawai'i, and the name means "long back," most likely referring to long generations of Hawaiian *ali'i* going far back in time, who were affiliated with the area. Hōkūle'a, the sailing canoe that re-created the ancient feat of navigating from Hawai'i to Tahiti and back without instruments, came ashore at Kualoa upon its return.

Kualoa has two separate campgrounds, each one considerably different from the other. Campground A is a relatively large site, completely separated from the rest of the park on its own road. It is partly wooded, with palms, ironwoods, large *kamani* trees, and a few monkeypods providing a fair amount of shade. A long, sandy beach fronts the campground, with a panorama of the bay offshore.

Campground B is an extension of the main beach park, sharing its beach, young palm trees, and wide, grassy expanses. The setting is just as spectacular as at Campground A, with the added feature of Chinaman's Hat looming directly offshore. Campground B is much more open than A, with only skimpy shade afforded by the young palms and some young *hala* and *milo*.

FACILITIES: Tent camping only. Campground A is primarily for group camping, but it has seven "family" sites that can accommodate two to ten persons each. It has a large rest room building with showers, lots of picnic tables, dishwashing sinks, drinking water, and a volleyball court. A kitchen building, with an attached covered pavilion, contains four picnic tables and a cold-drink machine. The kitchen is available by reservation only for large groups, but the pavilion may be used by anyone when the kitchen is not operating.

Campground B has two separate rest room buildings with showers, picnic tables, drinking fountains, and a public telephone. Gas and some groceries are available in Ka'a'awa, 2.5 miles north. More extensive shopping is available in Kāne'ohe, 9 miles south.

CAMPGROUND ACTIVITIES: Swimming is excellent and safe, but caution should be exercised when entering the water because the shallow area just offshore contains some rocks, coral pieces, and small holes. Snorkeling is good off the beach, between Chinaman's Hat and the park. It is better around the island itself, particularly on its seaward side, where caution

Weekend campers at Kualoa Beach Park, Campground A.

must be observed on windy days or during periods of high water. Shoreline fishing is not as good here as at other places on the windward coast, but sometimes goatfish, milkfish, and bonefish can be hooked.

PERMIT/RESERVATIONS: Permit applications are accepted no earlier than two Fridays before the period requested. Except as listed below, requests for permits are not taken over the phone, nor are reservations accepted. Applicants for Campground A "family" permits must appear in person at the following address: Department of Parks and Recreation, 650 South King Street, Honolulu, HI 96813; phone, (808) 523–4525. Groups may make reservations for Campground A up to 6 months in advance by calling (808) 237–8525. Campground B permits may also be obtained at the department or at any satellite city hall listed at the beginning of the section on O'ahu.

TIME LIMIT: Five nights; Fridays, 8 a.m. to Wednesdays, 8 a.m. (no camping Wednesdays and Thursdays because of maintenance).

COST: Free.

SPECIAL COMMENTS: Campground A, although available to all campers, is primarily used by large groups, often with young children. This is particularly true during the summer months. If quiet is what you are looking for, you may prefer Campground B. Both areas have their own charm, however. If possible, look them both over and then decide. A permit can then be obtained in the satellite city hall in Kāne'ohe.

NOTE! Gates to the park close at 8 p.m. and do not reopen until 7 a.m. Vehicles cannot leave or enter the campground during this period.

HOW TO GET THERE: From Honolulu (25 miles), take the H-1 Freeway west to Exit 20, Likelike Highway (Highway 63). Continue north on Highway 63 through the Wilson Tunnel to the intersection of Highway 83 on the left (Kahekili Highway). Proceed on Highway 83 another 9 miles to Kualoa Beach Park on the right. Campground A is reached by driving to the end of the paved road in the park and going straight ahead through a gate onto a dirt road. Campground B is reached by staying on the paved road that curves past the gate to Campground A and following it to a large parking lot near the water.

Swanzy Beach Park

LOCATION: The park is on the windward shore, in the town of Ka'a'awa, on Highway 83.

DESCRIPTION: Swanzy is a rectangular, grassy field, directly on the ocean and with a dramatic mountain backdrop. The park is mostly open, with some palm, *hala,* and *kamani* trees. The campground is located at the north end of the field. The narrow sand and rock beach is separated from the park by a seawall, which has steps leading down to provide access to the water. Swanzy suffers from being close to a busy highway, and its location within the town of Ka‘a‘awa is not conducive to camping privacy.

FACILITIES: Tent camping only; no vehicle camping. Rest rooms, outdoor showers, picnic tables, and a public telephone are provided, and the water is drinkable. The beach park contains a baseball field, basketball court, and a playground. Limited groceries and gas can be purchased directly across the street from the park. More extensive shopping can be done at Hau‘ula, 6 miles north.

CAMPGROUND ACTIVITIES: Conditions for swimming are only fair, because of the lack of a true beach, the shallow water, and the rocky bottom. But it is almost always safe. Snorkeling is fair to good, especially out near the fringing reef, where caution must be observed because of possible swift currents. *Pāpio,* milkfish, bonefish, and goatfish are taken here.

PERMIT/RESERVATIONS: Permit applications are accepted no earlier than two Fridays before the period requested. Requests for permits are not taken over the phone, nor are reservations accepted. Applicants must appear in person at the following address or at any satellite city hall listed at the beginning of the section on O‘ahu: Department of Parks and Recreation, 650 South King Street, Honolulu, HI 96813; phone, (808) 523–4525.

TIME LIMIT: Camping is permitted only on weekends and holidays that adjoin weekends. Hours are from noon on Friday to 8 a.m. Monday.

COST: Free.

SPECIAL COMMENTS: Very few people camp at Swanzy, probably because of its mediocre beach and its sports facilities, which can bring noisy groups to the park. The ball field can be floodlit at night, which is another disadvantage to campers.

HOW TO GET THERE: From Honolulu (28 miles), take the H-1 Freeway west to Exit 20, Likelike Highway (Highway 63). Proceed north on Highway 63 through the Wilson Tunnel to the intersection of Highway 83 on the left (Kahekili Highway). Continue on Highway 83 another 12 miles to the park on the right.

Kahana Valley State Park

LOCATION: The park is on the windward shore, 1.5 miles north of the town of Ka'a'awa on Highway 83.

DESCRIPTION: Kahana, which means "cutting" in Hawaiian, is a pretty crescent beach framed by a dramatic mountain backdrop. The sandy beach is fringed by ironwood and *kamani* trees. The peaceful bay, the tree-lined beach, a coconut grove across the road, and the striking mountains give the bay a "South Seas" atmosphere. The water in the bay is gentle, and the bottom is sandy and shallow, making it a good place for small children.

FACILITIES: Tent and vehicle camping. Rest rooms, picnic tables, and public telephones are available. Water is drinkable. The rest rooms are located quite far from the camping area, at the north end of the beach. A boat-launching ramp is also in this vicinity. Limited grocery shopping and gas may be obtained in Ka'a'awa, 1.5 miles south. For more extensive shopping, go north 4.5 miles to Hau'ula.

CAMPGROUND ACTIVITIES: Kahana Bay is a safe swimming area all year, although somewhat shallow and murky near shore. The bay is noted as

Shaded waterfront campsite at Kahana Valley State Park.

one of the best places to catch *akule* (big-eyed scad). Other possible catches are *pāpio* and goatfish. Kahana Valley, directly across the highway from the beach park, contains hiking trails and stream-fed pools for refreshing dips.

PERMIT/RESERVATIONS: Permit applications will be accepted no earlier than thirty days prior to the period requested. A permit may be obtained from a state parks office on any island. The address below is for the office on O'ahu: Division of State Parks, P.O. Box 621, Honolulu, HI 96809; phone, (808) 587–0300.

TIME LIMIT: Five nights; Fridays, 8 a.m. to Wednesdays, 8 a.m. (no camping Wednesdays and Thursdays due to maintenance). Another camping permit for the same park will be issued only after 30 days.

COST: Free.

SPECIAL COMMENTS: Although a very pretty campground, Kahana Bay suffers from being close to a busy road and from having no showers.

HOW TO GET THERE: From Honolulu (29 miles), take the H-1 Freeway west to Exit 20, Likelike Highway (Highway 63). Proceed north on Highway 63 through the Wilson Tunnel to the intersection of Highway 83 on the left (Kahekili Highway). Continue on Highway 83 another 13 miles to Kahana Bay on the right.

NEARBY POINTS OF INTEREST: An easy 2.2-mile hike takes you to Sacred Falls State Park, which has a very pretty waterfall and a great pool for swimming. The trail follows a pretty, wooded stream, and, as an added benefit, guava and mountain apple grow along the way. From the campground drive north about 3.5 miles, watching carefully for the parking lot on the left.

For information on the Polynesian Cultural Center, see the section on Mālaekahana State Recreation Area.

Hau'ula Beach Park

LOCATION: The park is on the windward shore, in the southern outskirts of the town of Hau'ula, on Highway 83.

DESCRIPTION: Hau'ula, which means "red *hau* tree," is situated on a thin strip of land between the highway and a narrow sandy beach. The campground is in the south part of the park, just after crossing a small stream. *Kamani* trees and ironwoods provide shade. Because of an offshore reef the ocean is usually calm all year, with very little shorebreak. The bottom off the beach is shallow, with some rocky places. The campground is very close to a busy highway and almost within a populated area.

FACILITIES: Tent and vehicle camping. Rest rooms, picnic tables, and a public telephone are available in the beach park section. Water is drinkable. Groceries and gas can be obtained in Hau'ula, just north of the park.

CAMPGROUND ACTIVITIES: Shallow water and a partly rocky bottom make swimming conditions only fair, but it is almost always safe. Snorkeling is very good along the edge of the coral reef. Goatfish, bonefish, and milkfish are likely catches here, and *pāpio* are sometimes hooked in the small channels on both sides of the park.

PERMIT/RESERVATIONS: Permit applications are accepted no earlier than two Fridays before the period requested. Requests for permits are not taken over the phone, nor are reservations accepted. Applicants must appear in person at the following address or at any satellite city hall listed at the beginning of the section on O'ahu: Department of Parks and Recreation, 650 South King Street, Honolulu, HI 96813; phone, (808) 523–4525.

TIME LIMIT: Five nights; Fridays, 8 a.m. to Wednesdays, 8 a.m. (no camping Wednesdays and Thursdays because of maintenance).

COST: Free.

HOW TO GET THERE: From Honolulu (29 miles), take the H-1 Freeway west to Exit 20, Likelike Highway (Highway 63). Proceed north on Highway 63 through the Wilson Tunnel to the intersection of Highway 83 on the left (Kahekili Highway). Proceed on Highway 83 another 17 miles to the park on the right.

NEARBY POINTS OF INTEREST: For information on Sacred Falls, see the section on Kahana Valley State Park. From the campground drive south for 1.3 miles, watching carefully for the parking lot on the right.

For information on the Polynesian Cultural Center, see the section on Mālaekahana State Recreation Area.

Hau'ula Trail System

LOCATION: These trails are on the northern end of the windward shore, behind the town of Hau'ula.

DESCRIPTION: In the hills behind this coastal town are three trails that are well worth exploring, even if you do not plan to camp.

The Hau'ula Loop Trail is a wide, well-maintained loop that passes through a pretty ironwood forest and a grove of high Norfolk pines. The trail is 2.5 miles long, gains about 600 feet elevation, and has fine views of the coast and the mountains. Camping is permitted along the trail, but it is difficult to find a place to pitch a tent on the steep slopes and in the dense forest growth. A ridge about 30 minutes into the hike is wide enough in some places to allow a tent alongside the trail. About 10 minutes farther on, a steep, poorly defined path on the left (if you began the loop by going left, otherwise on the right) leads upslope to a knoll where a small, grassy flat spot with a fine view is just big enough for one tent. Near the end of the loop the underbrush clears somewhat, making it possible to pitch a few tents on ground that, although not level, is not as steep as the terrain on the earlier parts of the trail.

The Ma'akua Ridge—Papali Trail is also a loop with excellent views of the mountains, the coast, and Hau'ula town. It is about 2.5 miles long and gains about 800 feet in elevation. As on Hau'ula Loop Trail, camping is permitted, but finding tent sites off the trail is equally difficult. There is a flat, clear spot with a good view that can hold one tent about 15 minutes into the hike, but it is practically on top of the trail. The first half of the hike traverses a medium forest of *hau, hala, ti,* and strawberry guava. After reaching the ridgeline, the trail enters a forest of young *koa* trees, and their crescent-shaped leaf stalks blanket the ground. As the trail begins to descend, the *koa* trees become larger until they finally disappear as the trail reaches an open slope near its end. There are two small stream crossings along the way, and water should be treated before drinking.

The Ma'akua Gulch Trail is completely unlike the others. Instead of ascending a ridge, it enters a gulch and follows a streambed to a lovely waterfall with a small pool at its base. The trail crosses the stream numerous times, and the last half mile or so requires rock-hopping and wading in the stream itself. Near the end, the steep walls of the valley come so close together you can almost touch them. The trail is 3 miles long one way and rises gradually about 1,100 feet. Camping is permitted at the mouth of the gulch. There is an open area at the end of the dirt road just before the trail narrows and enters the woods. The ground is hard-packed dirt, and it resembles a parking lot, but tents can be pitched easily here. Farther on along the trail are a few small clearings just big enough for one or two tents. After the trail enters the gulch, it is almost impossible to find a tent site.

FACILITIES: None. Stream water is available on all the trails, but it should be treated before use. The stream that crosses the Hau'ula Loop Trail often has an unattractive, milky color. Although my dog drinks it without any problems, I always bring my own water when hiking here.

PERMIT/RESERVATIONS: Permits are obtained from the Division of Forestry and Wildlife, 1151 Punchbowl Street, Honolulu, HI 96813; phone, (808) 587–0166.

TIME LIMIT: Two weeks.

COST: Free.

SPECIAL COMMENTS: A permit is needed for camping only. No permit is necessary for day hikes on any of these trails.

HOW TO GET THERE: From Honolulu (29 miles), take the H-1 Freeway west to Exit 20, Likelike Highway (Highway 63). Proceed north on Highway 63 through the Wilson Tunnel to the intersection of Highway 83 on the left (Kahekili Highway). Continue on Highway 83 another 17 miles to Hau'ula Beach Park on the right. Turn left on Hau'ula Homestead Road, proceeding two-tenths of a mile to Ma'akua Road, a dirt road on the right. Park on Ma'akua Road or in a small dirt parking area on the right, and you will see a wooden sign for "Hau'ula Trails" straight ahead. Walking along this dirt road, follow signs for the trail of your choice. Disregard any chain or cable across the road. This is to prevent access to vehicles, not people.

NEARBY POINTS OF INTEREST: For information on Sacred Falls, see the section on Kahana Valley State Park. From the Hau'ula trailhead, return to the highway, turn right, and drive south for 1.3 miles, watching carefully for the parking lot on the right.

For information on the Polynesian Cultural Center, see the section on Mālaekahana State Recreation Area.

Kokololio Beach Park

LOCATION: The park is on the windward shore, between the towns of Lā'ie and Hau'ula, on Highway 83.

DESCRIPTION: Kokololio, which means "gusty," probably refers to the brisk trade winds that often cool the shores of this large, lovely park with a long white sand beach. The park, wide and grassy, is naturally landscaped with mature ironwood and *kamani* trees, palms, and some clumps of *hau*. Spider lilies and philodendron grow in some of the shaded areas. The campground is at the north end of the park, shaded by some of the ironwoods and *kamani*. It is well separated from the picnic area and other day-use sections of the park. The beach is backed by trees, mostly ironwood, affording optional shade all along its length. It is narrow in places at low tide, and curves in a pretty arc to the north. The shorebreak is almost always small, and the bottom offshore is mostly sandy, with some broken coral.

FACILITIES: Tent camping only. Rest rooms, picnic tables, outdoor showers, drinking water spigots, and dishwashing sinks are provided in the campground section, and additional restrooms, tables, showers, and water spigots can be found in the beach park section. Water is drinkable throughout the park. Groceries and gas can be obtained in Lā'ie, 1 mile north of the park.

CAMPGROUND ACTIVITIES: Swimming is good directly offshore from the beach and is usually safe. Trade winds sometimes whip up small whitecaps on the water, but they rarely interfere with swimmers close to shore. Goatfish, bonefish, and milkfish are sometimes hooked here.

PERMIT/RESERVATIONS: Permit applications are accepted no earlier than two Fridays before the period requested. Requests for permits are not taken over the phone, nor are reservations accepted. Applicants must appear in person at the following address or at any satellite city hall listed at the beginning of the section on O'ahu: Department of Parks and Recreation, 650 South King Street, Honolulu, HI 96813; phone, (808) 523–4525.

TIME LIMIT: Five nights; Fridays, 8 a.m. to Wednesday, 8 a.m. (no camping Wednesdays and Thursdays because of maintenance).

COST: Free.

SPECIAL COMMENTS: At the time of writing, Kokololio was not quite ready to receive campers. Check at above address for latest status.

HOW TO GET THERE: From Honolulu (30 miles), take the H-1 Freeway west to Exit 20, Likelike Highway (Highway 63). Proceed north on Highway 63 through the Wilson Tunnel to the intersection of Highway 83 on the left (Kahekili Highway). Proceed on Highway 83 another 18 miles to the park on the right.

NEARBY POINTS OF INTEREST: For information on Sacred Falls, see the section on Kahana Valley State Park. From the campground drive south for 1.3 miles, watching carefully for the parking lot on the right.

For information on the Polynesian Cultural Center, see the section on Mālaekahana State Recreation Area.

Mālaekahana State Recreation Area

LOCATION: The park is on the windward shore, seven-tenths of a mile north of Lā'ie, on Highway 83.

DESCRIPTION: Mālaekahana is a beautiful park in a wooded grove on one of the finest sandy beaches on O'ahu. Ironwoods, *kamani, hala,* and sea grape combine to provide this grass and sand site with lots of shade, while allowing the beach plenty of sun. *Naupaka* lines the shore, and the view from the beach sweeps from Lā'ie Point to the sharp spine of the Ko'olau Mountains beyond. Several offshore islets complete a majestic seascape. The largest of these is Moku'auia (Goat Island), a bird sanctuary.

Shaded grove at Mālaekahana State Recreation Area is only steps from a long sandy beach.

FACILITIES: Tent camping only; no vehicle camping. There are two separate camping areas here. Campsite A has individual, numbered campsites, each containing a picnic table and a smaller table to hold a portable stove or barbecue. Rest rooms, showers, and three dishwashing sinks with drinkable water are within this campsite area. Campsite B also has individual, numbered campsites similar to Campsite A, except that Campsite A is larger and closer to the ocean. There are rest rooms, showers, drinkable water, and telephone. Unfortunately, many of the tables at both campsites have been damaged by vandalism. Groceries and gas are available in Lā'ie.

CAMPGROUND ACTIVITIES: The park has an excellent swimming beach, which is almost always safe. You can wade to the island offshore, Moku'auia, on calm days at low tide. The water is about waist high for the average adult. Keep in mind that the island is a bird sanctuary and do not disturb nesting birds, their eggs, or offspring. Do not bring a dog or other animal with you. Snorkeling is good on calm days off Moku'auia and near other rocky areas. Good surfing conditions sometimes exist off Moku'auia for body board and sailboarding, with waves of 3 to 7 feet. A surfer was attacked by a shark here in June 1993. *Pāpio* is the most common fish caught along the northern part of the windward coast. Other possible catches are milkfish, bonefish, and goatfish. The long, sandy beach stretching north from the campground offers good opportunities for shell hunting, especially after storms or other periods of high surf.

PERMIT/RESERVATIONS: Permit applications are accepted no earlier than 30 days before the period requested. A permit may be obtained from a state parks office on any island. The following address is for the office on O'ahu: Division of State Parks, P.O. Box 621, Honolulu, HI 96809; phone, (808) 587–0300.

TIME LIMIT: Five nights; Fridays, 8 a.m. to Wednesdays, 8 a.m. (no camping Wednesdays and Thursdays because of maintenance). Another camping permit for the same park will be issued only after 30 days.

COST: Free.

SPECIAL COMMENTS: The park gate is closed between 6:45 p.m. and 7 a.m. Vehicles cannot enter or exit during that period.

HOW TO GET THERE: From Honolulu (37 miles), take the H-1 Freeway west to Exit 20, Likelike Highway (Highway 63). Proceed north on Highway 63 through the Wilson Tunnel to the intersection of Highway 83 on the left (Kahekili Highway). Continue on Highway 83 another 20 miles to Lā'ie. After passing through town, watch for the park sign on the right. After turning off the highway at the park entrance, proceed to the second parking lot, because the first lot is for the picnic area.

NEARBY POINTS OF INTEREST: The Polynesian Cultural Center is only 1 mile south of the campground and offers a complete "tour" of the South Pacific, with authentic reconstructions of typical villages, cultural demonstrations, dances, canoe rides, and a *lū'au,* with a spectacular Polynesian show in the evening.

The major surfing beaches of the north shore, Sunset Beach, the Banzai Pipeline, and Waimea Bay, lie 8 to 12 miles north.

Kahuku Section: Mālaekahana State Recreation Area

LOCATION: The camp is on the windward shore, off Highway 83, almost 2 miles north of Lā'ie and about 1 mile north of the main section of Mālaekahana State Recreation Area.

DESCRIPTION: This concessionaire-operated camp is an attractive, wooded park on one of the most beautiful beaches on O'ahu. It has much the same environment as Mālaekahana State Recreation Area to the south. Ironwoods, *kamani,* and palm trees afford ample shade, while the *naupaka*-lined beach has plenty of sunshine.

FACILITIES: Cabins, tent, and vehicle camping. Tent camping is permitted at twenty-nine numbered sites. Rest rooms are portable chemical toilets, and showers and sinks are outdoors. Picnic tables and some outdoor grills are also provided for the use of campers. Camping vehicles are limited to several parking areas on the site. There are six cabins of different sizes, numbers 4 and 5 being the best located. The cabins are furnished, but occupants must provide their own bedding and cooking and eating utensils. A public phone is available at the manager's office. Recreational equipment can be rented at the office.

CAMPGROUND ACTIVITIES: The park has an excellent swimming beach, which is almost always safe. Snorkeling is good on calm days off Moku-'auia Island to the south and near other rocky areas. *Pāpio* is the most common fish caught along the northern part of the windward coast. Other possible catches are milkfish, bonefish, and goatfish. The long, sandy beach stretching north from the campground offers good opportunities for shell hunting, especially after storms or other periods of high surf.

PERMIT/RESERVATIONS: Cabins should be reserved as early as possible, particularly for weekends. Write or call Friends of Mālaekahana, P.O. Box 305, Lā'ie, HI 96762; phone, (808) 293–1736.

TIME LIMIT: Seven nights within any 30-day period.

COST: Tent and vehicle camping is $4.50 per person, per night, $5 for a single camper. One cabin sleeps six and costs $50 per night, five cabins sleep eight and cost $60, and a large cabin sleeping fifteen costs $250 per night. In addition, a tent cabin is available for $35 per night.

SPECIAL COMMENTS: Kahuku Section is an excellent place to camp if you don't mind the fee, if Mālaekahana State Recreation Area is full, or if you want to camp on a Wednesday and Thursday (which you cannot do at any other state or city and county campground). The park gate is closed between 6 p.m. and 8 a.m. and no vehicles can enter during that period. However, a 24-hour parking lot is located just outside the gate at the manager's office.

HOW TO GET THERE: From Honolulu (38 miles), take the H-1 Freeway west to Exit 20, Likelike Highway (Highway 63). Proceed north on Highway 63 through the Wilson Tunnel to the intersection of Highway 83 on the left (Kahekili Highway). Continue on Highway 83 another 20 miles to Lā'ie. After passing through town, watch for the Mālaekahana park sign on the right. Stay on the highway, continuing past the park entrance for about 1 mile, to the Kahuku Section sign on the right.

NEARBY POINTS OF INTEREST: For information on the Polynesian Cultural Center and north-shore surfing beaches, see the section on Mālaekahana State Recreation Area.

NORTH SHORE

Pālama Uka Camp

LOCATION: The camp is upslope from the coast on the north shore, above the town of Hale'iwa.

DESCRIPTION: "Upland wood enclosure," its translation from Hawaiian, is an apt description of Pālama Uka. Situated on a plateau above the north shore, where the cane fields meet the forest, it is one of the more isolated campgrounds accessible by car. A pretty, grassy site, with some medium-sized trees and sweeping views, Pālama Uka can be soggy and windswept in rainy weather.

FACILITIES: Tent and cabin camping only. The camp is divided into two sections, separated by a slight rise. The lower section contains a large, covered pavilion housing five long picnic tables. Rest rooms with flush toilets are nearby, as is an outdoor shower enclosure. The water is cold, but the pressure is good and so are the shower heads. Four very basic cabins contain nothing but wooden platforms for bedding, each of them able to hold eight persons. A smaller rest room and shower is located closer to the cabins. The upper section contains four similar cabins, a much smaller pavilion, and a small rest room and shower. Screening on several of the cabins is torn, and on my last visit (December 1992) one of the cabins was missing its walls. There is no electricity, and water should be treated before drinking. Shopping, restaurants, groceries, and gas are available in Hale‘iwa, 8 miles down the hill.

CAMPGROUND ACTIVITIES: The camp contains a flat, grassy field large enough for ball playing. Although several trails are close by, hiking is difficult without local knowledge. The military uses the area to the east for training, and former cane fields sprawl north and west. Pālama Uka is best suited for people who bring their activities with them or just want to kick back far from the crowds.

PERMIT/RESERVATIONS: Reservations should be made 1 month in advance, if possible. Call or write Pālama Settlement, 810 North Vineyard Boulevard, Honolulu, HI 96817; phone, (808) 845–3945.

TIME LIMIT: None.

COST: Tent camping is $2 per person per night. Cabins rent for $30 per night and sleep up to eight.

SPECIAL COMMENTS: Care should be taken to watch out for large cane-hauling trucks and other heavy equipment after you have left the highway. The 8-mile-long dirt road to the camp is in good condition, but it can be slippery and muddy in wet weather.

HOW TO GET THERE: From Honolulu (35 miles), take the H-1 Freeway to the H-2 exit, following H-2 to its end. Continue on Highway 99 to the traffic circle and bear right into the town of Hale‘iwa. Watch for a Pizza Hut on the left, then for a traffic light that permits traffic from a cane road to enter the highway. Turn right on this dirt road and bear sharp left at the **Y**, which comes up quickly. Turn left at the first opportunity (about four-tenths of a mile) and follow this road, which goes gradually uphill for 8 miles, to a rustic sign announcing the camp. The road, although unmarked, is called 'Ōpae'ula, which you may wish to confirm with workers along the way. Do not confuse the 'Ōpae'ula Lodge about 5 miles in with Pālama Uka.

NEARBY POINTS OF INTEREST: Waimea Bay, Sunset Beach, and the other north-shore surfing beaches are reasonably close by. Kawainui Trail, which leads to the largest natural freshwater pool on O'ahu, is not far from the camp. The trailhead is not marked and is difficult to see from the road. Continue on the road past Pālama Uka just over 4.5 miles, where the road reaches its lowest point in a gulch. To the right, a trail begins, which follows the left side of the Kawainui Stream. You will pass several smaller pools and make quite a few stream crossings en route.

Kaiaka Bay Beach Park

LOCATION: On the north shore, just west of the town of Hale'iwa on Hale'iwa Road.

DESCRIPTION: Kaiaka, which means "shadowed sea," is situated in an ironwood grove on a pretty peninsula with a rocky shoreline. It has sweeping ocean views from Hale'iwa to Ka'ena Point. Providing a backdrop is Mount Ka'ala, the highest point on O'ahu. The campground is in a flat, grassy area at the west end of the park. The shoreline that fronts the campground is rocky, but a nice sandy beach adjoins it on the east.

FACILITIES: There are seven numbered campsites, each with its own picnic table and trash barrel. The sites are all in an open, grassy area, and only numbers 1, 2, and 4 afford partial shade. Rest rooms, showers, and drinking water fountains are provided. The picnic tables and barbecues in the general use area have been badly vandalized, but so far those in the camping area have escaped.

CAMPGROUND ACTIVITIES: For swimming, it is best to enter the water from the sandy beach east of the camping area. The bottom here is sandy, with some rocky patches. Snorkeling is fair to good on calm days off the rocky shoreline. *Pāpio,* menpachi, and goatfish are the usual catches, but you might hook an *ulua.*

Kaiaka Bay Beach Park, on O'ahu's north shore, is rarely crowded.

PERMIT/RESERVATIONS: Permit applications will be accepted no earlier than two Fridays prior to the period requested. Requests for permits are not taken over the phone, nor are reservations accepted. Applicants must appear in person at the address below, or at any satellite city hall listed at the beginning of this section: Department of Parks and Recreation, 650 South King Street, Honolulu, HI; phone, (808) 523–4525.

TIME LIMIT: Five nights; Fridays, 8 a.m. to Wednesdays, 8 a.m. (no camping Wednesdays and Thursdays because of maintenance).

COST: Free.

SPECIAL COMMENTS: Because there are only seven campsites at Kaiaka, the campground is rarely crowded, nor is the park itself, except on weekends. Gates to the park close at 6:45 p.m. and do not open again until 7 a.m. Vehicles cannot enter or leave the park during this period.

HOW TO GET THERE: From Honolulu (28 miles), take the H-1 Freeway to the H-2 exit, following H-2 to its end. Continue on Highway 99 to the traffic circle just before Hale'iwa. Exit the traffic circle on Waialua Beach Road and proceed six-tenths of a mile to Hale'iwa Road on the right. Turn right and drive another eight-tenths of a mile to the sign to the park on the left.

Mokulē'ia Beach Park

LOCATION: The park is on the ocean 4 miles west of Waialua on Highway 930.

DESCRIPTION: Mokulē'ia, which means "isle of abundance," is an open, grassy campground on one of the most isolated and uninhabited beaches on O'ahu. The beach in front of the park itself is sandy, but there are some rock outcroppings between the sand and the water. However, pockets of sand lead all the way to the water on both sides of the park, making entry easier. The few young trees in the park afford no protection from the sun for campers or other park visitors.

FACILITIES: Tent and vehicle camping. Rest rooms, outdoor showers, picnic tables, drinking fountains, and public telephones are provided. Groceries and gas are available in Waialua, 4 miles east.

CAMPGROUND ACTIVITIES: A broken offshore reef, rock outcroppings, and patches of rock and coral on the bottom all make for care in entering the water and while swimming. High surf and dangerous currents are frequent during the winter months. Very good snorkeling is possible around the many sections of broken reef near shore. Cracks and crevices hide all kinds of fish, but a calm day is essential, because wave action drastically reduces visibility. It's hard to imagine with all the rock out there, but Mokulē'ia is a favorite spot for short board and sailboarders. Surf can run 3 to 8 feet. Observe where others are surfing and beware of the sharp, shallow reef. *Pāpio,* goatfish, and menpachi are the most frequent catches here. With miles of beach to explore in either direction and with lots of pocket beaches, coves, and crevices along the shore, Mokulē'ia can produce a bonanza for shell collectors. Cowries and cones are found most frequently, but many will be damaged from the pounding they take in and out of the water on this rocky coastline. Glider rides and parachute jumping are offered at Dillingham Airfield, just across the highway.

PERMIT/RESERVATIONS: Permit applications are accepted no earlier than two Fridays before the period requested. Requests for permits are not taken over the phone, nor are reservations accepted. Applicants must appear in person at the following address or at any satellite city hall listed at the beginning of the section on O'ahu: Department of Parks and Recreation, 650 South King Street, Honolulu, HI 96813; phone, (808) 523–4525.

TIME LIMIT: Five nights; Fridays, 8 a.m. to Wednesdays, 8 a.m. (no camping Wednesdays and Thursdays because of maintenance).

COST: Free.

SPECIAL COMMENTS: Mokulē'ia can be a hot campsite, mostly because of the lack of shade. If you don't mind spending the money, you will find a similar campground with shade and a nicer beach at Camp Mokulē'ia, less than half a mile away.

HOW TO GET THERE: From Honolulu (30 miles), take the H-1 Freeway west to the H-2 exit. Follow H-2 to the end, continuing on to where the road forks. Bear left toward Waialua (Highway 803), which turns into Highway 930 toward Ka'ena Point. Watch for the beach park on the right 4 miles past Waialua.

NEARBY POINTS OF INTEREST: Ka'ena Point Natural Area Reserve, 5 miles west, is worth a visit. See the section on Kea'au Beach Park.

Camp Mokulē'ia

LOCATION: The camp is on the north shore, 4 miles west of Waialua on Highway 930.

DESCRIPTION: Situated on a quiet, isolated beach, Camp Mokulē'ia is a 9-acre site with a combination of modern and older buildings. Although it has a crowded appearance from the road, the ocean side of the camp is spacious and lovely. Ironwoods and *naupaka* line a pretty, white-sand, crescent-shaped beach. The tent campground is separated from the main camp and consists of six flat, grassy acres. Some shade is provided by ironwood trees. The beach directly in front of the tent site is rocky, but fine sandy beaches border it on both sides.

FACILITIES: Cabins, lodge, and tent camping. Facilities at the tent site are somewhat sparse. There are two portable chemical toilets, a water spigot, and outdoor showers, but no picnic tables or barbecues. Cabins contain bunk beds and hold either fourteen or eighteen persons. The lodge offers rooms with twin beds, sink, table and chairs, and ceiling fan. On the lower floor, two rooms share a bath, but rooms on the upper floor have private baths. A suite is available, which contains a living room, kitchenette, and private bath. Meals can be provided for large groups, but individuals may sometimes join with a larger group by prearrangement. Groceries and gas can be purchased in Waialua, 4 miles east.

CAMPGROUND ACTIVITIES: The crescent-shaped beach is beautiful, affords excellent swimming conditions, and is usually safe. For information about snorkeling, surfing, shore fishing, and beachcombing in the area, see the section on Mokulē'ia Beach Park. Glider rides and parachute jumping are available immediately across the highway at Dillingham Airfield.

PERMIT/RESERVATIONS: Write or call Camp Mokulē'ia, 68–729 Farrington Highway, Waialua, HI 96791; phone, (808) 637–6241.

TIME LIMIT: None.

COST: Tent camping is $7 per person per night. Cabins are $125 per night (fourteen beds) and $160 per night (eighteen beds). Lodge rooms with shared bath are $45/50, rooms with private bath are $55/60, and the suite is $90/100. Meal service for breakfast is $5.00, lunch is $5.65, and dinner is $6.85. Meals for children under 11 are slightly less.

SPECIAL COMMENTS: Camp Mokulē'ia is used primarily by groups, but it is relatively quiet, and the tent area is separated from the other activities, affording a fair degree of privacy. Its beautiful grounds make it the best of the four campsites on Mokulē'ia Beach. Although the tent area has few facilities, tent campers may use all the grounds and facilities of the main camp.

HOW TO GET THERE: From Honolulu (30 miles), take the H-1 Freeway west to the H-2 exit. Follow H-2 to the end, continuing on to where the road forks. Bear left toward Waialua (Highway 803), which turns into Highway 930 toward Ka'ena Point. Follow the road to a long green fence on the right. A small sign at a driveway at the end of the fence reads, "Camp Mokulē'ia, Episcopal Church of Hawai'i."

NEARBY POINTS OF INTEREST: For information on Ka'ena Point Natural Area Reserve, 4 miles to the west, see the section on Kea'au Beach Park.

Mokulē'ia Army Beach

LOCATION: The beach is on the north shore, off Highway 930, just past Dillingham Airfield.

DESCRIPTION: This is a long, beachfront site on an isolated sandy shoreline. Vegetation is mostly *naupaka,* with ironwood trees providing shade in some places. The beach gets its name from the fact that it was formerly operated as a campground for military personnel. That facility has since closed. The beach is the same one shared by the other three Mokulē'ia campgrounds, and it reaches its widest point here.

FACILITIES: None. Tent and vehicle camping.

CAMPGROUND ACTIVITIES: See section on Mokulē'ia Beach Park.

PERMIT/RESERVATIONS: None.

TIME LIMIT: None.

Mokulē'ia Beach Park fronts miles of isolated sandy shoreline.

COST: Free.

SPECIAL COMMENTS: Camping here is for those who want privacy, enjoy primitive camping, and are willing to forego all facilities. If that is not for you, Mokulē'ia Beach Park shares the same beach and water activities and is only 1.5 miles away.

HOW TO GET THERE: Proceed as for Mokulē'ia Beach Park and continue to just past Dillingham Airfield. You will see campsite numbering signs on the ocean side of the road, and an abandoned wooden building marks the western end of the campground.

NEARBY POINTS OF INTEREST: For information on Ka'ena Point Natural Area Reserve, see the section on Kea'au Beach Park.

Camp Erdman

LOCATION: The camp is on the north shore, 6 miles west of the town of Waialua, on Highway 930.

DESCRIPTION: Camp Erdman is a YMCA camp situated in one of the most isolated areas on O'ahu, with a dramatic mountain backdrop. Only fishermen and a few bathers can be seen on the miles of wild and lonely beach. The grounds are flat and grassy, with several groves of ironwood trees. There are quite a few buildings here, but there is still lots of open space, and the beach is wide and spacious.

FACILITIES: Tent and cabin camping only. The tent campground is located in an ironwood grove at the west end of the camp, providing shade for most of the tent sites. Six cabins are located on the ocean side of the highway. Four of these contain bunk beds for up to eight persons and a bathroom. Each cabin has its own picnic table outside. The remaining two cabins are kitchenette units, complete with stove, refrigerator, and sink, but no cooking or eating utensils. They also have a private bath and can accommodate up to eight persons. Fifteen newer cabins are located across the highway, each with a private bathroom and accommodating sixteen persons. Bed linen is provided with the cabins. Groceries and gas are available in Waialua, 6 miles to the east.

CAMPGROUND ACTIVITIES: Swimming, snorkeling, shoreline fishing, and beachcombing are the same as described for Mokulē'ia Beach Park. The camp contains a swimming pool, basketball and tennis courts, and an archery range. Glider rides and parachute jumping are available at nearby Dillingham Airfield.

PERMIT/RESERVATIONS: Camp Erdman is a busy place. During the school year facilities usually are available to the public only on weekends. In the summer, youth programs may tie up all accommodations. Check with the camp administration well in advance. Erdman is not a place to arrive on the spur of the moment. Write or call Camp Erdman, P.O. Box 657, Waialua, HI 96791; phone, (808) 637–4615.

TIME LIMIT: None.

COST: Tent camping costs $7 per person per night, which includes use of community bath and all facilities. Cabins range from $50 to $150 per night depending upon capacity and facilities. Meals are available and the cost is quite reasonable, averaging about $5 per meal.

SPECIAL COMMENTS: Camp Erdman caters to large groups, often of young children, and can therefore be quite noisy. For a quieter and cheaper campsite, go to Camp Mokulēʻia, 2.5 miles back to the east, or for free tent camping use Mokulēʻia Beach Park, 2 miles east. The beach is nicest at Camp Mokulēʻia. As with most north shore beaches, swimming and snorkeling should be undertaken with care. Winter storms can cause dangerous high surf, and tricky currents can occur at any time.

HOW TO GET THERE: From Honolulu (32 miles), take the H-1 Freeway west to the H-2 exit. Follow H-2 to the end, continuing on to where the road forks. Bear left toward Waialua (Highway 803), which turns into Highway 930 toward Kaʻena Point. Follow the road past Dillingham Airfield to a large sign for the camp on the right.

NEARBY POINTS OF INTEREST: For information on Kaʻena Point Natural Area Reserve, 3 miles to the east, see the section on Keaʻau Beach Park.

Peacock Flat Campground

LOCATION: The campground is in the Waiʻanae Mountains, at the northwestern point of Oʻahu, above Mokulēʻia Beach and Dillingham Airfield.

DESCRIPTION: Peacock Flat is a partly wooded, partly open campground on relatively level terrain in an otherwise steep mountain environment. The campground proper sits in a pretty eucalyptus grove; about a mile farther along the jeep road is another, more primitive camping area. These are both favorite camping spots for organizations such as the Boy Scouts and the Sierra Club.

FACILITIES: The main campground contains a small covered pavilion housing a picnic table, which has a windscreen on two sides. There is an enclosed, composting pit toilet in good condition, but no water or electricity. The upper campground, about a mile away, contains only a roofed, two-sided structure, suitable only for partial rain protection.

CAMPGROUND ACTIVITIES: Hiking in the Mokulē'ia and Mākua forest reserves affords spectacular views over the valleys of the Wai'anae coast.

PERMIT/RESERVATIONS: Permits are required to camp, to access the road from the Wai'anae side, and to use the three trails to the campground, which are described below. A permit is not required to hike to the area via Peacock Flat Access Road, unless you intend to camp. Contact the Division of Forestry and Wildlife, 1151 Punchbowl Street, Honolulu, HI 96813; phone, (808) 587–0166.

TIME LIMIT: Two weeks.

COST: Free.

SPECIAL COMMENTS: Peacock Flat may be reached on foot or bike from Mokulē'ia on the north shore or via four-wheel-drive road from the Wai'anae side of the island. Two trails lead in from Mokulē'ia on the north shore: the Peacock Flat Trail and the Mokulē'ia Trail. Both cross private land and require those permissions in addition to the Forestry Division permits. The Forestry office can advise you on securing these permissions. The fastest access, requiring only the Forestry camping permit, is via the Peacock Flat Access Road, about 3.5 miles. Although this is a paved road all the way, only hikers and bikers may use it, and a locked gate bars the way to vehicles. The other access is from the Wai'anae side of the island.

HOW TO GET THERE: Via Mokulē'ia (on foot or bike only), from Honolulu (34 miles), take the H-1 Freeway west to the H-2 exit, following H-2 to its end. Continue on Highway 99 to the traffic circle and bear left into the town of Waialua, following the signs to Ka'ena Point. At 2.3 miles past Waialua Intermediate and High School, a road enters the highway from the left, at the corner of a coconut tree farm. Turn left and park in the small lot immediately on the right. Continue on this road on foot, passing around or over several locked gates, to the campground, about 3.5 miles.

Via Wai‘anae, from Honolulu (42 miles), take the H-1 Freeway to its end, continuing on Highway 93 to Yokohama Bay, about 38 miles. Turn right on the road up the mountain leading to the Ka‘ena Point Tracking Station, first stopping to check in at the security gate. Proceed up the road to an intersection, turning right and passing the tracking station. The road becomes a dirt road for the remainder of the way, and four-wheel drive is recommended, especially if it has been raining recently.

If you wish to hike in, you may take the Kuaokalā Trail, which begins at a dirt parking lot with a CONEX container serving as a small office. A trail sign is located across the road. This trail is about 2 miles long to a point where it joins the road described above, continuing on to the campground.

NEARBY POINTS OF INTEREST: For information on Ka‘ena Point Natural Area Reserve, see the section on Kea‘au Beach Park.

LEEWARD SIDE

Kea‘au Beach Park

LOCATION: The park is on the ocean 2.5 miles north of the town of Mākaha, on Highway 93.

DESCRIPTION: Kea‘au is an open, grassy park, with *milo, hala,* and palm trees scattered throughout its length. A long rock ledge makes up the shoreline, becoming a sandy beach only at the northern end. Even here, the reef comes up to the water's edge, and the bottom is rocky. The surrounding area is relatively undeveloped, giving the park a feeling of isolation, despite its closeness to the highway. The Wai‘anae Mountains provide a dramatic backdrop, and sunsets are great.

FACILITIES: Tent and vehicle camping. There are two rest room buildings in the park. Both were in bad shape at this writing, with sinks and toilet seats removed. Outdoor showers provide the only source of water, which is drinkable. Picnic tables and a public telephone complete the facilities. Groceries and gas are available in Mākaha, 2.5 miles south.

CAMPGROUND ACTIVITIES: The rocky ledge and wave action make water entry for swimming difficult except at the north end of the park. High surf and strong currents are common from October to April. Snorkeling is good on calm days. *Pāpio,* goatfish, and menpachi are the usual catches here, although you might be able to hook an *ulua*. Beachcombing is fair to good, especially after high surf.

PERMIT/RESERVATIONS: Camping applications are accepted no earlier than two Fridays before the period requested. Requests for permits are not taken over the phone, nor are reservations accepted. Applicants must appear in person at the following address or at any satellite city hall listed at the beginning of the section on O'ahu: Department of Parks and Recreation, 650 South King Street, Honolulu, HI 96813; phone, (808) 523–4525.

TIME LIMIT: Camping is permitted during summer months only. Five nights; Fridays, 8 a.m. to Wednesdays, 8 a.m. (no camping Wednesdays and Thursdays because of maintenance).

COST: Free.

SPECIAL COMMENTS: A fatal shark attack occurred here on 5 November 1992. An 18-year-old bodyboarder died when he was bitten by a large tiger shark in shallow water, only about 30 feet from shore. The attack defied all conventional wisdom, in that it took place in clear water, close to shore, at midmorning. State shark hunters caught six sharks in the area 2 days later, including a 13-foot tiger.

HOW TO GET THERE: From Honolulu (35 miles), take the H-1 Freeway west to its end, continuing along Highway 93 to Mākaha. Watch for the sign to the park about 2.5 miles north of town on the left.

NEARBY POINTS OF INTEREST: The world-famous surfing beach at Mākaha Beach Park is less than a mile south of the campground.

Ka'ena Point Natural Area Reserve. Sand dunes, sea birds, and endangered plants mark this isolated preserve, where motorized vehicles are prohibited. Tourists are often surprised that no road goes around O'ahu, linking its north and west shores. They are even more surprised to learn that a railroad *did* go around Ka'ena Point before it ceased running in 1948. From the campground, drive north about 4.5 miles to the parking area in Mākua–Ka'ena Point State Park. From here it is a 2.5-mile walk to the point.

Wai'anae Army Recreation Center

LOCATION: The facility is on the ocean in the town of Wai'anae, off Highway 93.

DESCRIPTION: Wai'anae, which means "mullet water," is a full-service recreational facility for the use of members of the armed forces, active and retired, Department of Defense (DOD) civilian employees, and certain other authorized personnel, and their guests. It is very attractively located on a long, sandy beach, with a mountain backdrop. Palm trees, *kamani,* and monkeypod dot the area. Wai'anae, with its many facilities, has the feel of a miniresort and has great sunsets.

FACILITIES: Cabins only; tent and vehicle camping not permitted. Accommodations range from standard rooms without kitchens to deluxe three-bedroom cabins. All cabins (except standard units) have complete kitchens, cooking and eating utensils, dishes, and linens. Each cabin also has its own sun deck, barbecue, and picnic table. An oceanfront restaurant provides meals and/or snack bar service Friday through Sunday. A bar is open 7 days per week. A separate pavilion area is available for group activities. Twenty-four-hour military police protection is provided.

CAMPGROUND ACTIVITIES: Swimming is excellent year-round right off the sandy beach that fronts the center. Snorkeling is very good at the north end of the beach, along the rocky point. For surfing, low waves break nicely along the northern end of the beach, which is mainly of interest to beginners. *Pāpio* and goatfish can be caught off the beach, with menpachi and parrotfish frequenting the rocky shore at the northern end. Recreational equipment for rent includes surfboards, sailboards, windsurfers, snorkeling and fishing gear, and various items of beach equipment.

PERMIT/RESERVATIONS: DOD ID card or other authorized identification is required. Reservations can be made in person, or by writing or calling the Wai'anae Army Recreation Center, 85–010 Army Street, Wai'anae, HI 96792; phone, (808) 696–4158. From the mainland, call toll free 1–800–333–4158. Reservations are accepted on a first-come, first-served basis, according to the following priorities: (1) active-duty Army personnel, 90 days in advance; (2) other active-duty and retired personnel, 80 days in advance; (3) DOD civilians and reservists, 60 days in advance; (4) other federal employees, 30 days.

TIME LIMIT: Fourteen days.

COST: Fees are on a sliding scale, beginning with $20 per night in standard rooms for pay grades E-1 through E-5, up to $65 per night in the three-bedroom cabins for pay grades O–4 through O–10.

SPECIAL COMMENTS: Wai'anae is an excellent, modernized facility and is by far the best place to stay on the Wai'anae coast if you are eligible. IDs are checked when entering the center and when paying for goods and services.

HOW TO GET THERE: From Honolulu (32 miles), take the H-1 Freeway west to its end and continue on Highway 93 to the town of Wai‘anae. Turn left on Army Street to the Recreation Center entrance.

NEARBY POINTS OF INTEREST: For information on Mākaha Beach Park and Ka‘ena Point Natural Area Reserve, see the section on Kea‘au Beach Park.

Lualualei Beach Park

LOCATION: The park is on the ocean at the south end of the town of Wai‘anae, on Highway 93.

DESCRIPTION: Lualualei is situated on a shoreline fronted by a low sea cliff and a raised coral reef, making water entry almost impossible. Palm trees and bush-sized *milo* are scattered throughout the grassy and sandy park. The campground suffers somewhat from being close to a busy highway, but it has great sunsets. A fine sandy beach lies just half a mile south of the campground.

FACILITIES: Tent camping only; vehicle camping not permitted. Rest rooms, outdoor showers, picnic tables, and drinking water are provided. At this writing, the rest room sinks and toilet seats had been removed. Groceries and gas are available in Wai‘anae.

CAMPGROUND ACTIVITIES: *Pāpio* and goatfish are most frequently caught here. If you are lucky, you might hook an *ulua*.

PERMIT/RESERVATIONS: Permit applications are accepted no earlier than two Fridays before the period of use. Requests for permits are not taken over the phone, nor are reservations accepted. Applicants must appear in person at the following address or at any satellite city hall listed at the beginning of the section on O‘ahu: Department of Parks and Recreation, 650 South King Street, Honolulu, HI 96813; phone, (808) 523–4525.

TIME LIMIT: Camping permitted summer months only. Five nights; Fridays, 8 a.m. to Wednesdays, 8 a.m. (no camping Wednesdays and Thursdays due to maintenance).

COST: Free.

HOW TO GET THERE: From Honolulu (30 miles), take the H-1 Freeway west to its end, continuing on Highway 93 to the outskirts of the town of Wai'anae, watching for the sign to the beach park on the left.

Nānākuli Beach Park

LOCATION: The park is on the ocean at the south end of the town of Nānākuli, just off Highway 93.

DESCRIPTION: A grove of mature *kiawe* trees fringing a curved sandy beach makes Nānākuli an attractive campsite. The camping area is at the south end of the park, where there is some partial shade from the trees. The ground is both grassy and sandy. There are great sunsets. Nānākuli means "look [appear] deaf," and is believed to have come from the habit of the former residents of the area of appearing to be deaf when questioned by travelers, so that they would not have to share their limited food supply with them.

FACILITIES: Tent and vehicle camping. Rest rooms, outdoor showers, and picnic tables are provided, and water is drinkable. The park also contains a ball field, basketball court, and a playground. It has a public telephone. Groceries and gas can be purchased in Nānākuli.

CAMPGROUND ACTIVITIES: Swimming is good at most times, but high surf and strong currents can occur from October through April. Snorkeling is good on calm days when the water is clear. Like most of this coast, frequent catches here are *pāpio,* goatfish, and menpachi.

PERMIT/RESERVATIONS: Permit applications are accepted no earlier than two Fridays before the period requested. Requests for permits are not taken over the phone, nor are reservations accepted. Applicants must appear in person at the following address or at any satellite city hall listed at the beginning of the section on O'ahu: Department of Parks and Recreation, 650 South King Street, Honolulu, HI 96813; phone, (808) 523–4525.

TIME LIMIT: Five nights; Fridays, 8 a.m. to Wednesdays, 8 a.m. (no camping Wednesdays and Thursdays because of maintenance).

COST: Free.

SPECIAL COMMENTS: Homeless people sometimes camp at Nānākuli, which can interfere with recreational camping. Check with city and county officials for the latest situation.

HOW TO GET THERE: From Honolulu (25 miles), take the H-1 Freeway west to the end, continuing on Highway 93 to the park sign on the left.

Kahe Point Beach Park

LOCATION: The park is on the ocean on Highway 93 about 4.5 miles south of Nānākuli.

DESCRIPTION: A pleasant, mostly open, grassy area, Kahe is partly shaded by some *kiawe,* sea grape, and palm trees. The campground is situated at the south end of the park, stretching along a rocky beach, where a low sea cliff makes entry into the water difficult. However, a small sandy cove affording easy access is located at the north end of the park. Kahe means "flow" in Hawaiian.

FACILITIES: Tent and vehicle camping. Rest rooms, outdoor showers, picnic tables, and a water fountain are located in the camping area. Additional rest rooms and a covered pavilion can be found in the beach park section, as is a public telephone. Limited groceries and gas can be obtained in Nānākuli, about 4.5 miles north, and more extensive shopping is available in Wai'anae, another 5 miles north.

CAMPGROUND ACTIVITIES: For swimming, enter the water from the cove at the north end of the park. Caution should be observed from October to April, when high surf can bring dangerous conditions. Snorkeling is good on calm days, along the rocky shoreline right and left of the cove. Typical catches along this coast are *pāpio,* goatfish, menpachi, and sometimes *ulua.*

PERMIT/RESERVATIONS: Permit applications are accepted no earlier than two Fridays before the period requested. Requests for permits are not taken over the phone, nor are reservations accepted. Applicants must appear in person at the following address or at any satellite city hall listed at the beginning of the section on O'ahu: Department of Parks and Recreation, 650 South King Street, Honolulu, HI 96813; phone, (808) 523–4525.

TIME LIMIT: Five nights; Fridays, 8 a.m. to Wednesdays, 8 a.m. (no camping Wednesdays and Thursdays because of maintenance).

COST: Free.

SPECIAL COMMENTS: The campground is frequently used by homeless people, which can interfere with recreational camping. Officials at the Parks

Department may be able to advise you about this. A large electric power plant is located just beyond the park turnoff. An excellent, safe sandy beach is located here.

HOW TO GET THERE: From Honolulu (23 miles), take the H-1 Freeway west to its end and continue on Highway 93 to the sign for the beach park on the left.

Camp Timberline

LOCATION: The camp is in the mountains on the southwest coast, about 20 miles west of Honolulu and 2 miles north of Makakilo.

DESCRIPTION: Timberline is a privately owned, quiet, 10-acre mountain retreat 2,000 feet high in the Wai'anae Mountains. It is used primarily by large groups, but others are welcome. Its forested area includes many native and non-native plants and trees. The camp is noted for its sweeping views and beautiful sunsets.

FACILITIES: Tent and vehicle camping, and cabins. Eight cabins are available, and a small area is set aside for tent camping. The cabins are furnished, and some have bathrooms and kitchens with utensils. Occupants need to bring their own bedding, including blankets and pillows. Vehicle camping is permitted on a space-available basis. Other facilities include a lodge with fireplace, a dining hall, a snack bar, and fire pits.

CAMPGROUND ACTIVITIES: The camp has a swimming pool; miniature golf course; basketball, volleyball, and badminton courts; ball field; and hiking trails.

PERMIT/RESERVATIONS: Reservations may be made by contacting Camp Timberline, P.O. Box 700308, Kapolei, HI 96709; phone, (808) 672–5441.

TIME LIMIT: None.

COST: Tent camping is $7 per person per night. Cabins cost $30 per person per night with three meals. Without meals cabins are $18 per night per person. Pole House Cabin (one to four persons) is $55 per night. Food service is as follows: breakfast, $4; lunch, $5; dinner, $6. Food service is available for individuals only when a group is using the dining hall. Persons wishing to take advantage of food service must notify the dining hall in advance.

HOW TO GET THERE: From Honolulu (20 miles), take the H-1 Freeway west to Makakilo (Exit 2). Proceed about 2.5 miles along Makakilo Drive, turning left on Kīkaha Street. At 'Umena Street, turn left at the stop sign to the locked security gate (you will have received the combination to the lock at the time you made your reservation). Continue to drive up winding Pālehua Road to the camp entrance.

Barbers Point Naval Air Station

LOCATION: This military installation is on the ocean, 2 miles southwest of the town of 'Ewa and 1 mile south of Makakilo.

DESCRIPTION: The naval base offers a waterfront campground and cottages for the use of members of the armed forces, active and retired, and their guests. It is attractively located on a long, sandy beach, with a coastal view clear to Diamond Head. It is well landscaped and maintained.

FACILITIES: Tent camping and cottages. Individually numbered tent sites are located along a dirt road directly on the beach, some in open areas, others in wooded shade. A modern building provides rest rooms and cold showers. Most sites have picnic tables. Accommodations consist of completely furnished two-bedroom cottages, with full kitchens, cooking and eating utensils, dishes, and linens. Each cottage sleeps up to six persons. Groceries can be purchased (military ID card required) from the base commissary and gas from the exchange service station.

CAMPGROUND ACTIVITIES: Good, safe swimming can be enjoyed all year. The ocean bottom near the shore is shallow and sandy, with patches of rock and coral. Snorkeling is fair when the water is clear, but there is not much to see. For surfing, this is a good place for beginners. Goatfish, *pāpio,* threadfin, and bonefish can be taken here.

PERMIT/RESERVATIONS: Department of Defense ID card is required. Campsite reservations may be made 30 days in advance, by phone or mail; cottage reservations can be made by written application only and are accepted up to 60 days in advance. Write to Cottage Reservations, Building 19, Barbers Point Naval Air Station, Honolulu, HI 96826; phone, (808) 682–2019.

TIME LIMIT: Seven days: Monday to Monday or Friday to Friday.

COST: Tents: $10 per site, per night, up to ten persons allowed. Cottages: enlisted, $35; officer, $50.

SPECIAL COMMENTS: Barbers Point Naval Air Station is one of the military bases selected for closure by Congress. The date of closing and the status of its recreation facilities had not been determined as of the date of this writing.

HOW TO GET THERE: From Honolulu (19 miles), take the H-1 Freeway west to Makakilo (Exit 2). Turn left on Fort Barrette Road (Highway 901) and proceed to base entrance.

Kaua'i

If Kaua'i didn't exist, Hollywood would have had to invent it. As early as the 1950s films such as *Pagan Love Song, Naked Paradise,* and *Miss Sadie Thompson* were made here. *South Pacific* was filmed on Lumaha'i Beach. Later, Elvis Presley starred in *Blue Hawaii* and John Wayne in *Donovan's Reef.* Kaua'i substituted for a prehistoric lost world in *King Kong,* for South America in *Raiders of the Lost Ark* and *Jurassic Park,* for Vietnam in *Uncommon Valor,* and for Australia in *The Thorn Birds.* Why all this movie-making activity? Quite simply, the beauty of Kaua'i is breathtaking.

One of the reasons Kaua'i is so scenic is that nature has had longer to work on it. It is the oldest of the inhabited Islands, between 3.8 and 5.6 million years old. Wind, rain, and ocean have had time to sculpture its massive sea cliffs and deep hanging valleys. The majestic rock towers of the Nā Pali coast, the lush rain forests of Kōke'e, and the arid reaches of Waimea Canyon (the Grand Canyon of the Pacific) all attest to the skill of these natural artists. All of these wonderful places are accessible to the camper, as are some of the loveliest beaches to be found anywhere in the world.

Another reason for the lush, green splendor of Kaua'i is that it receives more rainfall than the rest of the state. Mount Wai'ale'ale, in the center of the island, is not only the wettest spot in Hawai'i, but one of the wettest in the world. The average rainfall here is 451 inches, with a record 665 inches falling in 1982. Soaking up most of this moisture like a huge sponge, the Alaka'i Swamp distributes it to dozens of waterfalls and to the island's five rivers. Paradoxically, only a few miles away Waimea Canyon is as dry as its counterpart in Arizona.

Fourth largest of the main Islands, Kaua'i is almost circular, about 33 miles long and 25 miles wide, and encloses an area of 558 square miles. Formed from a single shield volcano, its caldera was once the largest in the Islands. Its highest point is Kawaikini, 5,243 feet, a remnant of the caldera, as is its close neighbor, Mount Wai'ale'ale.

According to legend in some oral chants, the original Polynesian settlers first came ashore in the Islands on Kaua'i, although anthropologists today lean toward awarding Hawai'i that honor. In any event, the chiefs of Kaua'i had the purest bloodlines of all the *ali'i,* which indicates very close ties to their ancient homeland. Kaua'i was the first of the Hawaiian Islands to be visited by a westerner, when Captain James Cook came ashore at

KAUA'I

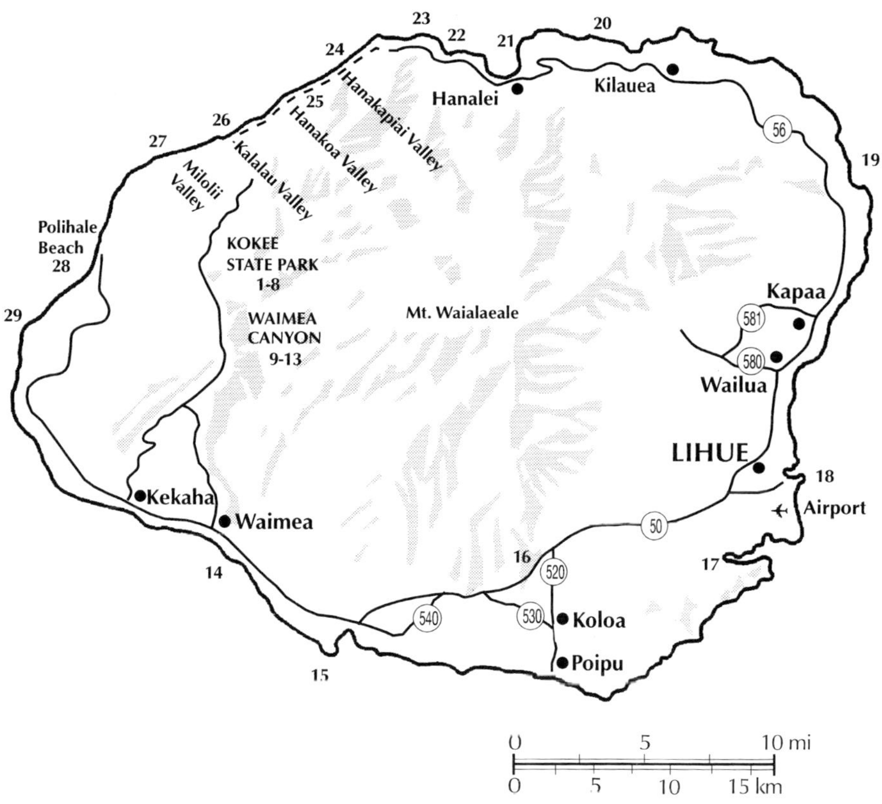

Kaua'i Campgrounds

1. Kōke'e State Park Campground
2. Sugi Grove Campground
3. Kawaikōī Campground
4. Kōke'e Lodge
5. Camp Sloggett
6. Kōke'e Methodist Camp
7. Hongwanji Camp
8. Wai'alae Cabin
9. Wiliwili Camp
10. Wai'alae Camp
11. Lonomea Camp
12. Kaluahā'ula Camp
13. Hipalau Camp
14. Lucy Wright Beach Park
15. Salt Pond Beach Park
16. Kāhili Mountain Park
17. Niumalu Beach Park
18. Hanamā'ulu Beach Park
19. Anahola Beach Park
20. 'Anini Beach Park
21. Hanalei Beach Park
22. Camp Naue (YMCA)
23. Hā'ena Beach Park
24. Hanakāpī'ai Beach
25. Hanakoa Valley
26. Kalalau Valley
27. Miloli'i Beach
28. Polihale State Park
29. Barking Sands Pacific Missile Range

Waimea in January, 1778. A monument to Cook stands near that spot today. Kaua'i was the only island not conquered by Kamehameha in his campaign to unify all the Islands. It finally came under his rule peacefully in 1810.

The first sugar plantation in Hawai'i was started here at Kōloa. Long the biggest industry on Kaua'i, sugar has now taken a distant second place to tourism, which is now the largest employer of the island's 51,000 inhabitants. Kaua'i has now exceeded the Big Island in coffee production and is experimenting with macadamia orchards. The island's tourist nickname is "the Garden Island," which probably refers to its lush, green environment, rather than its having more or better gardens than its neighbors. There is no public transportation. Hitchhiking is permitted, but you must stay off the paved section of the road.

On 11 September 1992, Kaua'i was devastated by Hurricane 'Iniki, which struck the island with torrential rain, monster waves, and winds gusting up to 160 miles per hour. Well over a thousand homes were destroyed, and several thousand more were damaged. Every hotel on the island was damaged severely enough to close its doors, rental car fleets were decimated, and hundreds of tourists were stranded in emergency shelters, along with many Kaua'i residents. Electric power to the entire island was lost for weeks, and even by the end of the year it had not been fully restored. Telephone service was out for several weeks, and air travel was temporarily disrupted.

Campgrounds and hiking trails also suffered damage, and many local residents, made homeless by the storm, moved into campgrounds throughout the island. The situation is now pretty much back to normal. As of January 1994 only two county campgrounds, Niumalu and Salt Pond, were still closed.

THINGS TO SEE AND DO. Descriptions of each of the points of interest listed below are found in the campground section indicated. Keep in mind that distances on Kaua'i are not great. Many of these locations are within easy range of several campgrounds.

Point of Interest	Nearest Campground
Captain Cook's Landing	Lucy Wright Beach Park
Fern Grotto	Hanamā'ulu Beach Park
Hanalei Valley and Lookout	'Anini Beach Park
Kalalau Lookout	Kōke'e State Park
Kīlauea Point National Wildlife Refuge	'Anini Beach Park
Kōke'e State Park	Kōke'e State Park
Maniniholo Dry Cave	Hā'ena Beach Park

Menehune Fish Pond	Niumalu Beach Park
Nā Pali Coast (Kalalau) Trail	Hā'ena Beach Park
'Ōpaeka'a Falls	Hanamā'ulu Beach Park
Russian Fort	Lucy Wright Beach Park
Sleeping Giant	Hanamā'ulu Beach Park
Spouting Horn	Salt Pond Beach Park
Waikanaloa Wet Cave	Hā'ena Beach Park
Waikapala'e Wet Cave	Hā'ena Beach Park
Wailua Falls	Hanamā'ulu Beach Park
Waimea Canyon	Kōke'e State Park

Kōke'e State Park

LOCATION: The park is at the north end of Waimea Canyon, near the end of Highway 55, about 43 miles west of Līhu'e.

DESCRIPTION: Kōke'e State Park encompasses 4,640 acres of beautiful forested wilderness at elevations from 3,600 to 4,000 feet. Native and introduced rain forests, pristine bogs, and spectacular lookouts over the Nā Pali Coast and Waimea Canyon make Kōke'e a must for anyone visiting Kaua'i. Majestic redwoods, rugged sugi cedars, and handsome Monterey cypress surround the lodge and the campground, planted in the 1930s as part of a reforestation effort. The park contains over 45 miles of maintained trails, providing some of the best hiking in the Islands. Kōke'e is also the ideal base for viewing and exploring Waimea Canyon (the Grand Canyon of the Pacific) and for venturing into the Alaka'i Swamp.

FACILITIES: There are several possibilities for camping at Kōke'e. The state maintains a campground adjacent to Kōke'e Lodge, as well as three backcountry campsites. Kōke'e Lodge has twelve cabins for rent at a moderate rate, and three private organizations offer their camp or lodge facilities for rent when not being used by their own members. Each of these facilities is described below.

The State Park Campground allows tent camping only. The campground is located on a hillside just past the lodge and museum area. Despite the sloping ground, numerous flat tent sites can be found. The campground is covered with high grass, and mature trees provide partial to full shade. A rest room building also contains showers and sinks. Drinking water can be obtained here or at a spigot in the small picnic area beside the campground parking lot. Two picnic tables are located here. A large pavilion sits between the campground and the Kōke'e Museum. The pavilion has two separate, identical sections; large picnic tables; rest rooms;

a barbecue; a dishwashing sink; and electric lights. This pavilion is a boon to campers for preparing and eating meals, especially during rainy weather. The campground is within easy walking distance of the Nu'alolo trailhead, which begins the spectacular Nu'alolo-Awa'awapuhi Loop described below. Permits may be obtained from a state parks office on any island. The following address is the state office on Kaua'i: Division of State Parks, 3060 'Eiwa Street Līhu'e, HI 96766; phone, (808) 241–3444. Time limit: Five nights in any one 30-day period. Cost: Free.

Sugi Grove and Kawaikōī are two primitive campgrounds across from each other on a jeep road about 4 miles west from park headquarters. The only facilities provided are pit toilets and picnic tables. Water is available from a nearby stream and should be treated before drinking. This is a good base for hiking the beautiful Kawaikōī Stream Trail and the Alaka'i Swamp Trail and for visiting Poamoho Canyon Lookout. From park headquarters drive north on the paved highway a short distance to the second dirt road on the right, about four-tenths of a mile. This is the Camp 10 road. Proceed another 3.5 miles to the campgrounds: Kawaikōī on the left; Sugi Grove on the right. Four-wheel drive is recommended, especially in wet weather.

Koaie Camp lies about 4.5 miles past Sugi Grove. It is a primitive camp with no facilities. An abandoned rain gauge shack may provide some shelter, if you don't mind sharing with the rats. Water is available from a nearby stream, which should be treated before use.

Wai'alae Cabin lies about another 4 miles past Koaie Camp. The cabin itself is for use only by Forestry personnel, but a lean-to and a small shelter are available for campers. Camping is permitted in the vicinity of the cabin, but there are no facilities of any kind. Water is obtainable from a nearby stream and should be treated before use.

Permits for the above four campgrounds are obtained from the Division of Forestry and Wildlife, 3060 'Eiwa Street, P.O. Box 1671, Līhu'e, HI 96766; phone, (808) 274–3433. Time limit is three nights. Cost: Free.

Kōke'e Lodge offers complete housekeeping cabins holding up to six persons. Older cabins consist of one large dormitory-style room with six beds, kitchen area, bathroom, and a wood-burning stove for heat. Newer cabins consist of two bedrooms, living room, kitchen, bath, and wood-burning stove and also accommodate six. Furnishings for both cabins include cooking and eating utensils, and bedding and linen is provided. Firewood for the stoves may be purchased at the lodge. A restaurant at the lodge offers a continental breakfast and lunch 7 days a week; hours 9 a.m. to 3:30 p.m. The lodge also contains a bar with a fireplace, and a gift shop. The lodge closes at 4 p.m. daily. The cabins are very popular and must be reserved far in advance—for some popular times, as long as a year. Cancellations are sometimes available. For reservations, write or call Kōke'e Lodge, P.O. Box 819, Waimea, Kaua'i, HI 96796; phone, (808) 335–6061. Time Limit: Five nights. Cost: $45 per night for the newer cabins; $35 for the older ones.

Camp Sloggett, consisting of a lodge and a bunkhouse, is available for rent when not in use by its owner, the Kaua'i YWCA. The lodge building contains a large central room with couches, dining tables and chairs, fireplace, and a big screened porch. It also includes two bedrooms (two single beds in each); a bathroom; and a commercial-style kitchen, complete with cooking and eating utensils. The bunkhouse is divided into two sections, with a large bathroom (toilets, sinks, showers, and private dressing rooms) located between the two sections. There are bunk beds for thirty-two persons, plus eight folding mattresses, and a private bedroom with a double bed is located at one end of the bunkhouse. Tent camping is permitted on the grounds. For reservations, write or call Camp Sloggett, Kaua'i YWCA, 3094 Ēlua Street, Līhu'e, HI 96766; phone, (808) 245–5959. Cost for the lodge and bunkhouse is $12 per adult per night. There is a minimum charge of $60 on weekdays and $96 on weekends. Tent camping is $5 per night per person for residents of Kaua'i, $7 for other Hawai'i residents, and $10 for others.

Kōke'e Methodist Camp is also available when not in use by church-affiliated groups. The lodge contains a central room with couches, piano, and fireplace. A large dining room leads out to an unscreened porch. Three bunk rooms accommodate up to eight persons each, in double bunks. There is a supply of blankets, but no other bedding is provided. Two bathrooms and a kitchen containing cooking and eating utensils complete the lodge building. An additional wash house contains toilets, hot showers, and sinks. Firewood can sometimes be purchased from the caretaker, but the tools and the supply are available to cut your own. A telephone is available for local, credit card, or collect calls. For reservations, call or write Kōke'e Methodist Camp, P.O. Box 905, Waimea, Kaua'i, HI 96796; phone, (808) 335–3429. Cost is $8 per person per night, with a minimum charge of $40 per night.

Hongwanji Camp consists of one large building with a fireplace, complete kitchen, tables and chairs, and a supply of foam-rubber mattresses. No bedding is supplied. Firewood is usually available. Four bathrooms with hot showers are also within the lodge building. A telephone is available for local, collect, or credit card calls. For reservations, write or call Hongwanji Camp, P.O. Box 999, Kalāheo, Kaua'i, HI 96741; phone, (808) 332–9563. Cost is $40 minimum charge for the first night, plus $3.50 per person over seven persons. Additional nights are $3.50 per person per night, regardless of the number of occupants.

CAMPGROUND ACTIVITIES: Hiking is the big activity at Kōke'e. One of the best hikes in the Islands, the Nu'alolo-Awa'awapuhi Loop, affords absolutely stunning views of the Nā Pali coast and into two of the dramatic "hanging" valleys of Kaua'i. Beginning in a tall rain forest, the trail soon breaks out onto an open ridge, with views of Ni'ihau and Lehua islands and a vast expanse of ocean. This 11-mile round-trip should be started early in the morning, so as to reach the overlooks before noon. Clouds tend to gather in the afternoon. The short hike to Waipo'o Falls skirts the edge of Waimea Canyon and ends at a lovely pool. Several trails lead into the Alaka'i Swamp, for a totally different hiking experience. Buy the inexpensive trail map or one of the Kaua'i trail guide books at the museum. Goats and pigs are hunted in certain sections of the park, and trout fishing is very popular. The season for trout is 16 days in August and all weekends in September. Permits are available at park headquarters. The farther you get from the road and the main streams, the better your luck will be.

SPECIAL COMMENTS: The restaurant at the lodge provides some meals, as mentioned above, but groceries and gas are only available in Waimea or Kekaha, a long 19 miles down the hill. Stock up before you come. Evenings at Kōke'e can be cold, especially during the winter months. Because open fires are not permitted, tent campers have little refuge except to huddle around the outdoor grill in the picnic area. Buying a drink in the lodge after dinner is a good investment, because you can then take a chair in front of the fireplace. Cabin and lodge occupants will appreciate their own fireplaces or wood stoves.

The water supply at Kōke'e has problems meeting state requirements governing turbidity and sometimes experiences biological contamination. Although many people drink the water with no problems, you may wish to treat or boil it before use.

Delicious plums are available for the picking at Kōke'e in midsummer. The best place to find them is along the south side of the road between the Kalalau Lookout and Pu'u o Kila, and on the Kauapuhi Trail. The Parks Department regulates plum picking, both the days and the hours you may pick them and the amount you may take. Check at park headquarters.

One of the features of Kōke'e is its "jungle fowl." These are feral Polynesian roosters and chickens, descendants of those brought to the Islands by the original Polynesians. Escaped long ago from captivity, they have made their home in the forests of Kōke'e. They have survived only on Kaua'i, because it is the only island that did not import the mongoose, which has wiped out virtually all ground-nesting birds on the other Islands. Many of the jungle fowl have now decided life is easier hanging around the lodge and cadging meals from tourists, but you will still hear roosters crowing deep in the forest as you hike the trails in Kōke'e.

HOW TO GET THERE: From Līhu'e (45 miles), take Highway 50 to Kekaha and the sign to Waimea Canyon (Highway 55). Follow Highway 55 along the rim of the canyon to Kōke'e Lodge, about 22 miles from Kekaha. The campground is located just past the lodge. Stay on the highway and make the first left turnoff after the lodge. For cabins, check in at the lodge. For Camp Sloggett, stay on the highway and make the first right turn past the lodge. Follow this dirt road for about a mile to another road to the right with a small sign for Camp Sloggett. Follow this road to the camp. For Kōke'e Methodist Camp and Hongwanji Camp, it is best to get directions at the time you make reservations. On your return trip, you might want to come down Waimea Canyon Road, which forks off to the left from Highway 55. Both roads are in about the same condition, but this one follows the rim of the lower canyon.

NEARBY POINTS OF INTEREST: Kōke'e Museum exhibits some of the flora and fauna of the area and sells books and pamphlets, mostly dealing with Kaua'i and Hawaiiana. It is located adjacent to the lodge.

The road to Kōke'e follows the west rim of Waimea Canyon almost from the moment it leaves the coast at the town of Waimea. There are two official overlooks along the way, and you will want to stop at several of your own choosing as well. It is easy to see why Waimea is called the Grand Canyon of the Pacific. Both were formed by erosion, and they look remarkably alike. Of course, the big brother in Arizona is much more massive and infinitely older, but you can still see the resemblance.

The Kalalau Lookout provides a dramatic view into the terminus of the Kalalau Trail, as beautiful Kalalau Valley unfolds its green splendor all the way to a cobalt-blue sea. This is one of the best views in Hawai'i. If you don't take the Nu'alolo-Awa'awapuhi hike, this will give you a small idea of what you are missing. It is just off the road about 2 miles northeast of the campground.

Hiking in the Alaka'i Swamp is a real swamp experience. Despite the trail, expect to be in deep mud most of the time. The plants and the environment are different from those on any other hike on Kaua'i. If you don't mind the effect on your clothing and you have a place to shower afterward, this is a unique experience. However, the state and several voluntary organizations are building a boardwalk along the Alaka'i and Pihea trails, which will afford less wear and tear on both swamp flora and hikers. Much of it will be completed by the time of this book's publication. Without a four-wheel-drive vehicle, the best way to enter the Alaka'i is via the Pihea Trail at the end of the Kōke'e Road. After 1.6 miles Pihea intersects the main Alaka'i Swamp Trail. If you have had enough, this is a good turn-around point. Or if the weather is good you could continue east to Kilohana for a great overlook into Wainiha Valley. I have been there three times and seen nothing but fog 10 feet in front of my face.

Waimea Canyon State Park

LOCATION: The campsites are at the bottom of the canyon, along the Waimea River and the Koai'e and Wai'alae streams.

DESCRIPTION: A series of five wilderness campsites is spread over a 6-mile stretch of the canyon floor, connected by trails that follow the watercourses mentioned above. The scenery is almost always dramatic, gazing up at the steep, eroded canyon walls and bright blue sky. Small pools provide refreshing places to cool off, and once down in the canyon, the trails are not strenuous.

FACILITIES: Only Wiliwili and Lonomea camps have pit toilets. Wiliwili, Hipalau, and Lonomea camps have roofed shelters and a picnic table. Water is only available from the streams and should be treated before drinking.

PERMIT/RESERVATIONS: Signing in at the trailhead is all that is required if you are day hiking. Camping (4-day limit) requires a permit from the Division of Forestry and Wildlife, 3060 'Eiwa Street, Room 306, Līhu'e, HI 96766; phone, (808) 274–3433.

TIME LIMIT: Four nights within any consecutive 30-day period.

COST: Free.

SPECIAL COMMENTS: Sanitation is important in the canyon, particularly at those campsites without toilets. Be sure to bury personal wastes at least 100 feet from the streams. Pack out everything you pack in. After you leave Waimea, there is no place to buy gas or groceries. Stock up before you come.

HOW TO GET THERE: Access to the canyon floor is via the Kukui Trail, about 7.5 miles north on Waimea Canyon Road from its junction with Highway 50 in Waimea. The trailhead is on the right side of the road, marked by a wooden sign. If you come to the Waimea Canyon Lookout, you have gone too far. A small parking area exists off the left side of the road. The sign-in kiosk is located a few hundred feet in from the road, near a picnic pavilion.

The Kukui Trail drops 2,000 feet in 2.5 miles. It begins with a series of switchbacks, snaking in and out of a forested area, with wonderful views of the canyon. The trail then turns north and makes its way over a long, eroded ridgeline before entering the forest again. The trail remains heavily wooded until it reaches the canyon bottom and the first of the wilderness campsites.

Wiliwili Camp, at the base of the Kukui Trail, consists of an open-sided, roofed shelter with a picnic table. Two portable-type pit toilets are located a short distance away. There is room to pitch tents, but high grass needs to be cut down or flattened. Camping in the shelter is permitted, if others are not using it for picnic purposes. A nice pool with great views is just a short distance from the camp. Cross the jeep road to the Waimea River and proceed downstream about 100 yards or so. This pool is usually deep enough for swimming, but even during periods of low water it provides a refreshing dip.

Wai'alae Camp is reached by following the Waimea Canyon Trail (jeep road) downstream about a mile. This camp has facilities similar to those of Wiliwili. The trail leaves the jeep road after about six tenths of a mile, crosses the Waimea River, and follows the Wai'alae Stream for about a third of a mile before reaching the camp.

The best campsite in the canyon is Lonomea Camp, which is 6 miles from the Kukui trailhead and can easily be reached in 1 day. The trail goes upstream from Wiliwili and crosses the Waimea River after about six-tenths of a mile at Kaluahā'ula Camp, an emergency shelter used when stream levels are too high to cross. The trail then follows the stream through Koai'e Canyon, passing the shelter at Hipalau Camp, and ends at Lonomea. A roofed, open-sided shelter covers a table, there is room for tents, and, best of all, two great pools with waterfalls are right beside the camp.

Lucy Wright Beach Park

LOCATION: The park is on the ocean on Highway 50 in the town of Waimea, 23 miles east of Līhu'e.

DESCRIPTION: Lucy Wright is a small park bordered by the ocean and the Waimea River. It is part grass and part sand, with some shade provided by medium-sized trees. A sandy beach fronts the park, which is often strewn with debris deposited by the Waimea River. The water offshore can be murky for the same reason.

FACILITIES: Tent camping only A small picnic area, rest rooms, outdoor showers, and drinking water complete the facilities. There is also a playground in the park. Groceries and gas are available in Waimea.

Weekend campers at Lucy Wright Beach Park, Waimea.

CAMPGROUND ACTIVITIES: Swimming is good on calm days, if the water is clear. Swimming is dangerous during periods of high surf, which generates rip currents and a pounding shorebreak. Surfing is good when conditions are right, especially near the mouth of the river. Waimea Bay is a fair fishing area for squirrelfish, goatfish, bonefish, and, sometimes, *pāpio*.

PERMIT/RESERVATIONS: Reservations for camping permits may be made by phone; however, all permits must be picked up in person at the following address (permits are not issued to persons under 18 years old): Department of Parks and Recreation, 4280A Rice Street, Building B, Līhu'e, HI 96766; phone, (808) 241–6660. Permits may be picked up after usual office hours and on weekends at the Kaua'i Police Deparmment, 3060 'Umi Street, Līhu'e. If you pick up your permit here, you must have the exact amount of the permit fee. Campers are permitted to go directly to the campground, where a roving ranger will collect the fee. In this case, the cost is $5 per person per night.

TIME LIMIT: Seven days. You may renew for the same area, but only after a full day's break in camping, with no more than 60 days camping per year.

COST: Free to Hawai'i residents, nonprofit groups, and for persons under 18. For all others, the cost is $3 per day per person.

HOW TO GET THERE: From Līhu'e (26 miles), take Highway 50 west toward Waimea. Just before entering the town, you will pass the Russian

Fort on the left and then cross a bridge over the Waimea River. Immediately after the bridge, watch for signs to the park on the left.

NEARBY POINTS OF INTEREST: A monument just west of the park commemorates Captain James Cook's first landing in the Hawaiian Islands in January, 1778.

On the opposite side of the Waimea River from the park lie the remains of Fort Elizabeth, a Russian fort built in 1815. Its crumbling black-rock walls give mute evidence of Russia's failed attempt to gain influence in the Islands.

Salt Pond Beach Park

LOCATION: The park is on the ocean 1 mile west of Hanapēpē, off Highway 50.

DESCRIPTION: Situated beside ancient Hawaiian salt beds that are still in use, Salt Pond is an attractive park with a small, crescent-shaped sandy beach fronting a wide, grassy field. Partial shade is provided by scattered palm trees.

FACILITIES: Tent camping only. Camping is restricted to the east end of the park. A large central pavilion houses the rest rooms and several long picnic tables. Water and electricity are available here. Screened outdoor showers are situated in front of the pavilion, toward the beach. Additional picnic tables in smaller covered pavilions are located throughout the park. Groceries and gas are available in Hanapēpē, 1 mile away.

CAMPGROUND ACTIVITIES: Swimming is excellent at the small sandy beach, which is partially protected by an offshore ridge. Snorkeling is good on calm days along the two rocky points on either side of the beach and in the vicinity of the offshore ridge. Several surfing sites are located offshore from the park, and it is a good sailboarding area, because of the relatively constant prevailing winds. Mullet is the most reliable catch, with an occasional *pāpio* or *ulua*.

PERMIT/RESERVATIONS: Reservations for camping permits may be made by phone; however, all permits must be picked up in person at the following address (permits are not issued to persons under 18 years old): Department of Parks and Recreation, 4280A Rice Street, Building B, Līhu'e, HI 96766; phone, (808) 241–6660. Permits may be picked up after usual office hours and on weekends at the Kaua'i Police Department, 3060 'Umi Street, Līhu'e.

Pitching camp at Salt Pond Beach Park, Hanapēpē.

If you pick up your permit here, you must have the exact amount of the permit fee. Campers are permitted to go directly to the campground, where a roving ranger will collect the fee. In this case, the cost is $5 per person per night.

TIME LIMIT: Seven days. You may renew for the same area, but only after a full day's break in camping, with no more than 60 days camping per year.

COST: Free to Hawai'i residents, nonprofit groups, and for persons under 18. For all others, the cost is $3 per day per person.

SPECIAL COMMENTS: The salt ponds adjacent to the park are the last ones still in use in Hawai'i. They are worked by members of an organization that has made salt here for generations. No Trespassing signs apply to all others.

HOW TO GET THERE: From Līhu'e (18 miles), take Highway 50 west to Hanapēpē (17 miles). After crossing the Hanapēpē River bridge, watch for the sign on the left to the park. Turn left for half a mile, make the first right turn, and drive another half mile to the park.

NEARBY POINTS OF INTEREST: Depending upon ocean conditions, the Spouting Horn blowhole can create a spectacular geyser complete with an accompanying roar, hence its name. The fountain is formed by water from a breaking wave rushing through an underwater cave and being forced out through a hole in its top. To reach the Spouting Horn from the campground, return to Highway 50, turning right toward Līhu'e. Turn right again at the junction of Highway 53 and right once more in Kōloa, away from Po'ipū. Watch for the Spouting Horn sign at a fork in the road in about 1.5 miles. Turn right at the fork and proceed to the parking lot on the left.

Kāhili Mountain Park

LOCATION: The park is off Highway 50, about 8 miles west of Līhu'e.

DESCRIPTION: The park consists of 215 acres in an attractive open meadow, backed by the dramatic, steep ridges and valleys of Mount Kāhili. A small lake is on the property, which is owned by the Seventh-day Adventist Church. The *kāhili* was the feathered scepter of authority carried by Hawaiian chiefs.

FACILITIES: Small houses, cabins, and cabinettes only; no tent or vehicle camping. All have electricity. Dishes and cooking utensils are provided, as are bed linen and towels. The houses have two bedrooms and two baths and are furnished with a double bed and two twin beds, table, chairs, and dressers. The cabins have one bedroom and bath, with a private outdoor shower, and the same number of beds. Cabinettes are essentially the same, but toilets and showers are in a separate building. Groceries and gas can be purchased in Kōloa, about 4.5 miles south. Laundry facilities are available, as is a public phone.

CAMPGROUND ACTIVITIES: Several hiking trails begin at the park, including one that climbs to the tower on Kāhili Ridge. Steep and strenuous, it affords a sweeping, but precarious, view.

PERMIT/RESERVATIONS: For reservations, write or call Kāhili Mountain Park, P.O. Box 298, Kōloa, Kaua'i, HI 96756; phone, (808) 742–9921.

TIME LIMIT: None, but the minimum stay is two nights.

COST: Small houses are $60 per night, for up to two persons, plus $6 extra per person for up to four. Cabins are $50 per night, double, plus $6 extra per person, up to four. Cabinettes are $37 per night, double, plus $6 extra per person, up to four.

SPECIAL COMMENTS: A school is located on the grounds of Kāhili Mountain Park, and recess periods can be noisy. That should not bother you, because your days are not likely to be spent hanging around the cabin. Quiet time is in effect at night.

HOW TO GET THERE: From Līhu'e (8.5 miles), drive west on Highway 50, watching for the Po'ipū cutoff, about 6.8 miles. Do not turn, but continue along the highway, watching for the 7-mile marker, about another half mile. Just after the marker will be a sign for the park on the right. Turn right and proceed through the cane field on a dirt road for about another mile.

NEARBY POINTS OF INTEREST: Po'ipū Beach is only about 8 miles south of Kāhili and is the most popular beach on the south shore. Swimming, surfing, bodysurfing, windsurfing, snorkeling, and shoreline fishing can all be enjoyed at Po'ipū Beach Park and its adjacent beaches, Po'ipū and Brennecke. To reach Po'ipū from Kāhili, return to the highway and turn left toward Līhu'e. In a little over half a mile, you will come to the turnoff for Po'ipū on the right. Follow the signs through Kōloa (a right, then an immediate left turn) to Po'ipū.

For information on the Spouting Horn, see the section on Salt Pond Beach Park. Follow the directions for Po'ipū Beach above until you reach the road fork south of Kōloa, marked left for Po'ipū, right for the Spouting Horn.

Niumalu Beach Park

LOCATION: The park borders the inner portion of Nāwiliwili Bay and the Hulē'ia River, in the southern outskirts of Līhu'e.

DESCRIPTION: Niumalu, which means "shade of coconut trees," is a small, grassy campground, bordered by ironwood trees on its bay side and a road on the other. Offshore, the water is calm and usually flat, covering a muddy tidal flat. Much of the nearby shoreline is covered with mangrove. Niumalu is attractive, but nearby houses give the feeling of being located in a suburban neighborhood. The camping area is close to the road, but there is not much traffic.

FACILITIES: Tent and vehicle camping. A large wooden pavilion contains rest rooms, seven tables, and electric lights. Behind the pavilion are outdoor screened showers, two barbecues, and two picnic tables. A small boat ramp is located in the park. Groceries and gas are available in Līhu'e.

CAMPGROUND ACTIVITIES: Because of the tidal flats, swimming is only fair, but it is almost always safe. *'Ōpelu,* mullet, and bonefish are caught here. It is also a good spot for crabbing.

PERMIT/RESERVATIONS: Reservations for camping permits may be made by phone; however, all permits must be picked up in person at the following address (permits are not issued to persons under 18 years old): Department of Parks and Recreation, 4280A Rice Street, Building B, Līhu'e, HI 96766; phone, (808) 241–6660. Permits may be picked up after usual office hours and on weekends at the Kaua'i Police Department, 3060 'Umi Street, Līhu'e. If you pick up your permit here, you must have the exact amount of the permit fee. Campers are permitted to go directly to the campground, where a roving ranger will collect the fee. In this case, the cost is $5 per person per night.

TIME LIMIT: Seven days. You may renew for the same area, but only after a full day's break in camping, with no more than 60 days camping per year.

COST: Free to Hawai'i residents, nonprofit groups, and for persons under 18. For all others, the cost is $3 per day per person.

SPECIAL COMMENTS: As of date of publication, Niumalu Beach Park was closed to camping due to renovation and repair of the pavilion. Check with the county for latest status. Niumalu is popular as a picnic and camping area with local residents, especially on weekends. The boat ramp is used by fishermen and water-skiers. The campground is attractive and well maintained, but lacks camping privacy.

HOW TO GET THERE: In Līhu'e, take Rice Street south to the junction of Highway 51 and follow Highway 51 to the junction of Highway 58 at the Matson Pier in Nāwiliwili. Turn right on Highway 58 and then make an immediate left at a sign to the Menehune Fish Pond. Follow the road about six-tenths of a mile to the park on the left.

NEARBY POINTS OF INTEREST: The Menehune Fish Pond is the best example of an inland fishing pond in Hawai'i, made by building a 2,700-foot stone wall across a bend in the river. The fish pond's true name is Alekoko, but tour guides try to convince you that it was built by the Menehune, a mythical race of small people. Don't you believe it.

Hanamā'ulu Beach Park

LOCATION: The park is located directly on the water in the town of Hanamā'ulu, just north of Līhu'e.

DESCRIPTION: Hanamā'ulu, which means "tired bay," is situated on a protected bay lined with a pretty, crescent-shaped beach. An attractive grove of ironwood trees backs the relatively narrow beach. The water near the shoreline is usually murky, because of silting from the Hanamāʻulu Stream, which empties into the bay, and debris sometimes washes ashore. The campground is a good location for those who want to be close to Līhuʻe. The grounds are flat and grassy, and tents can be pitched either in the shade or in the sun.

FACILITIES: Tent and vehicle camping. A modern pavilion with fluorescent lights occupies the center of the park and contains five picnic tables and a large barbecue. The rest rooms and screened outdoor showers are nearby. An older, wooden pavilion is located at the north end of the beach. It has electric lights and contains three picnic tables and attached rest rooms. Outdoor showers are also close by. A playground and two more picnic tables are located behind the pavilion. Groceries and gas are available in Līhuʻe.

CAMPGROUND ACTIVITIES: The bay is protected from the open ocean, and the bottom slopes gently from the shore. Swimming would be ideal except for the murky condition of the water, which puts off many people. Mullet, *ʻōpelu,* and bonefish are caught here.

PERMIT/RESERVATIONS: Reservations for camping permits may be made by phone; however, all permits must be picked up in person at the following address (permits are not issued to persons under 18 years old): Department of Parks and Recreation, 4280A Rice Street, Building B, Līhuʻe, HI 96766; phone, (808) 241–6660. Permits may be picked up after usual office hours and on weekends at the Kauaʻi Police Department, 3060 ʻUmi Street, Līhuʻe. If you pick your permit up here, you must have the exact amount of the permit fee. Campers are permitted to go directly to the campground, where a roving ranger will collect the fee. In this case, the cost is $5 per person per night.

TIME LIMIT: Seven days. You may renew for the same area, but only after a full day's break in camping, with no more than 60 days camping per year.

COST: Free to Hawaiʻi residents, nonprofit groups, and for persons under 18. For all others, the cost is $3 per day per person.

HOW TO GET THERE: From Lihue (2.7 miles), take Highway 56 north about 2 miles, watching for Hanamāʻulu Road on the right. Take Hanamāʻulu Road to Hehi Road and follow Hehi Road to the beach park.

NEARBY POINTS OF INTEREST: From the Wailua River Marina it is possible to take a boat ride up the biggest navigable river in Hawaiʻi to the Fern

Grotto, a fern-encrusted cave, where you will be serenaded with the "Hawaiian Wedding Song." You may find the tour guide's spiel corny and the singing mushy, but the scenery is pretty and the boat ride is nice. To get there from the campground, return to Highway 56, turn right, and proceed north for about 3.7 miles. Just before crossing the bridge over the Wailua River, a turn to the left leads to the Wailua River Marina.

Wailua Falls, an 80-foot falls on the Wailua River, can be reached by car. From the campground, return to Highway 56 and turn left. In just about a mile you will come to Mā'ala Road, where a sign points right to the falls, about another 3.5 miles.

'Ōpaeka'a Falls is another drive-in waterfall; this one is only half as high as Wailua, but well worth seeing. Across the road from the falls parking lot is a fine view of the Wailua River and the boats plying their route to the Fern Grotto. Leaving the campground, turn right on Highway 56 and proceed north for about 4 miles. Shortly after crossing the bridge over the Wailua River you will come to a stoplight and a sign to the falls. Turn left and drive up the hill to the parking lot on the right, about another 2.5 miles.

Nounou Mountain, called the Sleeping Giant, just west of the town of Wailua, resembles the form of a reclining man. It can be viewed best from a number of vantage points between Wailua and Kapa'a. A foot trail will take you to the giant's head, the highest point, if you are so inclined.

Anahola Beach Park

LOCATION: The park is on the ocean off Highway 56, about 5 miles north of Kapa'a.

DESCRIPTION: Anahola, which means "hourglass" in Hawaiian, is a scenic bay on the eastern shore of Kaua'i. An attractive white-sand beach curves around the bay. The beach park is located on the southeast end of the bay where a point of land offers some protection from strong winds, which frequently sweep the area. A grove of ironwood trees backs the beach and makes an excellent campsite. Offshore, a long, flat reef protects the shoreline from heavy surf.

FACILITIES: Tent camping only. Picnic tables, rest rooms, and showers are available, as is drinking water. Limited groceries can be purchased in Anahola, 1 mile north. More extensive shopping and gas are available in Kapa'a.

CAMPGROUND ACTIVITIES: Anahola is one of the safest places for swimming on the eastern shore except during periods of heavy surf, which occur mostly in the winter and spring. Surfing is prohibited in the beach park itself, but good bodysurfing and short and long board surfing can often be found just north of the park, with waves of 2 to 8 feet. Bonefish, threadfin, *pāpio,* and *ulua* are caught here. For beachcombing, the beach along the bay is a good area for glass balls and other flotsam and jetsam.

PERMIT/RESERVATIONS: Reservations for camping permits may be made in writing or by phone; however, all permits must be picked up in person at the following address (permits are not issued to persons under 18 years old): Department of Parks and Recreation, 4280A Rice Street, Building B, Līhu'e, HI 96766; phone, (808) 241–6660. After usual office hours and on weekends, permits may be picked up at the Kaua'i Police Department, 3060 'Umi Street, Līhu'e. If you pick up permits here, you must have the exact amount of the permit fee. Campers are permitted to go directly to the campground, where a roving ranger will collect the fee. In this case, the cost is $5 per person per night.

TIME LIMIT: Seven days. You may renew for the same area, but only after a full day's break in camping, with no more than 60 days camping per year.

COST: Free to Hawai'i residents, nonprofit groups, and those under 18. For all others, the cost is $3 per day per person.

HOW TO GET THERE: From Līhu'e (12 miles), proceed north from Kapa'a on Highway 56 for about 4 miles, to Anahola Road. Turn right and follow the signs to the beach, about another mile.

NEARBY POINTS OF INTEREST: For information on Kīlauea Point National Wildlife Refuge, see the section on 'Anini Beach Park.

For information on Fern Grotto, 'Ōpaeka'a Falls, and Wailua Falls, see the section on Hanamā'ulu Beach Park.

'Anini Beach Park

LOCATION: The park is on the ocean off Highway 56, midway between the towns of Kīlauea and Hanalei.

DESCRIPTION: 'Anini is a narrow sandy beach protected by one of the widest and longest fringing reefs in the Islands. Because of this, the water here is almost always glassy smooth. Tropical almond and ironwood trees line the beach, almost reaching the water's edge. The campground adjoins the beach park and provides tent sites both in an open, grassy area behind the beach and in a wooded grove right on the water.

Tropical almond trees at 'Anini Beach Park bent from the force of Hurricane 'Iniki.

FACILITIES: Tent camping only. 'Anini has two new rest room buildings. Hollywood buffs might be pleased to note that a bronze plaque on one of them indicates that it was a gift of Sylvester Stallone, who owns property nearby. Uncovered concrete picnic tables are located throughout the extensive camping area. Outdoor showers are available, as are two dishwashing sinks. Water is drinkable. Public telephones are located at the west end of the campground. A covered pavilion with two tables and electric lights is located between the campground and the beach park. Campers may use the pavilion, but may not camp around it. There is a faucet on the beach side of the pavilion, but it is often turned off. Additional facilities are available in the beach park proper, including rest rooms (public phone outside), showers, two pavilions, barbecue, picnic tables, and a dishwashing sink. Groceries and gas are available at Princeville, about 4 miles west.

CAMPGROUND ACTIVITIES: Although a safe and gentle swimming beach, 'Anini is very shallow close to shore. It is difficult to find a place to swim freely, and it is best suited for young children. The bottom reaches overhead depths about halfway to the outer reef, where it becomes shallow once more. Snorkeling is generally mediocre inside the reef, but is very good on calm days in the reef area, about 200 yards from shore, where the surf breaks. Board surfing can be good in the vicinity of 'Anini Channel, a

Tent at the north end of 'Anini Beach Park, with trees topped by Hurricane 'Iniki.

gap in the reef west of the beach park. Rip currents in the channel are dangerous during periods of heavy surf. Some sailboarding is also done in the channel, when the winds are right. *Pāpio,* goatfish, and bonefish are caught here.

PERMIT/RESERVATIONS: Reservations for camping permits may be made in writing or by phone; however, all permits must be picked up in person at the following address (permits are not issued to persons under 18 years old): Department of Parks and Recreation, 4280A Rice Street, Building B, Līhu'e, HI 96766; phone, (808) 241–6660. Permits may be picked up after usual office hours and on weekends at the Kaua'i Police Department, 3060 'Umi Street, Līhu'e. Here, you must have the exact amount of the permit fee. Campers are permitted to go directly to the campground, where a roving ranger will collect the fee. In this case, the cost is $5 per person per night.

TIME LIMIT: Seven days. You may renew for the same area, but only after a full day's break in camping, with no more than 60 days camping per year.

COST: Free to Hawai'i residents, nonprofit groups, and for persons under 18. For all others, the cost is $3 per day per person.

SPECIAL COMMENTS: ʻAnini is a fairly large campsite, but it can be very crowded with family groups, especially on summer weekends. The tropical almond grove at the water's edge was heavily damaged during Hurricane ʻIniki, and its effect will be evident for years to come.

HOW TO GET THERE: From Līhuʻe (30 miles), take Highway 56 north. After passing Kīlauea, about 26.5 miles, you will drive over a long bridge. Watch for Kalihiwai Road on the right (this will be the *second* Kalihiwai Road; you will have passed the first one before the bridge). Turn right and then make the first left on ʻAnini Road. Follow this road to the park.

NEARBY POINTS OF INTEREST: Just past the Princeville Shopping Center is a turnoff on the left side of the road. The lookout here provides a beautiful view of Hanalei Valley, its green taro fields and flowing river framed perfectly by towering mountains in the background. Hanalei Valley does double duty today. In addition to the growing of taro and other crops, it serves as a seabird refuge. If you are continuing west, the road drops down the hill and crosses the Hanalei Bridge, giving you a closer look at the valley and the taro fields. If you look off to your right you may see bison grazing in the fields. On the way back you can try a bisonburger in Hanalei.

Kīlauea Point National Wildlife Refuge, on the northernmost point of Kauaʻi, is a refuge and nesting place for many species of seabirds, including frigate and tropic birds, and the endangered Laysan albatross. It covers 160 acres of rugged seashore, including steep cliffs and offshore rocks. The lighthouse here is the largest in the Islands. Most of the area is inaccessible, and visitors must content themselves with viewing the birds and their aeiries from a distance. The grounds house a visitor center, a bookstore, and rest rooms. There is a small admission fee.

Hanalei Beach Park

LOCATION: The park sits directly on Hanalei Bay, on the northern coast of Kauaʻi, less than a mile off Highway 56.

DESCRIPTION: Hanalei, which means "crescent bay" in Hawaiian, lives up to its name, forming a beautiful, almost circular sandy beach. The park, also known locally as Black Pot Beach Park, is located between a large abandoned pier and the mouth of the Hanalei River. It is a dramatic setting, with the expanse of the bay framed by high, distant mountains. Ironwood trees back the beach and provide some shade, and there are a few grassy tent sites.

FACILITIES: Tent camping only. Picnic tables, rest rooms, cold showers, and drinking water are provided. Limited grocery shopping is available in Hanalei, less than a mile. More extensive shopping and gas at Princeville, 2.4 miles east.

CAMPGROUND ACTIVITIES: Swimming, bodyboarding, surfing, and windsurfing in the bay; canoeing and kayaking in the river. Fish that can be caught here include *ulua, papio,* squirrel fish, and scad. Excellent surfing spots include Hanalei Point and Hideaways near the campground, and Waikoko, on the other side of the bay. These breaks are for experienced surfers only.

PERMIT/RESERVATIONS: Reservations for camping permits may be made in writing or by phone, however all permits must be picked up in person at the address below (permits are not issued to persons under 18 years old): Department of Parks and Recreation, 4280A Rice Street, Building B, Līhu'e, HI 96766; phone, (808) 241–6660. After normal office hours and on weekends, permits may be picked up at the Kaua'i Police Department, 3060 'Umi Street, Līhu'e. If you pick up permits here, you must have the exact amount of the permit fee. Campers are also permitted to go directly to the campground, where a roving ranger will collect the fee. In this case, the cost is $5 per person per night.

TIME LIMIT: Weekend and holiday camping only.

COST: Free to Hawai'i residents, nonprofit groups, and those under 18. For all others, $3 per day per person.

HOW TO GET THERE: From Līhu'e, proceed north on Highway 56 to Hanalei. Upon entering town, turn right on Aku Road and right again on Weke Road until road ends at the park.

NEARBY POINTS OF INTEREST: See 'Anini Beach Park.

Camp Naue (YMCA)

LOCATION: The camp is on the ocean on Highway 56, about 4 miles east of Hanalei, just before Tunnels Beach.

DESCRIPTION: Naue, which means "to move" in Hawaiian, is a YMCA camp on four beautiful grassy and wooded acres, fronting a fine sandy beach. Ironwood trees line the shoreline, and tents can be pitched here or in an open grassy field behind the trees. High, steep ridges form a dramatic backdrop to the camp.

FACILITIES: Tent and bunkhouse camping. A large pavilion with several tables services primarily picnickers and tent campers. Two coed bunkhouses contain double-bunk beds and mattresses, but campers must furnish their own bedding or sleeping bags. Rest rooms are in two separate buildings and have hot showers. A large, completely equipped kitchen/dining room is available only to groups, but a refrigerator on the kitchen porch is available to others. Water is drinkable.

CAMPGROUND ACTIVITIES: Swimming is very good directly off the beach in front of the camp, but it is dangerous here during periods of heavy surf. Safer conditions exist at Tunnels Beach, several hundred yards west along the shore (see description in the section on Hā'ena Beach Park). Snorkeling is excellent at Tunnels Beach, which was named for cracks, holes, and arches in the reef in which many kinds of fish congregate. Tunnels Beach is also the site of good board surfing, and it is considered one of the best sailboarding sites on Kaua'i. *Pāpio, ulua,* and squirrelfish can be caught here. For beachcombers, the area between Tunnels and Kē'ē beaches is one of the best on the island for shelling.

PERMIT/RESERVATIONS: Reservations can only be made by groups, but individuals are accommodated on a space-available basis and can usually find a place unless the camp has been booked for exclusive use. It is best to call the following number to check on availability of the dates you wish to camp. Write or call Kaua'i YMCA Camp Naue, P.O. Box 1786, Līhu'e, HI 96766; phone, (808) 246–9090 or 4411.

TIME LIMIT: None, but space availability may limit individuals.

COST: For tent camping, one person plus tent is $10 per person per night. Each additional person in the same tent is $7 per person per night. The bunkhouses (coed) are $12 per person per night. YMCA members get a $1 discount; Kaua'i residents get a $1 discount.

SPECIAL COMMENTS: When calling about staying at Camp Naue, try (808) 246–9090 first. This is the caretaker's office at the camp. They are often more accommodating and have later information than the people in the Līhu'e office.

HOW TO GET THERE: From Līhu'e (40 miles), take Highway 56 north. About 3 miles past Hanalei, watch for the 7-mile marker on the highway. The sign for Camp Naue is on the right, between the 7- and 8-mile markers.

NEARBY POINTS OF INTEREST: See the section on Hā'ena Beach Park.

Hā'ena Beach Park

LOCATION: The park is on the ocean on Highway 56, about 4 miles west of Hanalei.

DESCRIPTION: Hā'ena, which means "red hot" in Hawaiian, is a very attractive park situated on a long, sandy beach. The area is flat and grassy, and partial shade is afforded from palms and other smaller trees. The beach, of fine white sand, slopes quickly at the water line and is exposed to the open ocean. Directly across the road from the park is the Maniniholo Dry Cave, which gives a dramatic backdrop to the campground.

FACILITIES: Two rest rooms with outside screened showers are located at each end of the park. A small pavilion containing two tables and electric lights is located in the center, near the beach. A dishwashing sink is nearby, and the water is safe to drink. Additional uncovered picnic tables and grills are found throughout the park. Groceries and gas can be purchased at Hanalei, 4 miles east.

CAMPGROUND ACTIVITIES: A sign on the park pavilion warns against swimming at Hā'ena, because of rip currents and a strong backwash. Despite that, some people do swim here when the ocean is calm, but it is for good swimmers only and definitely not for children. Safe swimming can be enjoyed during calm weather about a quarter of a mile east of the campground at Tunnels Beach, where an offshore reef provides protected but somewhat shallow conditions. Tunnels can be easily identified from Hā'ena, by the sunbathers on the beach and the swimmers and snorkelers in the water. Also, small boats and inflatables frequently anchor in the small lagoon created by the offshore reef. Safe swimming is also available at Kē'ē Beach, described below, about a mile west of the park. Snorkeling is excellent at Tunnels Beach, which was named for the many cracks, holes, and arches in the reef, where lots of different types of fish congregate. Tunnels Beach is also the site of good board surfing, and it is considered one of the best sailboarding sites on Kaua'i. *Pāpio, ulua,* and squirrelfish can be caught here. For beachcombers, the area between Tunnels and Kē'ē beaches is one of the best shelling areas on the island.

Hā'ena Beach Park, near the end of the road on Kaua'i's north shore, is the last campground for backpackers before the Nā Pali Coast Trail to Kalalau Valley.

PERMIT/RESERVATIONS: Reservations for camping permits may be made by phone; however, all permits must be picked up in person at the following address (permits are not issued to persons under 18 years old). Department of Parks and Recreation, 4280A Rice Street, Building B, Līhu'e, HI 96766; phone, (808) 241–6660. Permits may be picked up after usual office hours and on weekends at the Kaua'i Police Department, 3060 'Umi Street, Līhu'e If you pick up your permit here, you must have the exact amount of the permit fee. Campers are permitted to go directly to the campground, where a roving ranger will collect the fee. In this case, the cost is $5 per person per night.

TIME LIMIT: Seven days. You may renew for the same area, but only after a full day's break in camping, with no more than 60 days camping per year.

COST: Free to Hawai'i residents, nonprofit groups, and for persons under 18. For all others, the cost is $3 per day per person.

SPECIAL COMMENTS: Hā'ena is often windy and subject to frequent showers. The small roofed area of the pavilion provides little protection from slanting, wind-driven rain that can blow in from the sea. Unfortunately, as pretty as Hā'ena Beach Park is, it probably has the worst rest rooms on the island. They are usually dirty, in a poor state of repair, and heavily defaced by graffiti.

HOW TO GET THERE: From Līhu'e (40 miles), take Highway 56 north. About 4 miles past Hanalei, just after crossing a deep dip in the road that usually contains running water, you will see the dry cave on the left and the park on the right.

NEARBY POINTS OF INTEREST: Waikapala'e and Waikanaloa wet caves are just a short distance west of the campground. A rocky trail off the highway to the left leads upward to the Waikapala'e Wet Cave, a dramatic, deep cave with a watery bottom. Farther west, and practically on the left side of the road, is the Waikanaloa Wet Cave, in which it is possible to swim. If you have a waterproof flashlight, you can explore its inner chambers.

Kē'ē Beach, at the end of the highway and the beginning of the Nā Pali Coast Trail, is an excellent place to swim and snorkel safely, except during periods of high surf.

Hā'ena is the closest campground to the magnificent Nā Pali Coast Trail, and backpackers bound for Kalalau Valley often camp here the night before setting off. It is also a convenient overnight stopping place for day hikes along the trail, such as to Hanakāpī'ai Beach and Hanakāpī'ai Falls.

Nā Pali Coast State Park

Nā Pali is certainly one of the most beautiful parks in the world. Its 6,500 acres contain spectacular scenery and awesome views not found anywhere else. Nā Pali means "the cliffs," an apt name for a region where 2,000-foot valley walls plunge precipitously down to a restless sea. No roads disturb this lovely wilderness, and the only access is by boat or the single trail that follows the route ancient Hawaiians made to reach the former settlements in the coastal valleys.

Of the four campgrounds in the park, one can only be reached by boat. The others are accessible via the Kalalau Trail, which winds its way along the coastline to Kalalau Valley for a distance of 11 miles. Hiking the trail is an unforgettable experience. It passes through five valleys and descends to sea level only once before reaching Kalalau Beach, and every twist and turn reveals a view to boggle the mind. The trail penetrates lush forests, negotiates high ridges, and snakes precariously over narrow ledges, where ocean waves crash against the rocks far below. Mostly safe and well maintained, portions of the trail may be a problem for those with a fear of heights.

The following sections describe the Nā Pali campgrounds from east to west. This is the same order that those accessible by land are reached via the Kalalau Trail. Because camping permits for Nā Pali differ from those for other state campgrounds, such information is discussed here, rather than in the individual campground sections.

Hiking on the Nā Pali Coast Trail.

CAMPING PERMITS: As is the case at other state parks, camping in Nā Pali is limited to five nights in any one consecutive 30-day period. Within this five-night maximum, however, no two consecutive nights are allowed at Hanakāpī'ai or Hanakoa. Thus, you could spend a night at Hanakoa on the way to Kalalau, 3 nights at Kalalau, and a night at Hanakāpī'ai on the way out. Or, to maximize your time in Kalalau, you could hike in and out in 1 day and have five nights there. A further exception to the five-night rule is at Miloli'i, where the stay is limited to three nights. A permit can be obtained at any state parks office. The following address is for the office on Kaua'i: Division of State Parks, 3060 'Eiwa Street, Līhu'e, HI 96766; phone, (808) 241–3444.

Hanakāpī'ai Beach

LOCATION: The beach is on the Nā Pali Coast, off the Kalalau Trail, about 7 miles west of Hanalei.

DESCRIPTION: Hanakāpī'ai is supposed to mean "bay sprinkling food" in Hawaiian, which is probably a good example of my warning at the beginning of this book that in some cases, the true meaning of Hawaiian words has been lost. The beach lies at the end of the valley of the same name. In summer it is a fine white-sand beach, backed by large, black stones. In winter only the stones remain. At any time it is a lovely spot. Lush vegetation surrounds the beach, and steep valley walls isolate it from the rest of the coastline. Hanakāpī'ai Stream must be crossed to reach both the beach and the camping area. There is usually a rope strung across the stream, which aids rock-hopping, but, depending upon the water level, it is not always possible to keep your feet dry. Heavy rains can make the stream uncrossable. Camping is not feasible on the beach proper, which is not only surf-swept, but water from Hanakāpī'ai Stream often builds up behind the beach when sand blocks its access to the sea. Several tent sites overlook the beach, and more can be found in the forested area along the trail leading to Hanakāpī'ai Falls. *Hala, kamani,* and guava are the main trees in this area.

FACILITIES: Pit toilets are the only facilities offered at Hanakāpī'ai. Water is available only from the stream and should be boiled or treated before use. Because people wash and bathe here, take water from as far upstream as possible.

CAMPGROUND ACTIVITIES: Ocean swimming can be dangerous at any time of the year, but especially in winter and during periods of high surf.

Hanakāpī'ai Beach is the first campground on the Nā Pali Coast Trail.

The water is deceptive; drownings have occurred. Heed the signs and use caution. Hanakāpī'ai Valley was once inhabited, and the remains of many taro terraces step their way up the valley. Coffee was once grown here, and trees are still found a short distance from the beach, near the ruins of a coffee mill. Also a short way up the valley are huge mango trees, which drop hundreds of fruits during late spring or early summer. Unfortunately, the fruit is not reachable from the ground or by climbing, and most of it is smashed when it falls. But if you don't mind bruised fruit and are willing to fight the fruit flies and the ants, the results are delicious.

SPECIAL COMMENTS: Hanakāpī'ai Beach is heavily visited by day hikers, many of whom have just gotten off a bus. They make their way in everyday clothes and street shoes. Many of them underestimate the difficulty of the trail and turn back, but even so, the place can be crowded, especially on weekends. That may affect your willingness to camp here.

HOW TO GET THERE: From Līhu'e, take Highway 56 north to the end of the road at Kē'ē Beach, about 38 miles. The Kalalau Trail begins on the left side of the parking lot, just before the beach. A beautiful 2-mile hike, which crosses several small streams, ducks in and out of pretty forested glens, and offers dramatic views of the coastline, brings you to Hanakāpī'ai Beach.

NEARBY POINTS OF INTEREST: Hanakāpī'ai Falls is about 2 miles up the valley from the campground. This beautiful 120-foot-high falls boasts a pool at its base deep enough for swimming. It is even possible to swim behind the falls, climb up on a ledge, and view the world through a white veil of water. The trail generally follows the stream, crossing it three times en route. It ascends very gradually over many old taro terraces, passing a magnificent stand of bamboo, as well as guava, mango, and mountain apple trees. The last half of the trail narrows, becomes more difficult, and is dangerous in spots. Exercise caution.

Hanakoa Valley

LOCATION: The valley is on the Kalalau Trail, 4 miles west of Hanakāpī'ai.

DESCRIPTION: A wide, lush green valley, bisected by a stream, Hanakoa is frequently used as an overnight stop on the way to Kalalau. Unlike Hanakāpī'ai and Kalalau, Hanakoa is a "hanging valley," meaning that it does not end in a beach, but in a cliff that drops sharply into the sea. Hanakoa, which means either "bay of *koa* trees" or "bay of warriors," is a much wider valley than Hanakāpī'ai. The area around the trail is almost totally forested.

You will know you have arrived in Hanakoa by the appearance of a deteriorated shack on the left side of the trail. Directly across from the shack is a small, flat clearing that can accommodate several tents. A trail from this clearing leads down to a wonderful mountain pool, fed by a small waterfall. It includes a "Tarzan" rope that you can use to swing out over the pool and drop in. Even if you do not plan to camp at Hanakoa, don't miss the chance to cool off here.

A short distance from the shack the trail crosses Hanakoa Stream. Campsites can be found on old taro terraces along the left side of the trail.

FACILITIES: None. Water must be obtained from the stream and should be treated before use. Bury personal waastes at least 100 feet from the stream and pack out what you pack in.

SPECIAL COMMENTS: Hanakoa is noted for mosquitoes. Use repellent and zip up your bug screen. The shack just before the stream crossing is notorious as a garbage dump, including carcasses of dead goats that hunters have left. Please do not add to the mess. Boy Scouts and service organizations make periodic trips to clean it up. Let's try to put them out of a job. A hiker from Germany was swept away and killed in November, 1990, trying to cross the rain-swollen Hanakoa Stream. Do not attempt to cross if conditions dictate otherwise. Many moderate streams along this coast become torrents in rainy weather.

HOW TO GET THERE: From Hanakāpī'ai Beach, the Kalalau Trail rises in a series of switchbacks, reaching its highest point, 800 feet, about 3.2 miles from the start. A large boulder on the seaward side of the trail marks the location. If you venture around the boulder you will find a dizzying sheer drop to the ocean below. All kinds of "lover's leap" legends are told about this spot. Adopt one of them or make up your own. The trail then loses some altitude and winds in and out of two forested valleys before reaching Hanakoa, 4 miles from Hanakāpī'ai.

NEARBY POINTS OF INTEREST: Only about half a mile from the main trail, Hanakoa Falls is a slightly smaller copy of the falls at Hanakāpī'ai, with a shallower pool. It is much easier to reach. At the beginning of the trail, it can be difficult to stay on the correct path, because of other minor trails in the vicinity. But you will soon know if you have gone astray, and you can retrace your steps. To reach the falls, watch for a wooden sign shortly after crossing Hanakoa Stream. This sign marks a trail to the left, which begins at a walled agricultural terrace. The trail then drops down and crosses a fork of the stream, turns left, and follows along another fork of the stream. The trail is narrow and eroded in places, but the falls are a worthwhile detour.

Kalalau Valley

LOCATION: This valley is at the end of the Kalalau Trail, 5 miles from Hanakoa and 11 miles from the trailhead at Kē'ē Beach.

DESCRIPTION: Kalalau Valley is a very special place. Its beauty is both enchanting and awe-inspiring. I know of no more marvelous spot in all these Islands. If there was an Eden, it must have looked like Kalalau. The width of the white-sand beach, one of the widest in the state, can reach 300 feet or more in summer. Behind the beach, giant green spires pierce the sky—unreal, incredible shapes that prompted an artist friend to say, "If I painted this, no one would believe it." A lovely waterfall drops gently to the ocean near the west end of the beach, where steep cliffs and sea caves back the final stretches of sand. The beach ends in a massive rockslide, which closed forever a pretty double-ended cave from which people used to swim to Honopū, the next valley. On the opposite end of the beach,

Camping in the sea cave at Kalalau Beach.

Kalalau Stream exits a lush, green valley, surrounded by a high, semicircular wall and guarded by more green spires. It is a magical place. You may never want to leave.

FACILITIES: The camping area is long and narrow, stretching half a mile behind the beach from a point just west of the stream to the sea caves at its west end. Camping is not allowed in the valley itself. Two large composting toilet structures and several smaller pit toilets are the only facilities. Garbage pits are located at various points in the camping area, where refuse is burned; the residue is either buried or carried out. Water is available from Ho'ole'a Falls near the west end of the beach, which also serves as the community shower, and from Kalalau Stream. It should be treated before drinking.

CAMPGROUND ACTIVITIES: Swimming is safest during the summer months, but ocean swimmers should exercise caution at all times. The shorebreak can be rough, and certain parts of the beach drop sharply offshore. Observe where other swimmers are playing in the surf, and you should be okay. I have never seen anyone fishing at Kalalau, perhaps because no one wants to pack in fishing gear. But if you have it, you might be able to catch *pāpio,* threadfin, bonefish, and maybe a passing *ulua.*

SPECIAL COMMENTS: Due to heavy impact on the area, the Division of State Parks now restricts camping in Kalalau to sixty persons per day. This means that you must get a permit as far in advance as possible. It is not unusual for all summer permits to be gone by May.

Nudity is common but not universal at Kalalau. Although illegal in Kaua'i, it is tolerated here. The philosophy seems to be that the valley is inaccessible enough so that nudity is not a public nuisance, and people offended by it will not come all the way out here. Nudity, however, does not mean lewdness. People with or without clothes go about their business as they would at any other campsite and on any other beach. College professors, airline stewardesses, kids, and grandparents can all be encountered naked as the day they were born. But the days of wild beach orgies, fueled by marijuana, ended years ago when the last of the hippie population was forced to leave the valley.

The sea caves west of the waterfall are popular camping spots in summer (winter surf fills them with water). They afford protection from sun and rain, although they do drip a bit. If you camp here, be sure to note the zone of falling rock just outside the caves. Pebbles, stones, and even some fairly large rocks make a pattern in the sand as they drop from the cliffs above or are dislodged by goats. Cross this area quickly, and don't linger.

Sunsets at Kalalau are unforgettable. Watch for the "green flash," an aura that sometimes appears for a second or two just as the sun drops into the sea. Stargazing is probably better than you have seen it anywhere, although the cliffs behind the beach shut out the southern sky constellations. And if you should be surprised by "birds" fluttering with swift, jerky movements above the beach at night, they are not birds, but hoary bats, the only native land mammal in Hawai'i.

HOW TO GET THERE: From Hanakoa, it is 5 miles to Kalalau. The character of the trail changes markedly after leaving Hanakoa. Where the trail had been mainly forested, it now becomes mostly open. Vegetation is sparse, and narrow gullies replace the wide valleys traversed earlier. The trail stays closer to the sea now, close enough and high enough in some places to cause concern for those afraid of heights. The views are fantastic. The trail finally crosses a reddish brown saddle, and Kalalau Valley and beach appear below. At the bottom of the saddle is Kalalau Stream. Crossing is usually aided by a rope, but again, it will be difficult to keep your feet dry. By now, you probably won't care. Once on the other side, follow the right fork to the beach, and the trail will take you through the campground.

Another way to reach Kalalau is via propelled Zodiac rafts operated by Captain Zodiac from 15 May through 15 September. These inflatable boats can carry up to 20 people, and to put passengers ashore, they make a thrilling dash through the surf and run up high on the beach, where everyone races to debark before the next wave comes in. The view as you cruise along the Nā Pali coast is spectacular, and, seas permitting, the captain will take the boat into one or two caves along the route. Some people enjoy hiking in and rafting out, with the captain pointing out sections of the trail along the way. A word of warning: the Zodiacs cannot land on the beach if the seas are too rough, and it is possible to be marooned at Kalalau for 1, 2, or even 3 days, until the seas calm down. If you choose this option, have extra food along. To arrange a trip, call (808) 826–9371. The cost is $60 one way for you and your backpack, and *you must have your state camping permit for Kalalau in your possession.*

NEARBY POINTS OF INTEREST: No matter how wonderful the beach is, no visit to Kalalau would be complete without a trip up the valley. The trail, which begins just west of the Kalalau Stream, provides both a shaded forest walk and a fine view of the entire valley. It traverses a series of agricultural terraces, passes large mango trees, and, after 2 miles and an 800-foot elevation gain, reaches a great pool for diving, swimming, or just lounging. A smaller trail branches left off the main one and leads to Waimakemake Falls, which you may have seen if you visited Kalalau Lookout in Kōke'e State Park. It is difficult to find, but it lies between the pool described above and the stream crossing about 10 minutes back down the trail. It is near several terraces and makes its way over several of them en route to the falls.

Good swimmers can enjoy the special treat of visiting Honopū, the next valley west of Kalalau. Honopū, with its double beach, dramatic stone arch, and lovely waterfall, was the scene of the remake of the film *King Kong* with Jessica Lange. Honopū is sometimes called "The Valley of the Lost Tribe," especially by tour guides. One explanation for the name is that in 1922 a Bishop Museum archaeologist found several skulls in the valley that he thought were not Hawaiian, but belonged to an earlier primitive people. This was later proved wrong—the skulls were Hawaiian after all. But the name stuck, even though occupants of the Islands have never been referred to as "tribes."

To swim to Honopū, you need a calm morning. Walk to the western end of the beach, and make your way around and over the fallen boulders, staying close to the shoreline. You should soon be able to see Honopū Beach, which was not possible before the rock slide. In those days swimmers for Honopū took off from the now-buried double-entrance cave, without being able to see Honopū, which was hidden behind a rocky promontory. Personally, I always felt uncomfortable starting out for Honopū without being able to see where I was going. It is much better now, with the destination fully in view, although the rockslide has ruined the appearance of this end of the beach. Once you see Honopū Beach, you may enter the water or walk as far as you can, depending how long a swim you want to make of it. A reasonably good swimmer should reach shore in about 15 minutes. Allow a bit longer for the return, because you will be swimming against an offshore current. This current is very light in the morning, but increases in the afternoon. Thus, the earlier you start, the easier your trip back will be.

Miloli'i Beach

LOCATION: The park is on the west shore, 4 miles north of Polihale State Park. It is accessible only by boat.

DESCRIPTION: Miloli'i, which means "fine twist" (of rope) or "small swirling" (of a current), is an attractive, sandy beach backed by high cliffs. It is the westernmost of Na Pali's isolated beaches. Scattered ironwood trees provide shelter from the sun and from occasional afternoon winds.

FACILITIES: Three covered picnic shelters, pit toilets, running water, and showers make Miloli'i the most luxurious of Nā Pali's campgrounds. Warm showers are common, because the water is heated by the sun as it travels the pipeline from the valley. There is a cabin on the beach, but it is for park personnel only.

CAMPGROUND ACTIVITIES: Swimming is usually safe on calm days, but caution should be exercised during heavy surf and in the vicinity of the boat channel, where strong rip currents can occur. Snorkeling is excellent during calm seas, especially along the fringing reef on the east end of the beach. Local fishermen frequent the area, but I have no information on the catch here. You will probably find threadfin, bonefish, parrotfish, and possibly *pāpio*. For beachcombers, Miloli'i is noted as one of the best shelling beaches in Hawai'i. Cone shells, several kinds of cowries, and *momi,* the Ni'ihau shell made famous in necklaces, are all deposited during the winter surge. Sometimes other treasures wash ashore, such as glass balls from Japanese fishing nets.

SPECIAL COMMENTS: As at Kalalau, sunsets and stargazing are spectacular at Miloli'i.

HOW TO GET THERE: Most campers arrange to be dropped off and picked up by a commercial boat operator, usually out of Hanalei. Kayak clubs beach at Miloli'i, and if you are experienced, kayaks can also be rented for the trip, which is usually made from Kē'ē Beach, ending at Polihale, to take advantage of prevailing wind and currents. There is no land access.

NEARBY POINTS OF INTEREST: At the eastern end of the beach, a mile-long trail leads up Miloli'i Valley to a waterfall in a narrow, chutelike chamber, its sheer walls soaring up to the sky. It is an eerie place. The trail begins near the water tank and generally follows the stream. A small falls along the way provides a pleasant sit-down shower. As the trail passes taro terraces, *koa haole* gives way to *kukui* trees and some Java plum. The valley, not wide to begin with, narrows sharply toward its head, where an 8-foot waterfall feeds a small pool. Climbing around this falls brings you to the chamber described above, where a 100-foot falls drops down a steep face. The falls is often dry. Watch out for falling rocks.

Polihale State Park

LOCATION: The park is at the end of Highway 50, about 15 miles northwest of the town of Waimea, and 5 miles north of Barking Sands Pacific Missile Range. Polihale is as far as it is possible to go on the west shore of Kaua'i.

Polihale State Park boasts one of the widest beaches in Hawai'i.

DESCRIPTION: Polihale, which means "house bosom" in Hawaiian, has the distinction of being the westernmost beach in the United States. It boasts a dramatic setting, bounded on the north by the imposing sea cliffs of the Nā Pali coast, and rocky ridges and narrow valleys to its rear. The 140-acre park occupies the northern 2 miles of a 15-mile-long uninterrupted sandy beach, extending all the way to Kekaha. At Polihale, this beach is over 300 feet wide in summer, making it one of the widest, as well as one of the longest beaches in Hawai'i. The shorefront is backed by sand dunes as high as 100 feet. The islands of Ni'ihau and Lehua are clearly visible offshore, and the sunsets are spectacular. Polihale is one of the most beautiful and isolated beaches accessible by car in the state. A night spent here under a canopy of stars undimmed by city lights, or when the sea is turned to silver by a full moon, is an unforgettable experience.

The campground occupies the south end of the beach park, affording campers a separate and quiet place away from other park users and activities. Situated on high sand dunes overlooking the beach, it is one of the most appealing of the state's campgrounds. The site is divided into three numbered sections, each of which is spacious enough to provide privacy for a dozen or so individual tents. All three sections are directly on the ocean, on beach sand, with medium-sized *kiawe* trees affording partial shade. Tents may be located in this immediate area, near the trees and the picnic tables, or farther forward on the dunes, providing an unobstructed view of the sea and the sunsets.

FACILITIES: Tent and vehicle camping. Each of the three numbered campsites contains a rest room with screened outdoor showers, several picnic tables, barbecues, and a spigot providing drinking water. The beach park area is fairly well removed from the campground, but has additional rest rooms, showers, and picnic tables under covered pavilions. Groceries and gas are available at Kekaha and Waimea, 12–15 miles away.

CAMPGROUND ACTIVITIES: Swimming is safest in the summer, but swimmers should be cautious at Polihale at all times of the year, especially during high surf conditions. Rip currents and sharp dropoffs may be encountered. There are no lifeguards. A usually safe swimming area is known locally as Queen's Pond, a shallow area protected by a small reef. It lies about midway along the park's shoreline. Look for families with children in the water, and you probably have found the spot. Short board, long board, body board, and bodysurfing are possible here at times, but waves generally break quickly, thus rides are short. Wave height is 2–8 feet. *Pāpio,* bonefish, and threadfin can be caught here, and you may hook a wandering *ulua*. For beachcombers, shelling can be very good, especially after periods of high surf. But with 15 miles to pick from, you're bound to find something. An ancient *heiau* site is located at the northeast end of the park, in a gulch running back from the beach. A "sacred" spring is also supposed to be in the same vicinity, but I have never found it. When the tide is low, it is possible to rock-hop along the north shore to one of the narrow valleys north of the park. If you do so, make sure you check the tide tables and go and return only during low tide. Do not attempt this during high surf conditions and watch for slippery or unstable rocks.

PERMIT/RESERVATIONS: Permits may be obtained from a state parks office on any island. The following address is the state office on Kaua'i: Division of State Parks, 3060 'Eiwa Street, Līhu'e, HI 96766; phone, (808) 241–3444.

TIME LIMIT: Five nights in any one 30-day period.

COST: Free.

SPECIAL COMMENTS: Caution: *kiawe* trees are notorious for long, sharp thorns. Many of these thorns fall to the ground on small segments of branches that enable them to stand straight up. I have stepped on such thorns at Polihale that have gone through almost an inch of soft rubber sole and still penetrated my foot.

HOW TO GET THERE: From Līhu'e (38 miles), take Highway 50 west almost to its end at Barking Sands Pacific Missile Range, about 33 miles. Bear right on the paved road toward the mountains, watching carefully for small signs to Polihale. At the second sign, turn left onto the dirt road through the cane fields, for an additional 5 miles. The road to the campground forks to the left; the right fork leads to the beach park proper.

NEARBY POINTS OF INTEREST: Although the famous sands may be encountered outside its boundaries, Barking Sands Beach begins just south of Polihale and extends to Nohili Point. Under certain conditions the sand along this beach emits a "woofing" sound, which was known even to the ancient Hawaiians. The sound is usually produced from compressing the sand in some manner. The only way I have been able to make it perform is to run down from the top of a dune, letting my feet fall heavily into the steep bank of sliding sand. If you have done the same thing at the Great Sand Dunes in Colorado, you already know what the Barking Sands of Kaua'i sound like.

For information on Captain Cook's Landing and the Russian Fort, see the section on Lucy Wright Beach Park.

For information on Waimea Canyon, see the section on Kōke‘e State Park.

Barking Sands Pacific Missile Range

LOCATION: The facility is on the ocean about 10.5 miles west of Waimea, near the end of Highway 50.

DESCRIPTION: Barking Sands is a Navy installation with tent camping and beach cottages available for rent to military personnel, active and retired, and their dependents. It is situated on a continuation of the beach that begins at Polihale State Park, the longest and one of the most isolated beaches on Kaua‘i. For a more complete description of the area, see the section on Polihale State Park.

FACILITIES: Tent camping is permitted at Major's Beach, which has drinking water, rest rooms, and cold showers. Four two-bedroom beach cottages sleep up to six persons. The cottages are completely furnished, including one double bed, two single beds, and a sofa bed in the living room. Bedding is furnished, as are eating and cooking utensils. There is a small BX, with some basic food items, but for major grocery shopping and gas you will need to go to Waimea, 10.5 miles east.

CAMPGROUND ACTIVITIES: Caution should be observed in swimming, especially during spring and winter months. Heavy shorebreak, strong backwash, and rip currents can occur at any time. Short and long board surfing take place at several areas, known locally as Rocket Reef, Kinikini, Majors Bay, and Family Housing. *Pāpio,* bonefish, and threadfin are caught here, especially off the sections of beachrock south of Nohili Point.

PERMIT/RESERVATIONS: Department of Defense ID card is required. Reservations can be made at any time but will not be confirmed until 60 days in advance and must be by written application. It is best to call or write to the following address for the standard application form: Morale, Welfare, and Recreation, Pacific Missile Range Facility, P.O. Box 128, Kekaha, Kaua‘i, HI 96752; phone, (808) 335–4752 or Autovon (808) 471–6446.

TIME LIMIT: There is no time limit, but after 7 days cabin fee increases to $70 per day. An extension past 14 days requires approval of the base commander.

COST: There is no charge for tent camping. Cabins cost $55 per day for two persons, plus $5 per extra person per day, up to six persons.

SPECIAL COMMENTS: Barking Sands is in demand year-round. Weekends are particularly difficult to reserve. Best prospects are for weekday periods. If you want to spend some time in this area and Barking Sands is full, consider Polihale State Park, 5 miles north on the same beach.

HOW TO GET THERE: From Līhu'e (33 miles), take Highway 50 west to the entrance to the installation on the right side of the road. Ask directions to the beach cottages at the entry gate.

NEARBY POINTS OF INTEREST: See the section on Polihale State Park.

INDEX

ABOUT THE AUTHOR

Richard McMahon, a resident of Hawai'i for more than two decades, has taken hundreds of hikers and backpackers into the Islands' wilderness areas for adventure travel companies. He has also led trips to the mountains of Czechoslovakia and Turkey, on a bicycle tour of South China, and on an elephant safari in northern Thailand. He has hiked and climbed extensively in the Alps and in Japan.

Mr. McMahon retired from a career in the United States Army in 1979. He holds Masters degrees in English and history from the University of Hawai'i.